Sintra: A Glorious Eden

MALCOLM JACK has been a regular visitor to Portugal, where he has a home, for many years. He has written about eighteenth-century philosophy and literature and has edited the works of both Lady Mary Wortley Montagu and William Beckford.

Also by Malcolm Jack

The Social and Political Thought of Bernard Mandeville
Corruption and Progress: The Eighteenth-Century Debate
William Beckford: An English Fidalgo

As Editor
The Turkish Embassy Letters of Lady Mary Wortley Montagu
Vathek and Other Stories: A William Beckford Reader
The Episodes of Vathek

MALCOLM JACK

SINTRA

A GLORIOUS EDEN

CARCANET

in association with

THE CALOUSTE GULBENKIAN FOUNDATION

CALOUSTE
GULBENKIAN
FOUNDATION

This book belongs to the series *Aspects of Portugal*, published in Great Britain by
Carcanet Press in association with the Calouste Gulbenkian Foundation.

First published in Great Britain in 2002 by
Carcanet Press Limited
4th Floor, Conavon Court
12–16 Blackfriars Street
Manchester M3 5BQ

A CIP catalogue record for this book
is available from the British Library

ISBN 1 85754 587 7

The publisher acknowledges financial assistance from the Calouste Gulbenkian
Foundation and from the Arts Council of England.

Typeset in Monotype Bembo by XL Publishing Services, Tiverton
Printed and bound in England by SRP Ltd, Exeter

Contents

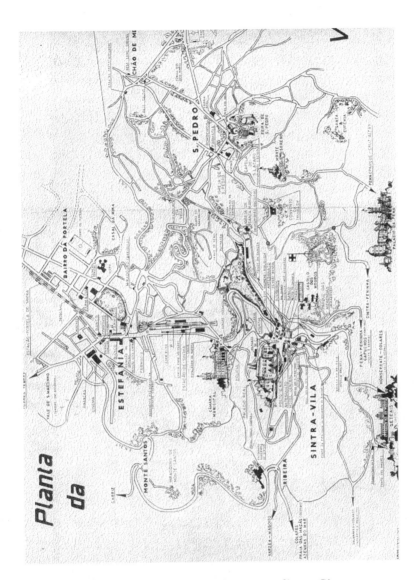

Map 1. Map of town and surroundings, Sintra

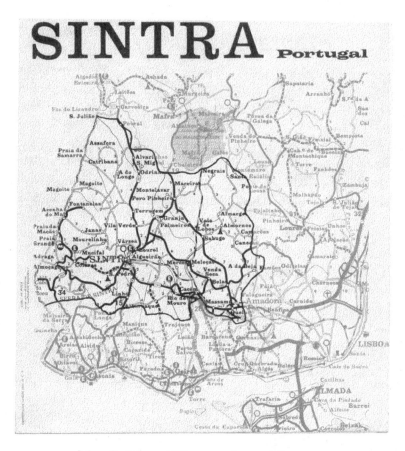

Map 2. Map of Sintra and coastal region

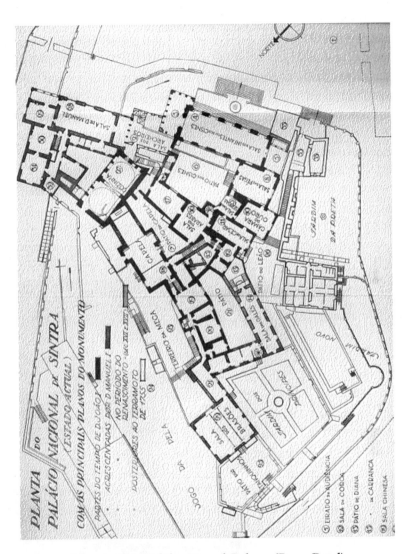

Plan 1. Plan of the Royal Palace (Paço Real)

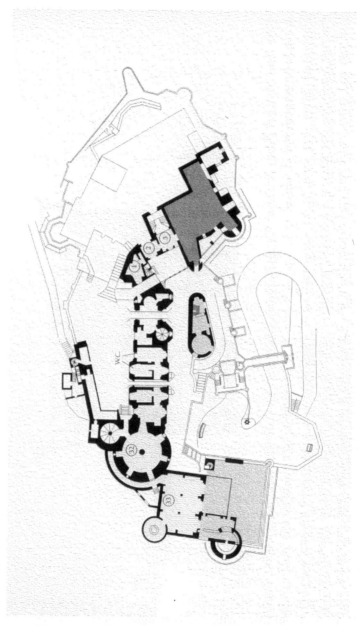

Plan 2. Plan of Pena Palace at entrance level (second floor)

List of Illustrations

Illustrations 1–9 will be found between pp.30 and 31; Illustrations 10–18 between pp.110 and 111; and Illustrations 19–26 between pp.174 and 175.

I am grateful to the owners of the following images for permission to reproduce them in this book.

1. Prehistoric Votive Offerings in São Martinho Valley. Drawing, F. Alves Pereira, Sintra 1957.
2. Inscription on a Roman tombstone in the Museum of São Miguel de Odrinhas. Inscribed by F. Alves Pereira, Sintra 1957.
3. General view of Sintra with Royal Palace (Paço Real), 1829. Lithograph by D. Schiopetta. Sintra, Historical Archive, Municipal Archive.
4. View of Royal Palace (from the south), 1507. Engraving by Duarte d'Armas, *Book of Fortresses*, 1510. Sintra, Historical Archive, Municipal Archive.
5. View of Royal Palace (from the south-east), 1507. Engraving by Duarte d'Armas, *Book of Fortresses*, 1510. Sintra, Historical Archive, Municipal Archive.
6. View of Royal Palace (from the west), 1507. Engraving by Duarte d'Armas, *Book of Fortresses*, 1510. Sintra, Historical Archive, Municipal Archive.
7. Cork Convent (Convento dos Capuchos), c. 1950. Photograph. Sintra, Historical Archive, Municipal Archive.
8. Convent of Peninha, c. 1960. Photograph. Sintra, Historical Archive, Municipal Archive.
9. View of old town with São Martinho Church. c.1960. Photograph. Sintra, Historical Archive, Municipal Archive.

Acknowledgements

Books of this sort are written over many years, perhaps even over a lifetime. I remember my first visit to Sintra vividly. It started on a crisp, sunny winter's afternoon. The romantic atmosphere of the town was added to by a chance encounter with a mysterious stranger. My mother, Alicia, and Clemente Demée, a family friend, accompanied me on that first journey so many years ago. I dedicate the book to their memory and to the memory of that afternoon.

Among many inspiring, if sometimes idiosyncratic English writers William Beckford's evocation of Sintra has been particularly haunting. Although the Portuguese Romantics have greatly entertained me, my real travelling companions on this journey have been the generation of earlier Sintrense scholars – Félix Alves Pereira, José Alfredo da Costa Azevedo, and Sergio Luís de Carvalho, the latter despite his sometimes baroque Portuguese. Francisco Costa's excellent monographs have been a source of delight as well as indispensable tools of research; João Rodil's evocations have been inspiring.

I am indebted to a host of friends and acquaintances. These include Professor João de Almeida Flor for advice and encouragement; Pedro de Almeida Flor for information about various aspects of art history; Eugénio Montoito, Élvio Melim de Sousa and Vitor Gomes of the Municipal Archive of Sintra where I was cordially received and greatly helped throughout the project; Robert Arnold for allowing me to visit the Quinta do Convento da Trindade and Betty Silveira for receiving me there; Keith Harris and Sidney Blackmore in London and Adriana Jones in Sintra for supplying books; Angela Delaforce for some unusual sources and ideas; Marcos Aurelio da Silva with whom I discussed many matters, some of an arcane linguistic nature; Carlos and Manuela Jorge, and Clive and Emma Gilbert for their enthusiasm and useful suggestions; Patricia Lamb of the British Historical Society of Portugal for helping arrange a visit to Ramalhão; Nuno Antunes for his fine photos; Laurent Chatel, Tom Sutherland and Morgan Webb, who all came up with some bright ideas and Robert Borsje for precise observations and considerable patience throughout the writing. I am also grateful for the support of Michael Collins with whom I discussed early plans and who started the book on its way; Felicity Luard of the Gulbenkian Foundation, London, and the Gulbenkian Foundation itself for its support. Finally I should thank my editors at Carcanet, Sarah Rigby, Liffy Grant and Judith Willson, for their careful and useful work and Michael Schmidt for actually producing the book.

Preface

Byron described Sintra as the most beautiful place in the world. His evocation of Sintra as a 'glorious Eden' has come to symbolise the mythical status that the town has acquired in the Portuguese and Anglo-Portuguese imaginations. There are a number of explanations for this. First comes the natural beauty of the place. High up on the *serra* along the Tagus estuary near Lisbon (see Map 2), Sintra's dramatic position has been enhanced by an eco-climate, which is damper and cooler than the capital's, and more hospitable to greenery, which makes it a pleasant retreat during the glaring summer months. Many exotic species of fauna and flora were added to the indigenous variety in the nineteenth century by Dom Fernando on the slopes of Pena and by Sir Francis Cook at Monserrate. These plantings changed the landscape, making it more lush and alluring, so that eventually, at the end of the twentieth century, it was declared a world heritage site.

In addition to this, the human habitation of Sintra can be traced back to prehistoric times. Archaeologists, beginning with Carlos Ribeiro in the nineteenth century, have uncovered Stone Age remains around the *planalto* north of the town. But even before this discovery, Renaissance writers like Francisco de Holanda who knew Sintra's complex oral history had written about Sintra's links with the classical age and the age of mythology. These writers, who were steeped in the classics, claimed that Cynthia, Goddess of the Moon, was worshipped on the sacred promontory of the Cabo da Roca, on the western edge of the European continent. From there to the valley of Colares where it is reputed that a monster, an ogre, had to be chained by Heracles, stretches an area which has become the subject of myth. Tritons, mermaids and monsters of various types inhabit the legendary landscape of Sintra and are so strongly associated with the area that they have found their way into the decorative features of its architecture over the ages.

Gradually, a sophisticated literature was added to an ancient, oral tradition. Portuguese writers of the Golden Age enthused about Sintra in verse and prose. Gil Vicente's plays, for instance, were produced for a courtly audience in the royal palace. These heroic, literary voices, which included Alexandre Herculano, Almeida Garrett and Viscount Juromenha, were heard by the great Romantics of the nineteenth century. In their turn they influenced new generations of writers, including the redoubtable Eça de Queirós. In the meantime a succession of British men of letters, including William Beckford, Robert Southey and Lord Byron visited Sintra and sang out its praises, ensuring that its name was widely known in England and elsewhere in Europe. Travel writing, Portuguese periodicals and then a generation of more serious but still aesthetically inclined, scholarly work took the story on into the twentieth century.

The fact that Sintra has long been chosen as the home of rulers has made its heritage. Admired by the Moors for its impregnable position and wonderful waters, it was the site of a governor's palace, which later became the favourite summer residence for Portuguese kings and queens (see Table of Kings and Queens of Portugal, p.215). Sintra has been associated with the crown since Portugal was established as a monarchy, and this has meant that not only grace and favours were bestowed upon its inhabitants but that the area around it became the fashionable residence of the aristocracy. Their *quintas* or country villas were embellished with rich ornamentation as overseas wealth enriched the upper classes as well as the crown. Chapels, cloisters, loggias and magnificent gardens were created out of rustic manor houses.

The changes that occurred in Sintra over the centuries

reflected the rich and varied blend of cultures – Phoenician,
Celtic, Roman, Germanic and Moorish – that characterises
the history of the Iberian Peninsula as a whole. This book sets
out to trace the way in which these cultural patterns changed
or added to the character of a place already notable for its
topography, climate and scenic splendour. On the one hand,
it is a story of palaces, castles and gardens, of ancient hermitages
and Gothic spires, but it is also an account of the different
aesthetic perceptions of Sintra, which has always been a
sanctuary for writers and artists. Its location, verdancy, rocky
heights and abundant streams have meant that Sintra has
been seen as almost Arcadian. But poets like Gil Vicente and
Byron and writers like William Beckford and Eça de Queirós
have invented the image of a terrestrial paradise. This story is
about the creation of an illusion as much as the history of an
actual *locale*.

For in truth, whoever intends to write a complete and impar-
tial history must first secure a long period of free time; next he
needs peace of mind and leave of all other activities, and finally
he must benefit from the favours of the most influential princes,
to encourage and reward his skills and research endeavours.

Damião de Góis

And Duarte Nunes, who was a poor pedant of a grammarian
without taste or imagination, went to work on a delicately carved
Gothic filigree and tracery of those monuments and shattered
them leaving only the historical facts, which amounted to little
and even then uncertain, and believed he had repaired a history,
when he had merely destroyed a poem.

Almeida Garrett

1

The Genius of the Place

High up on the dramatic promontory at the Cabo da Roca is
the very western end of the European continent, in the place
where Camões said the land ends and the sea begins. To one
side there is nothing to be seen but vast tracts of the Atlantic
which is at times flat across the horizon, but more often swells
in huge waves that roll unceasingly towards the land. The cliffs
rise steeply at the edge of the ocean, and even on calm days,
the water crashes against the rocks. The air is bracing and salty
to the taste, summer and winter alike. On the long coastline,
jagged promontories are battered by the relentless ocean and
the exposed rocks are twisted into mysterious shapes by the
pounding waves and by violent gusts of wind. Between the
jutting headlands are countless small coves, all but hidden from
view by the steep cliff tops, which are mainly inhabited by
large lizards and crabs. When the tide comes in, sandy beaches
are suddenly swallowed up by the torrent until the tide turns.
Water cascades over the cliffs and threatens the higher ground.
Through the spray, land appears and disappears, so that it is
impossible to make out what is real and what is imagined.
Often a sudden wind, presage of a storm, will whip up through
the boulders on the shore and tear at the moorland furze on
the barren headlands and the flinty, sloping hinterland beyond.
At other times, without warning, and even on a summer's
afternoon, a sea mist will rise and envelop the land, shrouding
trees and mounds in a mysterious haze.

It is not hard to imagine that here, in this isolated, primeval
place, prehistoric man chose to pay homage to his gods.

Everything around – the majesty of the ocean, as well as the bleakness of the terrain – inspires a sense of awe. This intuition is borne out by fact: traces of early man are found in markings on stones and rocks throughout the littoral area. However, it is at the rocky promontory – at the ancient *promunturium magnum* – that early man built his temple to the goddess of the moon, a shrine he erected in deference to the influence on his life of otherworldly powers. António Quadros tells us that the circle of stones found at the Cabo da Roca are in a familiar, lunar pattern.[1] The carefully placed pieces formed a temple to the Great Mother goddess of the moon, who was worshipped by a great number of ancient peoples, ranging in location from the Indian sub-continent to the Greek islands. The shrine was dedicated to a deity who represented womanhood, and above all fertility, through which the race was to be perpetuated.

Belief in the eternal mother, who was seen as the source of life as well as the protector of the young, was firmly established in the ideology of the ancient Iberians long before the cult of Cybele was formally introduced to Rome from Phrygia. Cybele, who embodied the power of nature, in the same way as the goddess of the Cape, was originally an Asiatic goddess. In Greek religious thought Cybele makes an appearance as Rhea, who personified the power of growth in the natural world. Indeed, she was hardly distinguishable from the earth itself (Ge).

The religions of this area greatly influenced one another during these long periods, and the close association that the Greeks made between the goddess and the earth could already be found in the religion of the early Iberians whose contact with Greek culture was established over many epochs. The Iberians took up the Greek tradition of building their temples in stone. At the principal shrine to Cybele, for instance, a sacred slab was central to all ceremonies, whilst at the Cape the lunar temple was a circular stone. Stone structures represent durability, a

---

1   A. Quadros, *Portugal: Razão e Mistério* (Lisbon, 1999) p.27.

permanence that will preserve the goddess's shrine indefinitely.

The symbol of a powerful, protective female figure, of the goddess' type, was to assume universal importance in Mediterranean culture, becoming idolised in pagan rites throughout the region. Eventually the image would be transformed, in the Catholic creed, to that of the Virgin Mary where, as the embodiment of purity and as the Mother of God, she became the object of widespread adoration.

Specially anointed priests would have performed sacrifices to the female lunar deity on the windswept Cape in Sintra. In the rituals and libations that took place, they were assisted by acolytes who were learning the rites of the priesthood which, in their turn, they would practise on the same promontory. The goddess the ancients of Sintra worshipped was Kinthia or Cynthia, whose name was derived from Cynthos, a mountain on the sacred island of Delos, the birthplace of the gods. This was the Greek Artemis or Roman Diana, goddess of the moon and of hunting, sister of Apollo, and god of light. From the word Cynthia came Chentra and finally Cintra, linking the *locale* inextricably to the deity.[2] Here, at the edge of the ocean,

---

2 We are told in Gabriel de Castro's epic poem, *Ulisseia ou Lisboa Edificada* (Lisbon, 1636), that 'from the celebrated Cynthia, Sintra took its name'. Canto V (ed. J.A. Segurado e Campos) (Lisbon, 2000) vol. 1 p.366. A considerable modern, scholarly literature has been written about the etymology of the word 'Sintra'. See E. Paxeco, 'Adraga, Alvidrar, Fojo, Sintra: Tentativa Justificatória de Etimologia' *Revista de Portugal, Serie A: Língua Portuguesa* vol XIV (Lisbon, 1949) where she traces the evolution of the names 'Selenitria-Seenitria-Sentria-Sintria'. For a discussion of various derivations in which the Arabic version 'Xentra' is mentioned, see E. Estrela *Sintra, nossa terra nossa gente* (Lisbon, 1997) p.159. C. Picard uses the form 'Shintara' in *Le Portugal Musulman (VIII–XII siècle)* (Paris, 2000), *passim*. E. Amarante says that 'Sin' is the Hebrew word for moon while 'tra' is an old Lusitanian word meaning three goddesses, including the goddess of the Moon. E. Amarante, *Portugal Simbólico* (Lisbon, 1999) p.117. A different derivation is that the name comes from 'Suntria', the first syllable of which is the Indo-European word for the sun. See J. Rodil, *Serra, Luas e literatura* (Sintra, 1995) p.16 and 'Sintra e a sua História' in *Sintra Património da Humanidade* (ed. J. Cardim Ribeiro) (Sintra, 1998) p.11. The spelling 'Cintra' was used in the eighteenth and nineteenth centuries and is associated with the Romantics and with English visitors. The letter 'C' is said to be a reminder of the Moorish crescent moon still to be found in the town's coat of arms. See Illustration 17.

her worship began in an appropriately Lusitanian setting, starting a long and unbroken association between the Portuguese people and the sea.

At the Cape, as at the jutting land of Espichel and Sagres to the south, we find communities which shared the same isolated background as those that inhabited other periphery areas of the continent, whether in Brittany or in the British Isles. From earliest times, their livelihood depended on the sea; mastering it was a test of survival. The funerary mounds or mausoleums of these Megalithic men, left as testimonials, are scattered over the whole region. Their piety is demonstrated in the votary relics found near these monuments, which signify a deep concern with the after life.

The lunar observations of the early Iberians were matched by an interest in solar eclipses – sun and moon formed a duality, and were the points of reference of the old eschatology. Apollo, god of the sun, balanced the luminous, feminine Artemis, his sister, with a masculine energy and virility. From the sun came warmth upon which life depended, while the moon was thought to impart a serenity that turned man into a cultural being, concerned with interpreting his existence and with creating images. Nevertheless, there was no simple distribution of qualities between the sexes. Artemis's pre-eminence was guaranteed by the fact that she had been born first and had even assisted at Apollo's birth. She could herself be a ferocious huntress, as much at home among the wild beasts as among men.

Prehistoric man struggled to reconcile the forces of solar and lunar energy; the duality they represented provided a dynamic in religious thought, which persisted throughout the pagan eras. The Celtic tribes, successors to the earliest inhabitants of the coastal areas, sought the same equilibrium in their worship of heavenly bodies. By the Middle Ages the sun and moon formed part of the element of fire, which had to be balanced by those of land, sea and wind. The last three elements are also present in the Sintra landscape.

Most of what we know about prehistoric Sintra is based on the accounts of the ancient Greek and Roman classical writers. The earliest reference to Sintra is made in Marcus Terentius Varro, who, according to Quintilian, was the most learned of the Romans, and who, as well as being a geographer, antiquarian and grammarian, was a poet, satirist and jurist. A patrician intellectual, Varro was at first an opponent of Julius Caesar. In the civil war, he fought on Pompey's side, serving for a time in Spain where he gained first hand knowledge of Iberian customs. Later, he was reconciled to Caesar and, appropriately for a man who wrote voluminously, was put in charge of the public libraries of Rome. His sardonic use of Menippean satire shows a distinct penchant for the satirical but Varro was also seriously interested in education and religion. Although he himself was a monotheist, believing that Jupiter was the source of all godliness, he nevertheless took a great deal of interest in the cultural development of religions. It is not surprising to find him talking about the *Mons Lunae*, the sacred Mount of Sintra where the ancient practices of moon worship had been performed since time immemorial.[1]

Varro's comments about Sintra and its earliest inhabitants are echoed by Pliny the Elder who, as procurator, had also seen public service in Spain as well as in other parts of the Empire. Pliny was a man of great curiosity and knowledge who devoted his considerable energy to works of ambitious scholarship. His *Naturalis Historia,* written in the first century AD, is a work of vast erudition in thirty-seven volumes. Its encylopaedic breadth encompasses surveys of philosophy, physics, the physiology of man, medicine and zoology. Indeed, it is an attempt to consider all that was known in his time, including subjects such as geography and the ethnology of Europe. Pliny travelled throughout Iberia in the course of performing his proconsular duties, gaining a detailed

---

1   Strabo, the Greek geographer (c. 64 BC–AD 19) calls Sintra 'hierna' linked to the Greek word 'hieros', meaning sacred. See J. Rodil, op. cit. p.9.

knowledge of the provinces of Baetica and Lusitania.[1]
Nevertheless, his geography could still be shaky. It is not clear
whether the great promontory he discusses (sometimes called
Artabrum) is our Cape (in Sintra) or whether it is Espichel,
which is situated further south.[2] In any case he suggests it is in
the north-western edge of the peninsula, with Sagres, the
Sacred Promontory, in the south. Even so, Pliny understood
the significance of finding ancient communities living at the
very periphery of Europe. He was an admirer of nature and a
believer in a beneficent deity, such as would have been
worshipped by early man at the Cape. He also included some
of the local myths of Sintra in his account.[3]

A century later the Alexandrine astronomer, Ptolemy,
refers to Sintra. Ptolemy developed a theory of the relative
movement of the sun, moon and planets around a static earth.
According to his geometrical theory, the motions of the
heavenly bodies are uniform or circular, or compounded of
circular motions, and spheres on which the planets are fixed
move as a whole. Ptolemy's astronomy, so lacking the sense
of force, a concept vital to modern physics, remained, with
some modification, standard scientific orthodoxy until the
time of Copernicus and Kepler. It is Ptolemy's system of
concentric spheres, which the nymph Tethys explains to
Vasco da Gama in the tenth canto of the *Lusiads* (1572). Best
of all spheres is the first, the Empyrean, from which a dazzling
light emits. In this radiant circle live the gods and the one, all-
powerful god who works in the world through his agents.

Ptolemy also wrote his *Geography,* which included a record

---

1   Livermore reminds us that the Roman province of Lusitania corresponds
neither to the tribal territory of the Lusitanians nor to the boundaries of modern
Portugal. H.V. Livermore, *Portugal: A Short History* (Edinburgh, 1973) p.4.
2   For a discussion of which promontory Pliny meant, see A. Guerra, *Plínio-o-
Velho e A Lusitânia* (Lisbon, 1995) p.86.
3   The 'sacred mount' is also referred to by Lucius Junius Moderatus Columella,
a contemporary of Pliny's who was born in Cadiz and who wrote the twelve-
volume *De Re Rustica*, praising cultivation, fish ponds, bees and gardens among
other things.

of all the principal places in the world as it was then known, including a promontory at the most westerly point of the European continent which may have been the Cape in Sintra.[1] He gave out the extravagant theory that the Cape once stretched far out into the Atlantic, as far as Madeira. When eventually Madeira was cut off by the ocean, he suggests, a substantial island, called Londobris, was formed off the coast, facing the promontory. This island, however, could not have consisted of the mere rocks that stretch outward from the Cape, known as the muzzle or snout (Focinho). Might Ptolemy have been mistaken in the location and instead have been referring to the island of Berlenga, off the Cape of Carvoeiro, much further north on the coast?

Whether or not this is the case, the theory of the extended headland is somewhat fanciful, reminding us of the enduring myth of blessed islands which has underpinned many reactions to Sintra. The myth centres on a combination of temperate climate, fertile soil, and plentiful food, which offers men the chance to exist in a peaceable, golden age. There were once thought to be at least ten of these islands, of which the three largest were dedicated to Pluto, Jupiter and Neptune. The islands were said to be inhabited by the descendants of the giants who lived in the legendary city of Atlantis, long sunk beneath the ocean waves. In Ptolemy's colourful account, the Lusitanians fled to the island of Londobris during their struggle against the Roman invaders. When the Romans laid siege to the island and landed there, a fierce battle ensued in which the indigenous people beat off the foreigners. Whether this was the occasion when the local leader, Viriatus, organised the resistance to the Romans, is not clear.

Classical myths of this sort became an important part of the associations surrounding the Cape, and the cosmopolitan Portuguese writers of the sixteenth century took them up

---

1   According to J.S. Ruth, Ptolemy was talking about Cabo Espichel (also known as Barbarum) not the Cabo da Roca. See *Lisbon in the Renaissance* (New York, 1996) p.44 n.30.

enthusiastically.[1] One of the most colourful of the Renaissance stories which were based on the myths comes from the pen of João de Barros who, in the humanist way, was also a historian and moralist. In his *Crónica do Imperador Clarimundo* (1522) the knightly hero, Clarimundo, defeats the nefarious giant Morbanfo, whose lair is the castle of Colir (Colares?). Morbanfo is a frightening character, addicted to sacrificing victims, and his death releases the whole area from a reign of terror. Clarimundo climbs to the summit of the *serra* with the wise Fanimor and there, bathed in the magical moonlight, proclaims the future of Portugal in epic verse. By now he is dressed for the part, in priestly robe and gown and, as he speaks, his own stature seems to assume the gigantic. There is no more melodramatic scene in Sintrense legend.

Shortly after João de Barros' outpouring, Gil Vicente, whose plays were performed in the royal palace at Sintra when the Court sat there, eulogised Sintra's Arcadian charms with his evocation of a 'terrestrial paradise'[2] (see pp.133–5). He inspired many Arcadian accounts of Sintra, and the area now became regarded as a magical place inhabited by nymphs and fairies and other fantastical creatures. One of these nymphs, Lisibeia, is closely connected with the origin of the nation: Vicente claims that a knight, named Portugal, made the long journey from Hungary in search of her celebrated nude figure in the caves of the Cape. They were eventually united, and the nation is said to have sprung from that amorous partnership. Other spiritual beings roam the *serra* in *Symtra* (1566), the work of the Castilian poetess Luísa Sigea. She and her sister, Angela, were true bluestockings, learned in ancient as well as modern languages and very capable tutors of the younger royals whose education they supervised.

1   B. Malinowski calls myths the 'secret motors' of society. For an interesting discussion of the 'reality' of myths and their cultural significance, see E. Amarante, op. cit. pp.21ff.
2   G. Vicente, 'Triunfo do Inverno' *Obras Completas* (ed. M. Braga) (Lisbon, 1971) vol.4 p.326.

Another of Sintra's most influential artists was the painter, architect and designer, Francisco de Holanda. De Holanda, who had had a sound Latin and Greek education, returned to Portugal, after living for many years in Italy, full of enthusiasm for classical culture and antiquities. On his way to Rome, he visited important historical cities, being content to read Petrarch and Dante as his guides to Italian culture. Once installed in the Eternal City, he mixed with artists and craftsmen and became known to Michelangelo himself. The great man was impressed enough with the young *fidalgo* to present him with a work of his own and kept up a correspondence with de Holanda after he had returned to Portugal.

Francisco was the son of Antonio de Holanda, a Flemish heraldic adviser to the Court, who had come to Portugal at the beginning of the sixteenth century. The family's royal connection had served it well, for Francisco was brought up in the style of the aristocracy, disdaining any association with the artisans who formed the artistic classes of the time. His patron was the distinguished diplomat, Alvaro de Castro. As a young man de Holanda roamed the Sintra forests in the company of the young Prince Dom Luís. His own talents soon attracted the attention of the Court. He began to provide miniaturist portraits and jewellery designs for the royal family and became a favourite of King João III, who granted him a generous allowance. Familiar with Pliny's *Naturalis Historia*, de Holanda records visiting the promontory from his home in nearby Belas in his work entitled *Da fábrica que falece à cidade de Lisboa* (1571). He describes a small, Roman temple of circular construction built at the same place as the temple of the indigenous Iberians. It was colonnaded and on the stones were inscriptions of distinguished Romans who had visited the site, as well as tributes to the solar and lunar deities. De Holanda's account rings true, not least because we know that the description is given by a man who understands buildings as well as appreciating antiquities.

Among contemporary scholars of the period was the

notable historian, Damião de Góis who both studied and saw
diplomatic service in the north of Europe. He spent some time
in Louvain learning Latin and there he met Erasmus, in 1532.
Steeped in contemporary humanism, de Góis, in his account
of Sintra, is prepared to spice up what might otherwise seem
too dry a history by speculating on the motivation of its partic-
ipants. This is a far cry from the historian merely chronicling
such facts as he regards as historically important. However, de
Góis' account might have been recognised as the beginning of
modern history if he had been able to resist adding anecdotes
to it! He blames a local man for telling him the following,
fanciful story about the Cape: there was once a man fishing
off one of the shoreline coves who threw his catch backward
into a small pool for safekeeping. Deciding to check on his
gains, he was surprised to find the figure of a nude youth who
had clearly been throwing his fish back into the sea. When he
tried to seize hold of the young thief, the nubile figure slipped
off into the surf and was never seen again.

All these stories were gradually incorporated into the
mythology surrounding Sintra. However, the seal was set on
the area's legendary status by the great epic poet Luís Vaz de
Camões, in his stately *Lusiads*. The poem describes Vasco da
Gama's journey to India as a Homeric Odyssey. By the third
canto, we find da Gama at the court of the Sultan of Malindi.
The Portuguese explorer is explaining the geography and
history of Europe, and the Sultan is told that beyond the
Pyrenees from France lies 'noble' Iberia. At the far end of that
peninsula, crushed up against the sea, is the little kingdom of
Portugal, the Crown on Europe's head! The Sultan does not
hear much about the centuries of Moorish occupation from
one who is intent on glorifying the early history of his
Christian nation. Instead, Camões concentrates on the exploits
of Afonso Henriques, who was still waging the campaign to
capture large areas of the country from Moorish hands some
three hundred years after Oporto (Portucale) had been secured
for Christendom. The future King of Portugal won decisive

battles at Guimarães (1128) and at Ourique (1139). A decade later, he was in the area of the Tagus estuary; and in 1147 Lisbon itself fell to his army after a siege. Then, moving along the coast, the poet tells us:

> Near the ancient
> Promontory of the moon [the King] brought
> Cool Sintra under his mighty arm,
> Sintra, where every pool and stream
> Has nymphs in its waters,
> Fleeing in vain from Cupid's tender fires
> While the cold depths burn with their desires[1]

Local legends about the sea were embellished as they were passed on, through the oral tradition. Pliny is the first to mention the story about a Triton or sea nymph that lived in a rocky cave on the ocean's edge. When the sound of the waves crashing into the cave were loudest, local belief was that the Triton was singing and using his conch. So well established was this tale that at the time of Tiberius Caesar a delegation of local dignitaries went to Rome to inform the curious and superstitious Emperor of the Triton's existence. Not everything about this curious hybrid creature – a man with scales like a fish – was frightening. When in a good humour, the Triton came ashore and played on the beach, eating fruit and talking to the natives. No less an authority than a distinguished Coimbra scholar and theologian, Frei Amador Arrais reports upon the domesticity of the Triton in his *Diálogos* (1589). By contrast, when the otherwise amiable creature was in pain, his moaning and groaning was heard along the whole length of the littoral.

The Triton was not thought to be the only inhabitant of this mythically populous coast. Mermaids and mermen were constantly sighted off the shore. Might they have come from the many fabled islands said to be lying far out in the ocean

---

1   L.V. de Camões, *The Lusiads* (trans L. White) (Oxford, 1977) p.59.

and peopled with descendants of the lost Atlantis, who were enjoying the benefits of a utopian existence? Another local story suggests that the caverns below the cliffs near the Cape are so deep that they go below the level of the sea. The sea-gulls screeching about by day and night were said to be spirits who, in their birdlike form, were allowed to revisit the earth but were, in fact, the souls of men. Their shrieks, mingled with the roar of the surf and the voices of demons coming from below, were piercing laments about the crimes and sins they had committed in human form.[1]

Further up the coast, past the strange bear-shaped rocks of Ursa is the ominously named Pedra de Alvidrar, the Rock of Judgement, which is so steep that no one could put a safe foot on it without risk to life and limb. To the north of that, off the peninsula of Peniche, sirens were heard singing in the swell. Fishermen returning from their nightly expeditions, reported evidence of weird monsters, the women of the sea (*mulheres marinhas*). But they were coy about specifying the women's particular, aquatic charms.

These fabulous tales were too good to be missed by Sintra artists of later ages: elements from both legends and historical facts are reflected in many decorative and architectural features in the palaces of Sintra.

The landscape of Sintra has greatly influenced the types of myth which have evolved around it. It has often been observed that the Sintra range seems to erupt from the coastline, giving the impression with its lofty peaks, which are often covered in mist, of being a quite separate, more northerly part of the country. The range's proximity to the ocean, and so to the humidity that comes off it, decisively influences the types of vegetation that can grow; but human interference in the form of afforestation in the nineteenth century softened the natural ruggedness of the landscape. The hinterland – known as the *terra saloia* – is a complex mixture of different geographical

---

1 Catherine Charlotte, Lady Jackson, *Fair Lusitania* (London, 1874) pp.209ff.

terrain as J. de Oliveira Boléo has shown in drawing up his comprehensive typologies.[1]

There are six types of relief. The mountain uplands (land over 500 metres high, with the highest point at Cruz Alta, 529 metres) are made up of different sorts of granite though various strains of marble (blue, rose and black) are also found in the rock. Below these ridges are hills, quite verdant in parts, with thicket and bush. Then come the flat plains, which have been desiccated by erosion. The moorland, with hardy furzes and alfalfa above the cliffs of the Cape, is a different type of terrain. In the valleys there is a wide variety of the fauna and flora for which Sintra is famous: this includes myrtle, cistus, rosemary, wild carnation, mimosa as well as the arbutus and luscious strawberry fruit. Finally there is the fertile meadowland where every kind of fruit can grow and where the vine is abundant.

Part of the mountain upland, or *serra*, consists of limestone and of hard granite, which is exposed all around as huge boulders. The majesty of these great rocks has long inspired visitors to the area.[2] Here the wind howls around the crevices and it is not yet sheltered enough for woodland growth. The rocks, strewn wildly around, show evidence of volcanic eruption. A series of seismic fault lines run across the area, the greatest in a northeasterly direction from the Focinho or 'muzzle' of the Cape. This is earthquake territory: at any time the earth may tremble. Records of minor quakes have been recorded throughout the history of Sintra and from time to time, there has been a more serious shaking. In 1356 and in 1531 there were earthquakes of sufficient strength to cause widespread damage. The earthquake that destroyed a great part of Lisbon in 1755 shook Sintra as well.

High up among the moss-covered peaks, hermits found ideal retreats. Isolated and remote, such places provided exhil-

1   J. de Oliveira Boléo, *Sintra e seu Termo* (Estudo Geográfico) (Sintra, 1973) p.39.
2   See *Arquivo Histórico de Sintra* (ed. J.M. da Silva Marques) 34 vols. (Sintra) (henceforth abbreviated as *AHS*), vol 8 p.19. Also see below p.73 n.1.

aration for those of spiritual tendencies. One such favoured site is situated at Peninha, at the western end of the Sintra range, with sweeping views of the ocean in one direction and the northward littoral in the other.

In 1673 the hermit Pedro de Conceição built a chapel on this prominence. There are several possible reasons for his choice: it was said to be situated on the exact spot where, according to one legend, a mute shepherdess was cured after seeing an apparition of a beautiful spirit, which was later taken to be the Virgin Mary. In another account, the shepherdess was searching for a stray sheep. Tired and distraught, she sank to rest when a beautiful young lady appeared before her, asking her why she wept. The shepherdess explained that she was exhausted from lack of food, for the crop of wheat had failed again causing severe famine. The beautiful lady told her to return home where she would find six loaves of bread in the larder. The loaves were found in exactly the place described. A search party which subsequently looked for the young lady found only images of the Virgin's face in the rocks.

In yet another version, sailors struggling to get ashore in a storm are supposed to have vowed to build a chapel if they survived. Maritime decorations in the interior of the building give credence to this seafarer's tale. But other variations about the origin of the place are also told – in one account, a miraculous fountain is said to have marked the spot where the monastery was built; while in another account, Peninha is considered to be part of a range of seven 'sisters' of the mountain. Combinations of these myths are told of other Marian shrines throughout the country.

The blue and white *azulejos* were fixed in the chapel at Peninha in 1711, whilst the retable is baroque and Florentine marble has been used on the walls. A small complex of simple buildings was added to the chapel to accommodate pilgrims who came to visit what had become a major Marian shrine. Inscriptions of their names are forlornly conserved for posterity. In 1781 the hermitage became Crown property since, unsurprisingly for an ascetic, Pedro de Conceição had failed to ensure its proper succession to his heirs. Peninha stands, looking like a fortress with battlements, grim in its grey, stark stone, with only hardy trees, bent by the wind, clinging to its edges. There is nothing there to distract attention from spiritual contemplation; even the sea in the distance looks false and surreal.

At the next, wooded solitude in the hills, Byron tells:

> Deep in yon cave Honorius long did dwell,
> In hope to merit Heaven by making earth a Hell.[1]

The cave of St Honorius, where he led his ascetic, isolated life, is set in a dell under the mountain ridge. Nearby is a monastic building, founded in 1560 by Dom Alvaro de Castro, (a diplomat and soldier), on the instructions of his illustrious father, Dom João de Castro, Viceroy of India. The Viceroy was, besides being a soldier and statesman, a scholar of no mean distinction, an historian and chronicler, and certainly another candidate for the accolade of 'last of the Romans'. He served with distinction in Tunis as a young man and in India, braving life and limb in service of the Portuguese Crown. When money for the expedition to the enclave of Diu was lacking, he gallantly offered his beard as guarantee against the advances made by the merchants of Goa. It was his heroic relief of Diu that gained him the vice-regal title. After these great adventures, he retired, in Horatian manner, to his modest plot in the Sintra hills granted to him by King João III. There he built a chapel dedicated to Our Lady of the Mountain. Later he added an unpretentious house at Penha Verde, an early example of the *villa rustica* (see p.105). In that idyllic surrounding he put the finishing touches to his famous travel accounts (*Roteiros*)

---

1   There is some confusion of location in Byron's account since Honorius' cave is described as being near 'Our Lady's house of woe' by which he meant Pena. Lord George Byron, *Poetical Works* (Oxford, 1945) p.184. Also see p.178 n.1.

of his first eastward voyage of 1536 which added so considerably to the geographical knowledge of the times.

Meanwhile, at his behest, Cork Convent, so named on account of the indigenous material used in its construction, was established for the Franciscan monks of Arrábida. Monks of the order, whose main duty was to console and help the poor, wore a habit or *capucha* from which was derived the more popular name of the convent, the Capuchos. Dom João's penchant for simplicity was well respected in the architecture of the buildings, as well as in the maintenance of the forest trees he loved. It was intended that the Convent should retain the feeling of a hermitage. Twelve, tiny, dank cells are cut out of the rock, which hangs in a low ledge. Each cell is sparse, containing little more in the way of furnishing than a bench. Indeed, the whole building is cut out of the rock, which still forms its roofing and gives the place a bleak aspect. Inside, on the ceilings, walls, and doors, cork is extensively used, softening the severity of the stone and providing insulation from extremes of climate. Time and inclement weather have damaged these surfaces; much of the cork has decayed, leaving bare, stark stonework. No wonder King Filipe II, of the united kingdom of Spain and Portugal said, on visiting Sintra in 1581, that Capuchos was the simplest monastery in the world. He admired its tranquillity and understood that a truly meditative life would be possible in its secluded surroundings.

Throughout the monastery, dark crosses adorn the walls. Even the eighteenth-century ceramics show gloomy preoccupations: Christ being flagellated; the crown of thorns; nails and mallet. There are penitential cells, images of saints being buried alive and a Capuchan monk being crucified; in fact everything to encourage those of a morbid disposition. Perhaps conscious of the overpowering effect that such images might have on the young novices, one or two softening touches were allowed. An elaborate altarpiece of three-coloured marble, in Renaissance style, decorates the chapel. Reassuring images of St Francis and St Anthony create a friendlier atmosphere in which a peaceful Virgin Mary slumbers between shells and *azulejos*. These familiar images might have helped calm the young novices who sat praying for the soul of Dom João, the illustrious patron of their order.

Grim though life at the Convent must have been, it seems that it was not severe enough for Honorius. In an account of her visit to Capuchos in the late nineteenth century, the redoubtable Lady Jackson relates the local story, which suggests Honorius' reason for moving to even more uncomfortable accomodation. One day, wandering in the Sintra hills, he encountered a young, comely girl who begged him to hear her confession at once. In refusing her, Honorius could not help noticing her nubile figure with a certain pleasure. Realising that she was Satan incarnate when she persisted in trying to win his attention, he invoked the power of prayer, whereupon the figure suddenly vanished. Despite his victory against temptation, Honorius believed that the presumably lustful glances he had conferred on the figure merited punishment. He decided to move out of the monastery and into the cave. Lady Jackson finds herself agreeing with the comment of her fellow traveller, a Frenchman, who finds this behaviour more foolish than saintly.[1]

Honorius was succeeded by another celebrated ascetic, Frei Agostinho da Cruz, in the late sixteenth century. He was the younger brother of the poet Diogo Bernades, one of the few survivors of King Sebastião's ill-fated expedition to Morocco who had sung the praises of Dom João de Castro in verse. Unlike his brother, Frei Agostinho was not a traveller. He arrived as a novice at Capuchos and, in all, stayed for a full forty years. Like Honorius, he also lived apart from the community, insisting that he could only achieve spiritual perfection by retreating entirely from communion with his fellow men. The Duke of Aveiro had a separate dwelling specially made for him. There, Frei Agostinho led the contem-

1 Catherine Charlotte, Lady Jackson. op. cit. p.203.

plative life and wrote his sonnets, elegies and eclogues on the passion and humanity of Christ and on other religious themes, including accounts of local legends and miracles. In some pieces he transforms the shepherd of the flock, the pastor, into a fisherman. This transformation was a spiritual symbol well suited to the Portuguese, whose seafaring experiences affected the thoughts of the lonely hermits who inhabited the Sintra hills. Frei Agostinho was no literary hack: his taste for contrasts and hyperbole links his style to the mannerism of the great Camões who, it has been suggested, may have read verses from his *Lusiads* to King Sebastião here at the Capuchos and not at the Royal Palace in Sintra itself.[1] At any rate the King, contemplating future glory, seemed inspired by the silent, austere beauty of Capuchos, which is shrouded in mist on many days of the year. The Convent survived down the centuries as a refuge for those seeking the contemplative life until the monasteries were closed in 1834.

Myths of sea and mountain give way to no less persuasive myths of gardens and valleys of fruits as one moves on towards Colares, which is sunk to the west of the *serra*, amid the hills. Camões' spirit hovers over the area. Was it an Adamastor-like creature that is supposed to have been chained up here with collars, hence the etymology of the name according to the poets?[2] One legend is that no less a personage than the god-like Heracles sought out and slaughtered a great ogre that lived in a nearby cavern. The local inhabitants, overjoyed that the terror of their lives was removed at a stroke, tied up its great corpse in hefty chains and dragged it away. A different story tells of the landing of a German princess who fell in love with the area and sought land rights from the Moorish ruler of

---

1   V.M.L. Pereira Neves, *O Convento dos Capuchos* (Sintra, 1997) p.110. After years of closure, Capuchos has recently been reopened.
2   E. Estrela considers the possible derivation of the name Colares from the word 'colinas' (hills). See E. Estrela, op. cit. p.123. Also see M.T. Caetano (*Colares*, Sintra, 2000, p.23), who says the name comes from 'Alaga Mares' or Galamers, a small village on the banks of the river. op. cit. p.23.

Lisbon, which she was granted in exchange for three gold necklaces (*colares*), the price which she had to pay for her estate.

Another legend about Heracles is based in Colares. In his eleventh labour, the god confronts the hundred-headed dragon, Ladon, who helps the 'daughters of the evening' to guard Hera's golden apples in the far-off Atlas Mountains. Heracles only gets the apples by tricking the god Atlas into helping him. William Beckford, wealthiest of the English grand tourists who came to Portugal and left descriptions of court life and of natural landscapes, feasting on golden apples in the Quinta Mazziotti in Colares remembers the legend and recounts it in his journal:

> The scenery is truly Elysian, and worthy to be the lounge of happy souls. The mossy fragments, grotesque pollards [and] rustic bridges, which occur at every step, remind me of Savoy and Switzerland. But the vivid green of the citron, the golden fruitage of the orange, the blossoming myrtle and the rich fragrance of the turf, embroidered with aromatic flowers allow me without a violent stretch of fancy to believe myself in the garden of Hesperides, and to expect the dragon under every tree.[1]

There is another connection with the Hesperidean myth that the learned Beckford does not make. Once the dragon Ladon was slain, he was transformed into the sky as the constellation of the serpent, a creature highly symbolic of the Portuguese nation from earliest times. It was the serpent's thirst for knowledge that the Portuguese identified with the impulse that drove the explorers to make the great overseas voyages of discovery. Sometimes regarded as a symbol of occult knowledge, the serpent has also been identified with the Sintra hills, which have appeared to those of poetical imagination to take the shape of a snake. Lying along the littoral, the serpent's

---

1 *The Journal of William Beckford in Portugal and Spain 1787–1788* (ed. B. Alexander) (London, 1954) p.237.

mouth is said to spit into the sea at the Praia das Maçãs.[1]

Beckford may have missed the associations Sintra has with serpents, but he did not fail to describe its Elysian charms. In the rich meadows and orchards of Colares he notes lemon as well as orange, bay and walnut trees. The noble vine has been cultivated since the time of Catullus' much-loved Falernian.[2] Apples are not the only golden fruit: there are golden plums and fragrant apricots as well. Flowers of every type abound, including carnation and jasmine in profusion and camellias of every hue. When the bountiful trees – oak, chestnut and cypress – are added to this, they create the perfect blend of orchard and woodland that was the Horatian idyll. In Horace's rustic settings, Roman heroes who had served the state passed useful days. The poet's description of them could easily fit a description of the brave João de Castro:

> They were a hardy generation, good
> Farmers and warriors brought to turn
> The Sabine furrows with their hoes, chop wood.
> And lug the faggots home to please a stern
> Mother at evening…[3]

The abundance of Colares is a Mediterranean abundance, found in fertile and well-watered land which is protected from inclement weather. It is not typical of the battered, bare soil of periphery peninsulas, where the early Iberians and Celts struggled to survive. Rather, Colares resembles the rich, generous lands of Tuscany. Joseph Barretti noticed this similarity with Italian landscape when he was on his tour of Spain and Portugal in the eighteenth century. His opinion is echoed, much later, in Sacheverell Sitwell's descriptions of Sintra. Sitwell suggests that the illusion of being in Italy is

---

1 J. Rodil *Serra, Luas e literatura* (Sintra, 1995) pp.7 & 119.
2 Eça de Queirós' characters often yearn for Ramisco, a Colares wine, regarding it as superior to any French import.
3 *The Odes of Horace* (trans. J. Michie) (London, 1964) p.165.

compounded by the appearance of charming villas tucked
away in the folds of the hills, with their cascading gardens and
running streams. There are 'languishing' views in every direction. Although he does not like every feature of local building
(Pena Palace, in particular, upsets his sense of architectural
purity) Sitwell acknowledges that the mixture of the natural
and the manmade provides, in Sintra, an ideal setting for the
creation of myth.[1]

1   J. Barretti, *Journey from London to Genoa* (intro. I. Robertson) (London, 1970)
p.179 and S. Sitwell, *Portugal and Madeira* (London, 1954) pp.101–2.

2

Caves, Celts, Romans and Suevi

The abundant valley of Colares has attracted human habitation since the earliest times but the exact sequence of its
ancient history is obscure. That prehistoric man settled here is
not in doubt – stones and other relics prove a long pre-history.
Nevertheless, the exact antiquity of the human occupation of
the Sintra area and, indeed, the rest of Portugal, is not easy to
establish. Archaeologists suggest that the western part of the
Iberian Peninsula may already have been inhabited in the
Paleolithic Age, as far back as 200,000 years ago, and perhaps
even in the time of *Homo erectus*, a million years ago, when
man moved from Africa to the hitherto deserted European
continent.

Definitive evidence of habitation, however, takes us back
to a much more recent period, between about 30,000 and
20,000 years ago. At the Coa Valley in north central Portugal
remains dating from about 25,000 years ago have been
unearthed though occupation might have gone back much
further into the Paleolithic Age. What has been specifically
dated, over an extensive area of seventeen kilometres of the
valley, suggests we are dealing with the Stone Age man who
subsisted as a hunter throughout the region of south-western
Europe. It is the period of cave culture when man, still
primarily a hunter, began to become an artist as well by
engraving images of the animals he hunted – bulls, bison, wild
boar, horse and stag – on the walls of his cave. Evidence of
these cave-dwellers spreads across an extensive area, which

includes France (Lascaux)[1] and the whole of the Iberian Peninsula.

Discoveries in the Tagus region suggest a similar dating although communities in the north and south of the country probably had little direct contact with one another. At the cave of Escoural (across the river from Lisbon at Montemor-O-Novo in the Alentejo) the evidence suggests occupation between 20,000 and 10,000 years ago. The types of decoration on the cave wall – which include up to fourteen pictures and three engravings, as well as other less clear markings – follow the general pattern of prehistoric cave drawings. But though the familiar animals are represented, there are also curious, hybrid creatures which have the bodies of men but the heads of horses or birds. Near to Escoural a small ceramic figure, probably a deity, which has been dated to about 17,000 years ago, has also been discovered. All this evidence suggests a culture of growing sophistication in which man was trying to interpret, as well as to understand, his environment and the forces that control it.

Closer to the Sintra area, remains have been dated to a more recent period, between the Megalithic and the Neolithic periods, around 5,500 years ago, though recent discoveries at Torres Vedras suggest an older dating (of 7,000 years ago). This was the time when man had left his solitary condition, that stage of society, which Rousseau was later to idealise as the benign 'state of nature'. Communities, in which members had rights to property, were beginning to form. Agriculture, hitherto hardly practised, was becoming a significant factor in survival. Metallurgy was making new instruments available, encouraging specialisation in different kinds of work. Religion played a significant role in the social evolution of these early societies. Evidence suggests that it often took the form of the

---

1   There has been a recent, spectacular discovery of prehistoric engravings, including images of bison, horses, rhinocerous and men in a cave at Périgueux dating from the same period.

cult of the Great Mother goddess because she symbolised fertility and the survival of society itself.

Fertile areas like Sintra, with easily worked volcanic soil and plentiful water supplies, were attractive to these early settlers, as has been shown by Alves Pereira, who followed in the footsteps of the great nineteenth-century archaeologist, Carlos Ribeiro, making detailed investigations of the remains scattered across the Sintra hills and valleys. He was particularly interested in the age of the stones and implements found near Santa Eufémia and Monte Sereno, to the east of the town of Sintra. The ceramic pieces he inspected at Santa Eufémia were cruder than those found at Monte Sereno. At the latter site, the implements included polished stone heads and blades cut from the local granite. Alves Pereira suggests that these more ornate pieces were not used for hunting or farming but instead served a votive purpose (see Illustration 1). He considers from his comparison of the two sites that the one at Santa Eufémia is the older. Indeed, on the basis of his evidence, he concludes that Santa Eufémia is the 'cradle' or the very origin of human habitation in Sintra.[1] In the 1970s Gustavo Marques continued Alves Pereira's exploration of the site, which had been started fifty years before. Marques did his own fieldwork: as well as examining the evidence of material on the surface, he dug a trench so that he could examine the substrata. He generally concurred with Alves Pereira's view that the site had been first settled in Neolithic times. Evidence of pottery and glass beads from the Eastern Mediterranean led him to the conclusion that there was already an eclectic cultural mix between 400 and 300 BC. He also found plenty of evidence of Roman remains.[2]

The rocks, which have been found in the valley of Colares, bear curious, elongated inscriptions, in some cases with diamond shaped crosses, circles or spirals which suggest they

1   F. Alves Pereira, *Sintra do Pretérito* (Sintra, 1957) pp.9–28.
2   See Gustavo Marques, 'Aspectos da Proto-História do Território Português. II Povoado da Santa Eufémia (Sintra)' in *Sintria I–II tomo I 1982–1983* (Mem Martins, 1984–87) pp.59–88.

were not for utilitarian but religious use. The markings, which may be a primitive form of writing, can be related to the long-established worship of sun and moon (see Chapter 1, p.6), indicating a growing sophistication in the local culture. At nearby Monserrate, similar prehistoric remains have been discovered, suggesting a deep intuition on William Beckford's part when he raised his 'primitive' cromlech or pile of unhewn stones in its grounds.

Evidence of Neolithic settlement throughout the area is confirmed by the existence of menhirs or large stone blocks set in upright positions. In more elaborate structures these blocks were brought together in dolmens. The dolmens consisted of tables or holes of stones, similar to those found in other parts of Portugal, such as the Alentejo, or abroad in Cornwall and other parts of the west of England. The blocks are poised on two supporting points, carving out an entrance space below. The dolmens serve as burial mounds, where the dead were laid to rest with proper respect to the gods. Each soul needed its own tumulus; rites of burial had to be carefully observed lest disturbed spirits of the dead returned to haunt the living. In their tombs, the dead are surrounded by their worldly possessions, indicating a belief in the continuity between life and the after-life, when the soul was journeying back to mother–earth. This passage of the soul back to earth was a version of the idea of the *regressum ad uterum*. The stone structures were the temples of an elaborate religion, common to a vast region which extended from the Near East to the Iberian Peninsula and which may have begun in either of these geographical areas.

In some cases the structures were of considerable size. At Capuchos the 'dolmen of the monk' consists of building on a significant scale. Here the central mausoleum or interior vestibule has been surrounded by walls and crowned by a cupola, possibly covered to provide greater protection against the elements. The circular enclosure, which is reminiscent of the circular temple at the Cabo da Roca, is once more the focal point of worship. The tripartite division of the structure is found again at the site of the tholos at the Praia das Maçãs. This has been identified as a considerable necropolis. The tholos faces the sea and acts as a barrier against the waves. In the structure of the mound, which is dug out of the rock as an artificial cave we find tumulus, false cupola and a long corridor. J.L. Marques Gonçalves adds that in addition to the early Neolithic structure, considerable remains in the forms of artefacts have been discovered, including engraved plates, fluted ware and idol figures and bell-beaker pottery. These ceramic and metal objects indicate occupation over a long period.[1]

Metal remnants suggest subsequent habitation in a later era, the Bronze Age. Implements such as axes and primitive chisels have been found in the valley of São Martinho, to the north of Sintra town. This is another city of the dead, another area of mausoleums, a necropolis stretching out over a large area. In the mounds where corpses were interred, implements for use in the after-life are also found. Not only does this indicate a belief in life after death, but more specifically, it shows that life and death were considered as a continuous process. Men would have the same needs and pleasures in the next life and would therefore need the implements they had used in the earthly one. The necropolis is also a sign of the growing importance of individuals; the grander graves in it are symbolic of the privileges which warlords and other leaders could by this stage claim over lesser members of the community.

Another important Neolithic site has been found at Catrivana, further north, near the Samarra creek. The artefacts uncovered there have included flints and polished stones, indicating a date of about 3,500 BC. At Terrugem, slightly to the south, a group of archaeologists have discovered a dolmen, which has been called the Pedra Erguidas. In the various levels

---

1 See J.L. Marques Gonçalves, 'Monumento pre-histórico da Praia das Maçãs (Sintra) Notícia Preliminar' in *Sintria I–II Tomo I 1982–1983* (Mem Martins, 1984–7) pp.29–58.

or strata which have been exposed, remains of prehistoric cultures have been identified. Nevertheless, a certain caution is needed in coming to conclusions about unusual rock formations. Alves Pereira sets out, with a discernible glee, to debunk one famous prehistoric myth. Near the lighthouse at the Cabo da Roca stands a huge monolithic pile of stones, known as the Adrenunes. In the nineteenth century many scholars spent a great deal of time in trying to determine when this dolmen was erected and in investigating its exact purpose. Learned tomes by leading archaeologists, antiquarians and other local luminaries began to fill the shelves. Subsequently, however, careful geological investigation has shown it to be a natural rock, not a man-made structure at all.

It is clear, however, that by the time of the Bronze Age, a plethora of tribes occupied the area that became Roman Lusitania. Oliveira Marques suggests that this was a period of violent conflict when invaders – Lusitanian, Carthaginian and Greek – added to the turmoil of the fighting that was already taking place among the local Iberian tribes.[1] Knowledge of this time is still sketchy but it can be dated from about 1,000 BC. Celtic influence was strongest in the north but would have permeated the south as well, a fact already noted by Pliny. The Celts were skilled in iron and gold work; they brought considerable sophistication to the ancient indigenous worship of the solar and lunar deities. Their *castros* or hilltop settlements were scattered throughout the territory. Sometimes, as in the Sintra area, they were built on the sites of already existing, prehistoric structures. In turn the Romans and then the Moors built upon the same fortress sites.

Greek and Phoenician communities were clustered around the coastal areas, with considerable agriculture in the hinterland. They brought with them a culture of the sea and a new cosmopolitanism, based on extensive trading links. Strabo in

---

1   A.H. de Oliveira Marques, *História de Portugal* 3 vols (Lisbon, 1984) vol. I p.16.

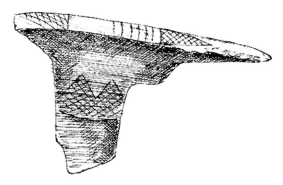

Fig. 17 — *Enxó votiva do Vale de S. Martinho*

1. Prehistoric Votive Offerings in São Martinho Valley.
Drawing, F. Alves Pereira, Sintra 1957.

L·AELIVS·L·F·GA·L·AELIANVS·H·S·E
L·AELIVS·SEX·F·GL·SENECA·PATER·H·S·E
CASSIA·Q·F·QVINTILIA·MATER·H·S·E
L·IVLIVS·L·F·GA·L·AELIANVS·ANN·XIIII·H·S·E
L·IVLIVS·L·F·GIVLIANVS·AN·XX·V·H·S·E
AELIA L·F AMOENA   H·S·E

2. Inscription on a Roman tombstone in the Museum of
São Miguel de Odrinhas.
Inscribed by F. Alves Pereira, Sintra 1957.

3. General view of Sintra with Royal Palace (Paço Real), 1829.
Lithograph by D. Schiopetta. Sintra, Historical Archive, Municipal Archive.

4. View of Royal Palace (from the south) 1507.

Engraving by Duarte d'Armas, *Book of Fortresses*, 1510. Sintra, Historical Archive, Municipal Archive.

5. View of Royal Palace (from the south-east), 1507.
Engraving by Duarte d'Armas, *Book of Fortresses*, 1510. Sintra, Historical Archive, Municipal Archive.

6. View of Royal Palace (from the west), 1507.

Engraving by Duarte d'Armas, *Book of Fortresses*, 1510. Sintra, Historical Archive, Municipal Archive.

1325 – Cintra – Portugal

Convento dos Capuchos

7. Cork Convent (Covento dos Capuchos), c.1950.
Photograph. Sintra, Historical Archive, Municipal Archive.

8. Convent of Peninha, c.1960.
Photograph. Sintra, Historical Archive, Municipal Archive.

9. View of old town with São Martinho Church c.1960.
Photograph. Sintra, Historical Archive, Municipal Archive.

his *Geography,* in the last years of the first century BC, alludes to the fierceness of the Lusitanians and to the considerable prosperity of Tartesso or Megalithic Lusitanian society, which was politically, as well as economically, sophisticated. He contrasts the prosperity of the central southern region with other parts of Iberia, where mountainous terrain or more extreme climate makes for more difficult cultivation. It is likely that Olisipo (Lisbon) was founded around this time (according to the legend, by Ulysses on one of his heroic journeys). However, it would be some time before Olisipo developed into a large city.

The area continued to develop when, in 218 BC, the Roman legions marched into Iberia, beginning a colonisation that was to have a profound cultural impact. There was widespread resistance to the Roman invasion in various parts of what has become modern Portugal from the remote mountain region of Trás-Os-Montes to the central province of Lusitania, in which the district of Scallabitanus covered the Tagus estuary and the Sintra area. Here the local Lusitani tribe was interbred with Celts and the Conii. The Celtiberians, as they are known, had established important trading links with North Africa, enjoying considerable prosperity, which was partly the result of a rich agriculture practised on the plains between the Tagus and the Douro.

The Lusitanians were a fierce, martial people who marched into battle chanting war cries and who were determined to cling on to possession of their lands. They were led by a military caste, rather like the Japanese samurai, who were separated from the commercial classes, the actual wealth-creators. Nevertheless, their leader, Viriatus, a shepherd and a huntsman, clearly had exceptional talents for leadership. Bringing disparate bands of tribesmen together, he managed to keep the Romans at bay for eight years until the Romans, unable to defeat him in battle, eventually bribed less honourable tribesmen to betray him. Viriatus was murdered in 139 BC during pretended peace negotiations.

Although this was a serious setback, however, it did not entirely quell local resistance. Both Strabo and Diodorus Siculus record the fierce resistance that the Lusitanians put up against Roman occupation, with renewed campaigns in 80–72 BC. Lusitania did not formally become a Roman province until 25 AD although long before that, the southern areas of modern Portugal had become Latinised. Guerilla warfare lasted longest in the remote, mountainous regions of the north.

The Romans had invaded Iberia for economic reasons. They had not been concerned, at least initially, with conquering territory, and whilst introducing a centralised administration they were tolerant of local customs and even of local religion. J. Cardim Ribeiro suggests that in Lusitania the worship of the Emperor co-existed and was mingled with the traditional worship of lunar and aquatic deities.[1] Other foreigners also worshipped in their own way. From Roman times, the gypsies gathered annually at Janas, in the month of September,

> for a great festival of singing and dancing, the guitars and accordions were never silent for a moment and the meals were prepared on great braziers at the foot of the hill. And at sunset, at the very moment the sun touched the horizon, when its rays reddened the whole plain down as far as the cliffs of Ericeira, the priest who had celebrated mass would come out of the chapel to bless the gypsies' livestock, the mules and the horses, the finest horses in the whole Iberian peninsula.[2]

José Saramago notes the curious, circular shape of the hermitage of São Mamede at Janas, where the festival took

---

1   See J. Cardim Ribeiro 'Estudos histórico-epigráficos em torno da figura de I Iulius Maelo Caudicus' in *Sintria I–II tomo I 1982–1983* (Mem Martims, 1984–87) pp.151–477.
2   A. Tabucchi, *The Case of the Missing Head of Damaceno Monteiro* (London 1990) p.27.

place, which is more reminiscent of a rustic home than a place of worship.[1]

During Roman occupation, particularly during the *Pax Romana*, the period which began with the reign of Augustus Caesar in the last part of the first century BC, Lusitania, like other parts of the Empire, flourished. This was a period of administrative consolidation, during which Roman law was increasingly applied and coinage, standards of weights and measures and the calendar became widely used. The introduction of Latin as the *lingua franca* meant easier conditions for trade and business; at the same time, the infrastructure was improved by the building of roads between vital points in the country. Particularly important was the position of Olisipo, facing the sea and the southern trade routes to North Africa. By the time the Roman grip on Iberia was consolidated, Rome had become mistress of the Mediterranean, having finally destroyed Carthage in 146 BC. Trade routes from the western part of the Empire could now be securely guaranteed. In 138 BC Decimus Junius Brutus undertook reinforcement of the walls of Olisipo, suggesting that the area to the north, inhabited by Celtiberians and Lusitanians, remained hostile to Roman occupation.

As we have seen, the area of Sintra had already become important for agriculture in Celtic times. Under Roman rule, wheat and olives were cultivated while wine and cattle production were also expanded. These products fed a growing population in the region but were also exported, on a considerable scale, to Italy, where Iberian olive oil and wine were popular. Garum, a rich fish sauce, also became an important gastronomic export. Meanwhile other sources of wealth –

---

1   J. Saramago, *Viagem a Portugal* (Lisbon, 1988) p.181. It is now thought to be the place referred to by D. Francisco Melo in his tract, *A Vista das Fontes* (1657) in which he referred to people wandering like cattle around the church of São Mamede. Cattle have always been blessed at Janas over the centuries. See L.P. Cardoso 'D. Francisco Manuel de Melo, "A Vista das Fontes" e a Ermida de São Mamede de Janas' in *Sintria-I–II tomo I 1982–83* (Mem Martins, 1984–87) pp.1029–65.

particularly the mining of metals – were also boosted by increased demand. Exports to Italy could be shipped from Olisipo. The abundance of water, an important feature of Roman civic life, added considerably to the attractions of Sintra and Colares as places to live in.

This economic expansion had a considerable effect on the Sintra hinterland, where the density and type of Roman building suggest that a prosperous city, with villas and baths, had grown up on the high plain, the *planalto*. Though the Romans kept the greatest wealth for themselves, there was also opportunity for indigenous inhabitants to prosper. These Romanised Lusitanians, now speaking the local version of Latin which eventually became Galaico-Portuguese, tended to come from the *decuriones,* or middle-class property owners, distinguishable from the *senatores* or Roman aristocratic administrators but considerably above the *plebs* or ordinary citizens. Service in the Roman army could lead to member-ship of the *equites,* a class just below the senatorial class from which advancement to the very highest social rank was a possi-bility. Gradually local people would also be admitted to the public service, eventually taking up even the important magis-terial positions. As in other parts of the Roman Empire, the entire economic system depended upon the institution of slavery. The slaves, drawn from the indigenous population, had no rights of citizenship, yet they were the source of cheap labour on which the prosperity of all well-established citizens, Roman or Luso-Roman, depended.

Evidence of the local prosperity in Roman times is spread across the Sintra region, particularly in the form of funerary monuments. At the Quinta da Cabeça, in the Colares valley, the remains of a tumulus typical of this sort are buried among groves of myrtle and box. The tumulus is dedicated to the memory of a member of the Galeria tribe, a notable Luso-Roman named Gaius Terentius Rufo. The epitaph is inscribed on a marble plaque, which is quarried from local stone in the area (see Illustration 2). The tumulus resembles any number of similar monuments that were erected at family tombs throughout provincial Italy. As the *pater familias*, Gaius Terentius Rufo would have presided over a large family, the basic social unit on which everyone, freemen and slaves alike, depended. The Emperor himself, by analogy, was given the title of Father of the Senate, or political family.

Despite our knowledge of social conventions, it is not always easy to be sure about the exact nature or purpose of the monuments which have been discovered. Alves Pereira, for instance, identified one large object, probably from Cascais but now in the museum at Odrinhas, as a funerary monument. It is inscribed with the name of the procurator of the province of Lusitania, Gaius Julius Celsus, a member of the Quirina tribe rather than of the apparently more populous and successful Galeria tribe. But more recent investigations, mentioned by da Costa Azevedo, have led to its re-classification as an altar dedicated to an unidentified god.[1]

At least thirty or more monuments, either of a funerary or sacrificial type, are scattered about the area. Of particular interest are the *stellae* (stone projections sometimes in the shape of stars) found on many of the graves in the Sintra area. Five different groups have been classified on an iconographic basis. There include: those bearing professional tool marks; cruciferous types; those decorated with geometric motifs; those with non-geometric but decorative motifs and, finally, the epigraphic *stellae*. Some interesting peculiarities have been observed. *Stellae* with representation of the pomegranate have been found only in the Portuguese territory and not in other parts of Iberia. There have also been a number of unfinished *stellae* found in the region, suggesting the existence of specialised workshops where they may have been finished. Archaeologists have guessed that such a factory was situated at São João das Lampas.

At São Miguel de Odrinhas there is something grander to

---

1   J.A. da Costa Azevedo, *Velharias de Sintra* 6 vols (Sintra, 1957) vol. 4 p.58.

be seen. Here lie the remains of a substantial Roman villa, with elegant mosaic floors indicating a considerable degree of wealth on the part of its owner. He probably belonged to the growing élite of Olisipo, and would have owned a farm area of over a thousand hectares. The building had its own bath and recreation area, once again illustrating the material benefits of life in Roman Lusitania. It also had a mausoleum, a regular shaped and considerable structure with circular walls, well enough made to be still standing. On top a cupola, long since collapsed, protected the tumulus beneath.

Inside the mausoleum a rectangular, sacrificial altar was found. It is made of marble, and is highly polished and decorated with ornate floral motifs. Inscriptions once again point to its being a monument to a member of the Galeria tribe, certainly a prosperous Luso-Roman citizen. Curious legends attach to this particular piece of stonework. One of them suggests that it was used by a bereaved mother to transport the body of her dead daughter from somewhere in the region of Ericeira. In another version of the story, a grandfather is said to have been trying to transport the corpse by the same method. Another monument, a huge funerary pillar, was thought to mark the grave of a saint. People flocked from afar to rub dust off it in the hopes that the dust itself would have curing powers.

The tombstone and many other Roman funerary remains are now housed in the elegantly restored museum at Odrinhas. The building is set out on the pattern of the old Roman villa complex, in sympathetic architectural style. Pavements of mosaic, peristyles and baths, well supplied by local streams, indicate considerable prosperity. Among the most impressive pieces in the collection within the museum are the highly decorated Etruscan sarcophagi, with their elaborate tops, which were brought to Portugal by Sir Francis Cook of Monserrate.

The archaeologist Scarlat Lambrino is convinced that the number and extent of the Roman ruins in the Sintra area enables us to conclude that there was a considerable settlement on the plain *(planalto)* to the north of the hills. The area occupied by buildings may have spread as far as Mafra and Ericeira. It would have been an area of rich agriculture, supplying the needs of Olisipo as well as the region around Sintra itself. The local landowners lived on their large estates or *latifundia,* comfortable in their enjoyment of the conveniences of Roman life. They may have served in the administration of Olisipo and, in some cases, have made the journey to Italy themselves. Their status was considerable, something that we can deduce from the inscriptions left on the grander funerary monuments, with their elaborate inscriptions and *stellae.* These stones, sometimes finely carved and engraved, sometimes in undistinguished heaps, lined up in rows in the main hall of the new museum, are an enduring reminder of the considerable success of the *Pax Romana* in the distant western province of Lusitania.

Roman occupation of the area lasted peacefully until the early 400s, but by the time Alaric the Visigoth sacked Rome in 410 the Roman *imperium* in Iberia was being challenged by the arrival of Alans, Vandals and Suevi from the north. These Germanic invasions of the Peninsula began in 407, according to Oliveira Marques, and were made by sea as well as by land.[1] They coincided with considerable local disturbances *(bagandas)* which had already upset the calm of Roman centres such as Braga. There is evidence that the local insurgents collaborated with the invaders. Nevertheless, although these barbarian incursions compromised Roman control, they did not altogether threaten the Roman way of life, particularly in the towns and cities. The invaders were more interested in the benefits of a rich, southern agriculture than in attempting to replace existing political and administrative institutions. Nor had they come in numbers sufficient to displace the indigenous populations. Instead they looked to the fertile soils of the northern parts of Iberia, including areas of what is now

---

1   A.H. de Oliveira Marques, op. cit. vol. 1 p.48.

northern Portugal and Galicia, as good productive land from which they could make a comfortable living. In due course, they moved south, toward Lisbon and the Sintra area but tended to avoid direct conflict with the inhabitants of the towns. The Roman style of life, already established to a considerable level of sophistication in the *planalto* to the north of Sintra, was thus allowed to continue more or less undisturbed in its civic form. This synthesis of Roman and barbarian occupation was still in place when the Moors invaded three centuries later.

In Portugal the leading barbarian invaders of the fifth century were the Suevi, as opposed to the Vandals who occupied Spain. The Suevi, who had come from the Rhineland, were a warrior people who had been constantly on the move and were now tempted by the gentle Luso-Galician *locale* they had reached. The capital of the Suevic kingdom was established at Dume, near Braga, in the north but they occupied Oporto as well. Much of the information about the Suevic kingdom comes from Hydatius, Bishop of Chaves, who acted as a negotiator between the Suevi and the Romans. He also had dealings with the Visigoths who had now become prominent in Spain.

The Suevi did not attempt to obliterate Roman customs where they existed, nor did they change the language, Galaico-Portuguese, which was spoken across the whole northern region. Their own language had, in any case, never been written down. When they moved further south, they practised the same policy of tolerance and alliance with the localised Roman communities. The Roman governor of Lisbon, one Lusidius, welcomed Suevic leaders to the city and formed a strong alliance with them.

These political developments encouraged the assimilation of Suevic and Roman culture at a time when Roman rule itself was collapsing. By 476 the Western Roman Empire went into extinction. This pattern of cultural integration was an early example of a toleration of foreigners that has been the common experience of the inhabitants of the Portuguese territory. It was not severely challenged under Moorish rule, where, in accordance with Koranic imperative, considerable tolerance was shown to believers of other religions, including Christianity and Judaism. Much later when Portugal itself became an imperial nation, assimilation with other cultures was practised overseas. Miscegenation was encouraged in many colonial territories, from Brazil to the Far East.

As the apparatus of Roman administration disappeared in the Iberian provinces, a power vacuum was created. The Catholic clergy seized the political initiative, particularly after the conversion of the Suevic kingdom to Christianity. The Suevi had, of course, by now had a continuous contact with the Romanised Christians of their own kingdom for a century or more. But it was with the arrival of St Martin at Dume, before 550, that the official conversion took place. It is said that St Martin saved the life of the son of the Suevic King, Theodemir and was duly installed in Braga as archbishop. At Dume he rebuilt the church dedicated to his namesake, St Martin of Tours, who in the Middle Ages was to become a great cult figure after whom many churches, including the church of São Martinho in Sintra, were named. St Martin had the vision of a secular kingdom but one that was Roman in its religion and culture. It would also have the capacity to absorb pagan features in its ritual. The authority of the Church was confirmed by the holding of religious councils at Braga in 563 and again in 572. The result of these councils was a re-organisation and strengthening of the Church by the re-arrangement of sees and synods, both within the Suevic kingdom and in neighbouring Galicia.

St Martin's political views were later reflected in the code of St Isidore of Seville, which similarly aimed to apply a system of law to Romans, Suevi and Goths alike. Within these basi-cally theocratic states, commerce was considered to be a morally dubious activity. Its practice was left to the Jewish minority. As in other parts of Europe, the exclusion of Jews from the professions meant that they became dangerously marginalised from mainstream Iberian society. Nevertheless, they were left to practice their own religion until the Inquisition was set up in the sixteenth century.

In Spain the Visigoths were beginning to forge a nation out of the disparate elements of society. In the north of Portugal, however, despite many vicissitudes and complex entanglements with this sometimes fragmented Visigothic Spanish state, the Suevic kingdom survived for another century and a half. In the south, the Church also filled the power vacuum created by the demise of Roman rule in the province of Lusitania. The new diocese of Ossonoba became the episcopal base of a new political and administrative union that held the area together, as well as maintaining good relations with the Suevic kingdom to the north. This state of equilibrium lasted until the arrival of the Moors.

3

The Moorish Legacy

Sintra, like the rest of Iberia, was to be significantly affected by the next invasion of the Peninsula. The Moorish occupation began in July 710, when a small group of ships under Berber command crossed the Straits of Gibraltar from North Africa. No doubt numerous vessels had made the short journey from Africa to Europe before but on this occasion, the seafarers had a different objective. They had been specifically sent, under the command of Tarif Ibn Malik, to reconnoitre and to report back on whether the fabled lands of Iberia might be ripe for occupation by the armies of the Prophet. To his surprise, Tarif Ibn Malik met with no resistance on Spanish soil when he landed his several hundred men. The party foraged in the countryside but did not linger. Soon it was on its way back to North Africa with a considerable booty that included highly prized Iberian slaves.

In the following summer of 711 Tariq Ibn Ziyad, Governor of Tangier, made another crossing, this time with the intention of occupying Spanish territory. The Governor had planned to wait at Gibraltar for the arrival of a larger force led by Musa Ibn Nusayr but events forced him to change plans. The Visigothic King of Spain, Roderick, was caught unprepared, being at that time engaged in a campaign against the Basques in the north. In an attempt to seize the initiative, he rallied his troops and marched south from Córdoba. His army was composed of different Iberian elements not used to fighting together. Meanwhile, Tariq Ibn Ziyad had taken up a strong position near Algeçiras, where he waited. Roderick led a frontal assault but the divisions within his forces showed. The Muslim invaders exploited every weakness in the Christian army, putting the Iberians on the defensive. Their early victory signalled the end of Visigothic Spain, for in a matter of months Tariq Ibn Ziyad had swept northwards into the heart of the Peninsula. When Musa Ibn Nusayr finally landed with his force of twelve thousand troops the following summer, the annexation of the whole of Iberia had begun in earnest. The combined forces of the two Moorish generals could not be stopped, despite their rivalry with one another: Seville, Mérida and Toledo fell to the invaders. Within another year Moorish troops were advancing into Galicia in the far north.

These Moorish landings in Iberia began a momentous chapter in the history of Spain and Portugal which only came to an end some eight centuries later with the fall of the Arab Kingdom of Granada to their Catholic Majesties in 1492. It would be misleading to impose too orderly a pattern on the history of this long period which, even more than the period of Roman occupation, was the subject of persistent wars, internal struggles and rivalries.[1] Sometimes these struggles were between the Moorish kingdoms of the south and the Christian states of the north; sometimes alliances formed across the religious divide so that Christian rulers, especially of smaller states, sought alliances with the powerful Caliph of Al Andalus. But the balance of power had irretrievably shifted. The Moorish caliphate was now the principal political power in the Peninsula, reversing the previous situation in which successive Europeans (first Roman, then Vandals) had occupied North Africa. Nevertheless, the fact that these previous occupations had taken place meant that the two cultures, European and African, had already coexisted under the same

---

1   For a good account of the history of Moorish Iberia, with details about the struggles between the various kingdoms, see J. Read, *The Moors in Spain and Portugal* (London, 1974). On the specific subject of the Moorish occupation of Portugal, see C. Picard, op. cit.

political authority. That background of contact made it easier for the Christian Iberians to adapt to the Moorish control of the Peninsula.

There can be no doubt of the immense significance of the occupation in every cultural area from language, science, law and architecture, to the practice of fine arts (particularly music and ceramics) and the practical sciences (like irrigation). The degree of influence was different in different parts of the Peninsula. The areas least affected were the Asturias, Galicia and the north of Portugal where Moorish occupation was either brief or never complete. Moorish rule was particularly consolidated in southern Iberia, in Spain in Andalucia (El Andalus) and in Portugal in the Algarve, where the city of Silves was of principal importance. The province of Balata stretched from Lisbon to Santarém and included Sintra. Sintra then, as always, was regarded as an important bastion of defence for Lisbon. Its Moorish period is part of the story of a string of towns and cities – Coimbra, Évora, Beja, Alcácer, Mértola and Silves – that constituted important centres of Moorish life in the Garbe (Moorish Portugal). Whilst there is considerable documentary evidence of life in Moorish Portugal, far fewer remains of Moorish buildings exist in the country than in Spain.

Certain characteristics of the early Moorish period – the Umayyad Caliphate centred on Córdoba – are important to bear in mind when attempting to understand the lasting influence of the Muslim culture throughout Iberia. In the first place there was a certain religious tolerance based on the Koranic precept 'Let there be no violence in religion'. According to this principle, Christians and Jews were left to practise their own religion without interference from the authorities since tolerance should be shown to anyone holding to a belief in one God. It may also have been politically expedient for the newcomers to practice this liberal policy for their numbers (estimated to vary between 40,000 in the early years to 300,000 at the end of the fifteenth century) would never have allowed them to dominate the indigenous population completely.[1]

Whatever the balance between principle and expediency, there is no doubt that a lenient policy encouraged Arabisation just as the Romans' initial tolerance of indigenous faiths and religious practices had encouraged the Romanisation of Iberia. The Moors were also pragmatic enough to adapt existing administrative structures to their own needs. In this way they became heirs to Visigothic/Suevic as well as Roman, traditions. The Moorish super-culture was therefore built upon highly eclectic foundations, mixing elements of Eastern and Western influences. The blend of different traditions explains why Mozarabic culture (the pattern of Christian assimilation to Moorish ways) took such firm root in the Peninsula. It was only in the later periods of the Caliphate, when fundamentalist puritans came from North Africa, that persecution began and some of the considerable early advantages were lost.

The Moorish occupation of Portugal was built on the same economic foundations of agriculture and trade as Roman Lusitania had been. Agriculture was greatly improved by the introduction of sophisticated systems of irrigation, which lasted through the centuries. Sintra, with its abundant water supply, was an extremely attractive place to North Africans used to much more parched territory. Its fertile soil made the production of several crops a year possible. Wheat and barley were grown, the vine continued to be cultivated (despite Koranic injunction wine-drinking was widespread in Moorish Iberia) and the olive, already famous in Roman times, remained a produce of high quality. All types of fruit – apples, pears and the orange, introduced by the Moors – could be produced in abundance in the Sintra area. Important crafts, based on the production of silver and copper, also flourished.

---

1   These figures are given by Jan Read, op. cit. pp.53 & 226. In the eleventh century the Berber and slave population is put at 40,000. See A. Borges Coelho, *Portugal na Espanha Arabe* 2 vols (Lisbon, 1989) vol. 1 p.95.

The impregnability of Sintra was very much in the minds of the Moorish rulers of Balata when they first took over the area in the eighth century. Almumine Alhimiari, an historian writing in the twelfth century and relying on earlier accounts of Al Bakri tells us that Sintra has two solid castles high up on the mountain ridge. Their commanding position gives excellent surveillance up the coast; the proximity of the sea is another military advantage. Sintra, as always, was vital in the defence of Lisbon itself. But Sintra's strategic importance was not its only attraction. No inhabitant of the arid plains of North Africa could fail to be impressed by its rich vegetation and Arcadian charms. Al Bakri notes the damp mists of the mountain; he admires the plentiful water supply provided by cascading streams above ground, which can be diverted in channels to every slope and dip of the mountain. He enthuses on the bountiful supply of apples and pears, which were distributed from Sintra all over the Garbe. Olives, already cultivated since Roman times, continued to be an important source of wealth for local agriculture. The vine also continued to be cultivated in the slopes and valleys despite warnings against the evil of alcohol in the Koran. The Moorish rulers of Iberia adapted to a culture in which wine was drunk, just as the Mozarabs under them assimilated many Eastern habits and practices.

The fertility of the land was another important asset. Sintra and Colares became the grain and fruit basket for the whole Lisbon area. The boast that wheat could be grown and harvested in forty days was made by a number of different Moorish inhabitants of Balata. The plentiful supply of water and cooler climate also allowed the cultivation of gardens, with the possibility of a wide variety of flowers, something that delighted the Moors. More than one Arab chronicler cites the plentiful supply of fuel that the trees of Sintra provided.

This material abundance made the rulers of the Garbe wealthy but it also made them less inclined to physical or manual work. The Moorish upper classes, which were always heavily outnumbered by the Mozarab population, came to rely on Berber workforces to produce essential commodities and local craftsmen to make the higher quality luxury goods that they increasingly demanded. At the same time, Slav mercenaries were relied upon to keep the peace. Inter-tribal struggles, sometimes mirroring rivalries in North Africa, continued to plague the caliphates. The Christian states of the north had constantly to be kept at bay, usually by a major summer offensive each year. The Moors controlled the Asturias for a very short period. Tracts of Galicia and northern Portugal proved impossible to subdue totally. Nevertheless, because the Christian states of the north were not always united among themselves, the Moorish caliphs retained control of a large part of the Peninsula without great difficulty. Within a decade of the first landing in Iberia, the Moors had crossed the Pyrenees into Gaul, occupying Narbonne and capturing Toulouse in 717. They remained on the French side of the mountains for half a century, despite suffering defeat at Poitiers in 732. It was not until 778 that they were finally driven back into Spain by Charlemagne the Great.

Despite the continuous warfare across Iberia, within Al Andalus there was an extraordinary renaissance of arts and sciences at this time. Music, poetry, philosophy and medicine all flourished, as did the manufacture of fine ceramics, most notably of tiles. All this activity made Al Andalus a significant cultural centre in the greater Islamic world, developing its own, cosmopolitan way of life. A talented circle of philosophers and poets held court at Córdoba, and the Garbe produced its own scholars and men of letters. Borges Coelho's collection of manuscripts gives an idea of the variety and excellence of this literary and scientific culture. He lists, among many others, Ibn Sara of Santarém, Ibn Alquaquid of Évora, Ibn Asside of Silves and Ibn Muçana of Lisbon.[1] Let us consider the contribution of just the last two writers in order to estab-

---

1   A. Borges Coelho, op. cit. vol. 1 pp.219ff.

lish a sense of the area's social and cultural development at this
time.

Ibn Asside lived in the flourishing, southern Arab city of
Silves in the eleventh century. His great work was the *Livro
dos Círculos* in which he deals with the lofty subjects of the
order of the universe and man's place in it as an intellectual
agent. His grand metaphysical theory displays all the signs of
an eclectic and sophisticated cosmopolitanism, incorporating
detailed knowledge of Indian philosophy and religion. Ibn
Muçana, who lived in the first part of the eleventh century,
is, by comparison, a rather homely figure who, when not
engaged in flights of literary fancy, happened also to be the
mayor of Lisbon. He specialised in eulogies and flourishing
outpourings, including the ode to Alcabideche, nestling in the
valley below the Sintra mountain range. The poem begins by
asking that the good citizen-farmers of that village never suffer
a lack of grain or onions or pumpkins! It celebrates both the
richness of the land (although in a good year it will not produce
more than twenty loads of cereals) and the sturdiness of its
inhabitants. There is a Horatian tone to the poem, celebrating
the bucolic delights of Colares. The poet speaks of a quiet
freedom which the tillers of the land, happy in their work,
enjoy above the easier but less rewarding lifestyle of their urban
cousins. Ibn Muçana is said to have recited this poem to a
friend *en plein air* while oxen were ploughing a nearby field.

The equilibrium of the Moorish rule gradually began to
disintegrate. The earlier more tolerant Moorish attitude may
have continued for much longer in Iberia if the Peninsula had
been isolated from the power struggles that took place in
North Africa. However, dynastic connections ensured that
disturbances there affected Iberian politics. By the twelfth
century, the puritanical Almoravids were in the ascendant.
They preached a sterner version of Islam than had previously
been taught, much less tolerant of other religions and scornful
of Iberian laxity, which had descended to allowing the
drinking of wine by the faithful. The Almoravids launched a

series of new campaigns against the Christian states of the north and for the first time made life uncomfortable for some of the Mozarab subjects of the Caliphate.

In the meantime events of considerable significance were taking place in the region of the Garbe. A new, formidable leader, in the person of the Burgundian prince, Afonso Henriques, had appeared as the champion of a new kingdom of Portugal which, as well as being liberated from the Moorish rule, was also to be entirely independent of any of the Christian domains of Spain. The origins of this national independence are entangled in the complicated legacy of Alfonso VI of León who, in 1095, left Galicia to his legitimate daughter, Donna Urraca and the countdom of Portucale (extending south of the Mondego) to Donna Teresa, his illegitimate daughter. Donna Teresa ruled Portucale after the death of her husband, Count Henry, with the title of Queen. She had ambitions to add Galicia to her realm, but it was left to her son, Afonso Henriques, to settle with the other side when they both met at the tournament of São Mamede, near Guimarães. Afonso Henriques emerged as the strong man from this encounter and, expelling his mother, took over the countdom of Portucale himself. In a proclamation dated 6 April 1129, he declared himself 'in possession of Coimbra and all other towns of Portugal'. His pretensions to kingship were quite clear and he soon began to style himself as the King of Portugal. His status was greatly enhanced by recognition from Rome after the so-called Treaty of Zamora (1143) by which Alfonso VII of León was elevated to the title of 'Emperor of Spain'.[1]

In 1147 Afonso Henriques captured Santarém, putting himself in strategic control of the rich agricultural area north of the Tagus. He was now in a position to challenge Lisbon, the jewel in the crown of Moorish Balata. After a twenty-month siege and with the help of English, German and French

---

1   We are told that there is no proof that such a treaty was ever made; nor are its terms recorded. J.H. Saraiva, *Portugal A Companion History* (Manchester, 1997) p.15.

crusaders, the self-styled King of Portugal captured Lisbon. The full story has been graphically told by José Saramago in his novel *The History of the Siege of Lisbon*. The historical action in the novel is centred on the Castle of São Jorge and is seen as much from the defenders' point of view as from the point of view of the attacking Christians. Saramago's evocation of Muslim Lisbon, with its mosques and calling to prayers is graphic and sympathetic while incipient Portuguese nationalism, under Afonso Henriques, is treated with gentle irony. Saramago is impressed by other features of Moorish culture, including the tolerance shown to Christians and the technological sophistication that enabled the North Africans to make the best use of local resources. Among the foreigners who helped the Portuguese prince and who stayed behind after the siege was the English priest, Gilbert of Hastings. He became the first Bishop of Lisbon, the first in a long line of Englishmen associated with the history of the emergent nation of Portugal.

In the same year of 1147, Afonso Henriques captured Sintra, apparently without any resistance on the part of its Muslim inhabitants despite its considerable stronghold position.

By this time, Moorish occupation had left a lasting impression on Sintra. One evident feature of the occupation, apart from the battlements of the castle, is in the layout of the streets that run up the slopes from the central square. There is no overall plan or grid pattern as there had been in Roman urban centres. Instead the streets twist and turn in all directions, crisscrossed by alleyways, small courtyards and staircases. They confirm the importance of the house as the main feature of Arab urban architecture, rather than the street. Some of the straight frontages, giving on to the steep paths, still have a very Moorish appearance. In the other direction, in front of the present day Hotel Tivoli (formerly the Nunes) was the Largo de Meca, with the Rua de Meca leading off it.

The outward façade of houses, especially if they are tiled, is deeply impregnated in the Portuguese imagination. (The contemporary poetess Sophia de Mello Breyner, for instance, says that the reflections from these tiled Moorish fronts are like mirrors of the imagination and have influenced her poetry.) Within the sturdy, wooden doors of the houses were interior spaces that formed courtyards which, in the case of the wealthy, were decorated with fountains. These hidden retreats were designed as refuges from the summer heat and would be decorated with plants and lush flowers such as the camellia. They also provided places for repose where the faithful might pray or meditate upon the wisdom of the Koran in peace. The inner courtyard, which was sometimes decorated with galleries and ornate balconies, was the centre of the domestic life of the inhabitants, especially the women, who would not venture out of the house alone or, in the case of the most orthodox, unveiled.

In the complicated unplanned streets there were many indications of a highly organised and sophisticated urban life. The mosque was the rallying point – we know that the sites of several Sintra churches were originally the location of mosques – sending out call to prayers throughout the day. Meanwhile in the schools and academies nearby, the art of calligraphy was taught alongside medicine, mathematics and literature, ensuring a high quality of intellectual life among the Mozarabs. The public baths, important places for ritual ablution, also acted as social venues as such institutions had done in Roman times. Along the streets, the Mozarab wandered, dressed in a rectangular, wide-sleeved tunic, turbaned or hatted, sometimes wearing a loose scarf. Numerous workshops producing carpets, jewellery and precious metals, as well as perfumes, added to the bustle of the town. Foodstuffs and spices were sold in the *souk*, or market place. Factories which needed more space (such as potteries with kilns or dyeing works for fabrics) were located on the outskirts of the urban centre, up near São Pedro.

One of the most important Moorish crafts, of which physical traces still survive, was ceramics. The evidence suggests that the art of Iberian ceramics was influenced from as far afield as Iran and China. Decorative motifs came from nature: the peacock, for example, symbol of cosmic energy and the lotus flower, which had symbolic importance in religions of the Far East. Other designs included mythological beasts, such as the dragon so popular in Chinese art, and the stylised geometrical patterns from Iran. Of particular importance was the production of glazed, encaustic tiles; Moorish skills in this fine craft were eventually used in the making of Portuguese *azulejos*. Tiles were prepared from clay, first hardened by firing into a 'biscuit', then painted with pigments (made by mixing metallic oxides and alkaline silicates with water). The tile was then immersed in a fluid glaze before being fired again, this time at a lower temperature. The pigment and glaze would become fused in the hard glass, producing a fine, smooth finish. Moorish tiles of rare quality are still intact in the royal palace at Sintra (see p.56).

By far the most dramatic Moorish legacy left in Sintra, however, is the old Moorish castle (Castelo dos Mouros).[1] Indeed, it is one of the few Moorish buildings left in the area, even though it has been considerably restored by various Portuguese monarchs through the ages. This sturdy structure, with towers and battlement walls, perches on two lofty summits about 450 metres above sea level. The five towers are connected by a serpentine wall, which encloses the entire fortified area. It is possible to walk right around it, an important military feature, which ensured that information about attacks could be relayed effectively to all parts of the castle. It was also easy to communicate with the *walis* or ruler who was installed in his residence on the site of the present royal palace in the old town below.

The castle was part of a defensive trio of fortifications, which included Lisbon and Santarém. Its position, on the high slopes of the mountain with steep ravines falling off from the walls, made it virtually impregnable. From the battlements

---

1   See Illustration 18.

there is a particularly good prospect of the land lying to the north, the direction from which a Christian attack was expected. Despite its impressive fortifications, however, Sintra was in fact given up to Afonso Henriques without a fight in 1147 after he had captured Lisbon.

The castle was built in the early decades of the eighth century not long after the arrival of the Moors in Balata. Legends suggest that, given its prominence, the site may have been used for lunar worship of the type practised at the Cabo da Roca. It is not difficult to imagine this given the height and drama of the location. In a later period the surreal appearance of the craggy cliffs in the mist appealed to the Romantics who saw magical qualities in the Sintra landscape. Nevertheless, there is no surviving evidence of any prehistoric or Roman structure on the summit. Rumours about a burial chamber full of precious objects and hidden treasures underneath the battlements persisted for many ages. Despite the existence of a subterranean passage under the first of the towers and the steepness of some drops of the battlements where a cavern might potentially have been cut out, no such chamber has ever actually been found. If a caliph lies buried there, guarded by demons and spirits, he has remained so, undisturbed, over the centuries.

Within the gates of the castle is a great cistern, known as the cistern of the Moors although it has been restored at a later date. The general restoration of the castle was carried out in early times by Portuguese monarchs including King Sancho I, son of Afonso Henriques. Later, at the beginning of the fourteenth century, King Dinis also improved the fortifications although the defensive use of the castle had by then become much less important. One of the romantic legends associated with the castle is that Bernardim Ribeiro, a scholarly poet, inhabited one of the towers, drawing inspiration from the isolated setting. Bernadim Ribeiro was a learned man who wrote in Hebrew, Latin and Castilian as well as in Portuguese. Though he was courtly and cosmopolitan, he also seemed to cut the figure of the isolated, Romantic poet *avant la lettre*. Dom Fernando was inspired by the legend of the Moorish castle to undertake restoration of its battlements whilst he was building Pena Palace on the other ridge.

Most historians of Portuguese architecture also allow for some kind of Moorish foundation for the Royal Palace of Sintra (Paço Real), a building closely associated with the Portuguese kings and queens who lived there over the centuries (see Plan 1). However, the extent of that influence has been the subject of considerable controversy. The boldest assertion that King João I built his palace on Moorish foundations was made by the Count of Sabugosa, in his courtly book *O Paço de Cintra* (1903). Although the Count acknowledges difficulties in being certain about exactly where the Moorish building lay in relation to the existing palace, he identifies clear Moorish features in it and asserts that the later reconstruction undertaken by the Portuguese monarchs was actually executed by Moorish workmen.[1] The view that the palace is Moorish in origin was flatly denied some twenty years later by the archaeologist, Professor Reynaldo dos Santos, who said that such an assertion had no basis in fact. He was writing, of course, in an era when acknowledgement of the Muslim influence on Portugal as a whole was muted; indeed it may even have been ideologically unacceptable to dwell on a period of foreign domination in the last era of Portuguese imperial pretensions. That might explain what otherwise appears a curious contradiction, for having made the assertion that there is no basis for calling the palace Moorish, Professor dos Santos goes on to consider which of its features were indeed Arabic.[2]

---

1 Conde de Sabugosa, *O Paço de Cintra* (Lisbon, 1903) pp.1–9.
2 See F. Costa, *O Paço Real de Sintra* (Sintra, 1992) p.21. Correia de Campos, who supports the theory of the Arabic origins of the palace, though admitting the physical remnants are small, claims that Professor dos Santos' powers as a writer and his authority as a scholar tended to overwhelm critics into accepting his views. See *Monumentos da Antiguidade em Portugal* (Lisbon, 1970) p.239.

A generation later, Raul Lino, in his book on the palace (1948) attempts a compromise theory about a building whose lack of symmetry contrasts with the more patterned plan of the Alhambra in Granada with which it has often been compared. He condemns the facile description of the palace as Moorish in the absence of any real evidence. He gives a warning that identifying the evidence is no easy matter, given the numerous changes made to the building. Columns used in the palace, for instance, were imported from North Africa but have been found to have originated in Italy. On the other hand, typical Moorish battlements are built over these columns whilst the arched windows have as much an Oriental as a Gothic feel to them. Lino accepts Sabugosa's assertion that much of the work done in the fifteenth century *was* the work of Moorish artisans, who were following traditional methods. In his terminology the palace is 'Moorified' rather than Moorish, in acknowledgement of the Moorish influence on the building rather than in any pretence that it was actually constructed at the time of Moorish rulers. Lino also perceptively draws attention to the influence of Castilian taste on Portugal. It is certainly the case that in Andalucia, Moorish architecture abounded. The splendours of Seville and Granada would have greatly influenced Portuguese monarchs when they chose the style of their new royal residence in Sintra.

In the 1970s the notable local historian Francisco Costa revisited the dispute about the Moorish origins of the palace. Sceptical of the direct link to the Moors made by the over-enthusiastic Arabist Borges Coelho, Costa himself acknowledged what Lino had earlier called an Oriental 'flavour' to the building. But Costa is concerned to be accurate about what actually is Moorish. Even the pepper pot chimneys of the kitchen, he says, are similar to structures in buildings in France and Italy rather than to Arabic ones in the Middle East. For Costa, the urge to create a myth connecting the royal palace to an exotic, distant period of Portuguese history was a dubious quest. It seemed that for some people it was enough that one of the rooms in the palace was known as the Sala dos Arabes (Arabs' Hall) for them to jump to the conclusion that it had been built by the Moors. In fact, as Costa asserts, it is known to have been added to the complex in the reign of King João I and was given the name because it was considered to be the oldest part of the palace.[1]

The distinction of the disputants and the complexities that surround a building which has been both damaged by natural causes and tampered with over the ages by its royal inhabitants, do not suggest an easy resolution to the problem of whether it is authentically Moorish. If the internal evidence, on a number of different points, confirms that little of the existing building was part of a Moorish palace, there can be no doubt that significant Moorish methods of construction and stylistic features have been used in its construction. It is likely that the Royal Palace was indeed built on the site of an older, Moorish building and that it was probably constructed by *Mudejar* workmen – in other words by Moorish builders and craftsmen living under the Christian kings of Portugal.[2] The most substantial evidence of Moorish influence is in the very bricks and mortar of the palace. W.C. Watson, writing in the first decade of the twentieth century, notes that the palace walls, once stripped of plaster, are found to have been constructed in the Arab manner – that is, they were made of layers of rubble bonded at intervals with thin bricks two or three courses deep.[3] A striking example of this method has been found in the inner wall of the Sala dos Cisnes (Hall of Swans). Originally that wall would have been the outer wall of the old palace of the *walis* or Moorish ruler. The Castelo dos Mouros can be seen from various vantage points in the rooms and courtyards, reassuringly defensive on the brow of the hill.

1   See F. Costa, op. cit. pp.42–9.
2   This has no doubt led one art historian to label the taste of King João I as 'Gothic-Mudejar', see A.M. de Brito Correia, *Palácio Nacional de Sintra* (Lisbon, 1993) pp.10 & 20.
3   W.C. Watson, *Portuguese Architecture* (London, 1908) p.117.

In several parts of the palace the tiles suggest Moorish work-manship. In early depictions of the building, the famous pepper pot chimneys are shown decorated in tiles rather than plastered in the existing manner. The tiles were green and white, traditional Moorish colours. Elsewhere, notably in the Sala das Pegas (Hall of Magpies), there are beautiful brown and white tiles in Moorish patterns which greatly enrich the deco-ration of the room, re-done in the time of King João I. Other Moorish-style tiles, once again in green and white, are to be found in the patio as well as in the Sala das Sereias (Hall of Mermaids), which was probably part of the original Moorish palace. Dark, black *azulejos*, rarities of the fifteenth century, decorate the thick walls of this small room.

The older Sala dos Árabes (Arabs' Hall) does have genuinely Moorish parts, but these seem confined to the walls (which, once again, were made in the manner already described). They are tiled in traditional blue and green, with some fine poly-chromatic flower patterns of blue, green and yellow over the doors. The tiles on the walls appear in diagonal waves, which add to the elegance of the room. A small round basin foun-tain in the middle is surrounded by a square of tiles, which are largely worn away. Although its decoration looks European, the concept of a basin in the middle of the room brings an Eastern feeling to the space. In earlier times other decorations added a different Oriental element to the amalgam. W.C. Watson describes Indian figures which he believes were spoils brought back from India for Dom Manuel by Vasco da Gama after his voyage of 1498.[1] That supposition would certainly add to the romantic and patriotic notions of the palace as a centre of national life at a time of significant overseas expan-sion. From the window there is another fine view of the Moorish castle, which seems particularly appropriate to the ambience of this room.

W.C. Watson says that the techniques of Moorish

---

1   Ibid. p.125.

carpentry used in the ceilings of the palace were handed down to generations of Portuguese architects.[1] As late as the seventeenth century, ceiling work, though no longer decoratively Oriental, still followed the Moorish principles of construction. Woodwork and panels display the same background of highly sophisticated craftsmanship. The two rooms of the Palace to have outstanding ceilings, the Sala dos Cisnes (Hall of Swans) and the Sala dos Brasões (Hall of Shields) are both examples of skilled craftsmanship. The first hall was painted in the time of João I. Additions were made by Dom Manuel. Even so the twenty-seven octagons, some of which are oddly shaped, are in the Moorish style. In the Sala dos Brasões, the cornices begin twelve feet from the ground, giving a more closed in feeling to the room than expected. The walls are tiled in *azulejos* of a later period. Yet again the shapes and construction are Moorish. The two rooms display skilled panelling; the wood is finely worked, giving a rich effect. They are embellished by the superb working of the ceilings, showing considerable aesthetic debt to a foreign style that had come to Portugal and Spain from North Africa.

The final but striking piece of evidence for the Moorish origin of the palace is, curiously enough, in the chapel. Beyond the chapel is the Terrace of Mecca. The popular view is that on this spot the *walis* had erected his private mosque. Such a story added to the glamour and romance of the building, emphasising its ancient and continuous existence. Once again, the most Arab aspect of the chapel is the ceiling, which is entirely Moorish in construction and design despite the fact that it was actually put up in the sixteenth century and made of chestnut and oak. The whole surface is covered in an intricate, patterned design of stars, triangles and octagons and figures of various other geometrical shapes. Its ornate, geometrical pattern, in hues of darkened red, add to the feeling of its being a mosque despite the white doves, symbolising the

---

1   Ibid. pp.136ff.

Holy Ghost, which flutter on the walls. On the floor is a large mosaic of tiles with a typically *Mudejar* feeling.

The Moorish influence in the chapel echoes similar influences in other churches across the country. In various parts of Alentejo, Christian churches were routinely built on the site of old mosques, using similar building techniques and sometimes even the same stones as the original constructions. A striking example is the church of São Francisco at Évora. The continued use of a site felt to be sacred is another example of the process of the assimilation of different elements in Portuguese culture. The decoration of the chapel at the Royal Palace shows, too, how Moorish features could be accommodated and indeed blended into European Gothic style, reaching a crescendo in the early Manueline style, which was unique to Portugal.

Tracing the evolution of Manueline art is an intricate undertaking. Various stages in the development of this indigenous style can be identified through the reign of King Manuel from 1495 to 1521 and indeed, beyond it. Dom Manuel, known as the Fortunate, benefited from the huge revenues that poured in from Brazil (discovered by Pedro Álvarez Cabral in 1500) on the one hand and the Far East on the other. The slave trade was initially centred in the north of Brazil. The port of Bahía rose in importance as the fine Portuguese mansions, which still adorn the old town centre, attest. In the East there was a lucrative commerce with Persia, India and even China. The Portuguese town of Goa, with its impressive churches and other public buildings, became the centre of an extended web of trading.

On the basis of the wealth that he acquired from these different parts of the world, Dom Manuel was able to endow buildings on a grand scale in Portugal; it is calculated that he sponsored over sixty projects across the country. The use of Manueline decorations extended to many other buildings already in existence. In some cases the additions of features in the Manueline style, such as at the Royal Palace of Sintra are quite extensive, while in other places they are confined to a smaller scale, perhaps to a window frame or a portal.

The Manueline style is distinctive in its mixture of Gothic and Eastern styles. The blend of these two elements is different in each example, which adds to the difficulty of describing them accurately. At its height the style is found mainly in solid, ecclesiastical buildings which embody Gothic cloisters and arches but are also highly ornate. Typical Manueline style features include decorative sculpturing, depicting exotic animals as well as fauna and flora. These naturalistic elements can sometimes become overwhelming. Columns are twisted into spiral forms; arches are adorned with mouldings in the form of nautical cables. Ribs of plain pointed arched vaulting are supplemented by heavy liernes in round or square relief; intertwining mariners' knots give bulk to decorative cables. Niches and turrets twist and twirl in intricate, Baroque patterns across elaborate doorways. The overall effect is of elaborate embellishment bordering on the wild.

The examples of Manueline style in the Royal Palace at Sintra tend to be from the early, less florid period. The works there began in 1508, as we know from notebooks belonging to the chief builder, one André Gonçalves, who also kept a careful account of the costs. Curved features with naturalistic embellishments – for example bent branches that resemble two artichokes face to face – can be found in the carriage entry which runs between Dom Manuel's additions and the older parts of the Palace. There are arched doorways within, with more examples of curved branch work, twisted and inter-twined.

However, the most striking part of the Manueline addition to the Sintra palace is the entire wing that was added to the eastern side. On the façade of this wing six windows, three on each floor, overlook the entrance court. The windows are all broadly similar in design though details of decoration vary on each. Their Manueline features are immediately visible, which include fine frames in twisted Baroque form, but the windows also exhibit clear links with the earlier Moorish-style windows in the older, western block. Each of the Manueline windows has two round-headed lights and a framing stand on corbelled-out bases at the side. The capitals are formed of wreaths of twisted foliage; on the lower floor one has twisted around it two branches, out of which grow the cusps. Decorative flowers are found engraved on them, sometimes in square shapes, sometimes round. Branches also intertwine on the sides, supporting three dramatic finials, capped with turban-shaped tops. While thus distinct in their exuberant naturalistic and exotic additions, the windows nevertheless have the same shape as the earlier Moorish ones and do not feel out of place when viewed with them.

There are many Manueline features in this part of the building. A number of doorways are in the florid style; at the end of a passage, a doorway has a half-octagonal head with curved sides. The door leading into the Sala dos Cisnes is also Manueline. Inside other rooms, such as the Sala das Duas Irmãs (The Hall of Two Sisters) there is evidence that the older struc-ture was embellished at the time of Dom Manuel. Two rows of columns and arches have been inserted below the ceiling. The arches are rounded and unmoulded; the thin supporting columns are also round with eight sided bases. The great hall of the Sala dos Brasões was completed at the end of King Manuel's reign.

One of the most significant cultural legacies of the Moorish period in Sintra was to add to the stock of myth and imagery which has been so important in defining the *locale*. The very image of the castle ramparts guarding an Arab town, with its mosque and minarets, in the extraordinarily lush setting of Sintra, fired the Romantic imagination and continues to exert a powerful hold, as can be seen in popular representa-tions of the town's history.[1] William Burnett's engravings,

---

1   For example in the children's book, charmingly illustrated by J. Ruys, *Sintra O Encantado Monte da Lua* (Sintra, 1997). The castle ramparts and crescent moon can be seen on Sintra's coat of arms. See Illustration 17.

which evoke Sintra in an Arcadian setting, depict the Moorish castle and ruins as stage props that make for an exotic effect.

There has always been a hint of Oriental glamour and mystery about Moorish figures in the Portuguese imagination. In popular fairy stories, such as *The Subterranean Passage*, for instance, Moorish rulers appear as devious characters who gain great mastery over the local population by their knowledge of magic. But the Moorish association has not always been represented in a sinister light. A legendary lovesick Moorish Princess, who languished at the departure of her knightly hero for the wars, is a sympathetic and engaging Sintra character. Her sighs were said to echo in the hills around the Palace of Seteais.[1]

Several nineteenth-century buildings in the town display Oriental features both architecturally and in their interior design. Pena Palace, the Quinta do Relógio and the fountains like the one in the Volta do Duche where passers-by stop to imbibe the clear, cold water pouring down the mountain cliff, all show Moorish influence. At Pena the Moorish theme is part of an elaborate mosaic of styles, which also includes the neo-Gothic, the neo-Manueline and the neo-Moghul. This gaudy, extravagant mixture is evident throughout the palace, although certain styles are more pronounced in some areas than in others. Elements of pastiche are blended into serious attempts at creating atmosphere. The jumble of styles, which is characteristic of the castle, has sometimes offended purists in search of classical harmonies. Accounts suggest that the Oriental features of the palace, which include Moghul as well as Moorish influences, were preferred by the architect, the Baron Eschwege, whereas the more Gothic and Manueline

1   This popular explanation of the origin of the name of 'sete-ais'(meaning 'seven sighs') is disputed by scholars who associate the word with 'centéais' or rye. Costa finds first mention of the name in 1340, see *Estúdios Sintrenses* vol. II p.79 and de Carvalho agrees that the name derives from 'field of rye'. S.L. de Carvalho, op. cit. p.13.

features were the choice of his patron, Dom Fernando, the Prince Consort.[1]

The Moorish features of Pena stand out even in the Hollywood-like backdrop of somewhat louche styles that surround it. The boundary walls outside the original monastery have typically Moorish arches, which at some points frame views of the valley around. Similarly, the belvedere is in the shape of an Arab minaret. It is covered with yellow tiles and topped by a cone. A fine horseshoe arch (a form the Moors inherited from the Visigoths) is cut out in the tunnel around the walls. These arches are multi-lobed and fan gracefully into elegant points. Twisted columns have been imported from Granada. The entrance gateway of the castle is a strikingly Arabic feature, cut out in a horseshoe shape and set in a wall surmounted by a row of merlons. Two columns, whose capitals are decorated with Egyptian motifs, hold up the arch. The tympanum is covered in decorative tiles.

Within the rooms of the palace there are many neo-Moorish features. The Sala dos Árabes has the interior design of a mosque; the atmosphere is accentuated by arches, grisaille and tiling. Neo-Manueline additions and Portuguese Indian furniture add to the exotic blend. It has a particularly theatrical feeling to it and evokes a sense of the *Arabian Nights* stories. The Sala Indiana, the work of the architect Domingos Meira, is a mixture of Indian and Moorish styles. There is elaborate plasterwork with geometric motifs and multi-lobed arches in relief, which define the space between the wall panels and the decorated wooden ceiling. As in the other rooms, like the Sala Nobre, there is an eclectic mixture of Oriental furniture and objects, including fine Chinese porcelain.

The most strikingly neo-Moorish façade of nineteenth-century Sintra is the Quinta do Relógio, which nestles in the shady grove across the road from the Quinta da Torre da Regaleira. In William Beckford's time the Quinta da Relógio

---

1   P. Pereira & J.M. Carneiro, *Pena Palace* (London, 1999) pp.33ff.

was the residence of Thomas Horne, his agent. Beckford talks of the great chestnut tree that shades Horne's square terrace, from where the most romantic views of Sintra may be seen.[1] António Tomas de Fonseca, the architect and painter, designed the existing house in the nineteenth century for the Count of Monte Cristo whose fortune, like so many others, came from trading interests in Brazil. Its front façade, raised at the centre, shows typically castellated battlements. At each end, it is decorated with a turban-like pinnacle, capped by a crescent moon, a symbol of the Moors. Below this high frontage is the plain tympanum; below that are three graceful arches in typically rounded style, held up by unadorned columns whose capitals are of elegant, naturalistic design. The polychrome is exuberant; the inner walls bear mottoes of the Kings of Granada in Arabic script. The doors below have the same Moorish shape as the windows to either side on the wings.

Another Sintra legend hangs over this somewhat neglected *quinta*. Crown Prince Carlos chose it for his honeymoon with Princess Amélia, who found Sintra and the house frighteningly exotic. After Carlos was assassinated in 1908, a ghostly image was said to be reflected in the waters of the lake, which stands in the overgrown and gloomy grounds. At Monserrate, down the road, although the exterior is in Moghul style, the long, arched gallery, which runs through the house, also has a distinctly Moorish feeling. Of all the Sintra interiors, it is most reminiscent of the Alhambra in Granada. Moorish remains, including a necropolis, have also been found in recent excavations in Colares, suggesting that the valley and its river were important points of transport seawards.[2]

Sintra has always been famous for its clear, running streams of cold water. These cascades add to the Edenic quality of the

1   *The Journal of William Beckford in Portugal and Spain 1787–1788* (ed. B. Alexander) (London 1954) p.142.
2   See M.T. Caetano, op. cit. pp.33ff.

place and were much admired by the Moorish occupants and used by them in their ritual ablutions. It is therefore not unfitting that several of the fountain niches, which are cut into the mountain side, should be constructed to resemble Arabic resting places. In the Volta do Duche, situated below the Municipal Park, at a point where the road sweeps round, is the neo-Moorish fountain of José de Fonseca. It is an elaborate structure, topped by battlement walls, and highly decorated, with an arched frame in the shape of a turban. Within the frame are to be found the traditional three arches in horseshoe shape. Below is the indented fountain area, entirely tiled in the *Mudejar* style, with decorative frieze and bricks above. A slight depth adds to the effect of a *trompe l'oeil* as one rounds the bend toward the fountain from the direction of the town hall. Not all visitors to Sintra have admired restoration of this type, however. The poetess Oliva Guerra considers it to be in extremely bad taste.[1]

To leave a discussion of the Moorish influence in Sintra without a mention of gastronomy would be remiss. A visitor to Portugal is much struck by the sweetness of Portuguese desserts and little cakes. The use of eggs and almonds immediately remind one of Arabic pastry delicacies. Sintra's special pastry is the *queijada* or cheesecake. It is certain that cheesecakes have been made in Sintra since the Middle Ages. *Queijadas* appear as a form of payment in medieval accounts. In 1369, for example, a half dozen cheesecakes and goats show up in the accounts of the Monastery of São Vicente da Fora.[2] In her exhaustive book on the complex history of *queijada* making, Raquel Moreira considers the question of their Arabic origins. She makes the telling point that they were produced in an area of the country which was entirely Arabised. She notes that the Arabs have traditionally enjoyed using white cheese in sweets, as well as blending almond and

---

1   O. Guerra, *Roteiro Lírico de Sintra* (Lisbon, 1940) p.15.
2   *AHS* vol. III p.125.

cinnamon.[1] One might add that elsewhere in the south of the country where *queijadas* are produced, the Moorish influence was strongest. The evidence of an Arab connection is compelling even if there is no final proof. By the nineteenth century *queijadas* were so identified with Sintra that Eça de Queirós had them sent to Paris so that, in a Proustian way, he could be reminded of the *serra* when nibbling them. By that time, no visit to Sintra was thought to be complete without enjoying the very Eastern taste of this delicacy.

---

1   R. Moreira, *Queijadas de Sintra* (Sintra, 1999) pp.27ff. The book is a delightful history of the making of *queijadas* from earliest times.

4

Royal Sintra

In 1154, only seven years after it had been captured from the Moors, Sintra received a royal charter (*foral*) from Afonso Henriques.[1] The granting of a charter by the first King of Portugal began a long association between the town of Sintra and the Crown, which was to continue for over seven hundred and fifty years until the expulsion of the Braganças in 1910. Sintra was not the only town to receive a charter from Afonso Henriques – he granted as many as forty – but it conferred upon Sintra privileges normally accorded to towns of greater importance or size, such as Guimarães, Coimbra and Leiria. The granting of the charter has therefore been rightly regarded as a landmark in the recognition of the unusual status of Sintra and its part in the history of the emerging Portuguese nation.

The *foral* is an extensive document, containing fifty-four articles, which sets out, on the one hand the privileges that were being granted to the inhabitants of Sintra and, on the other, the duties and the taxes that they would have to pay the King in return. It also regulated judicial and penal codes, defining the role of the magistracy and the execution of law within the borough. However, the *foral* is not only a document of legal significance but also one of considerable sociological interest. It sets out a code for social behaviour and prescribes penalties for those who choose to break it. In this way it is a highly prescriptive document, defining the social norms to be observed in the Sintrense community.

---

1   For the Latin original and a Portuguese translation and commentary, see F. Costa, *O Foral de Sintra* (Sintra, 1976). (Henceforth abbreviated as *Foral.*)

The *foral* of Sintra is written in Latin,[1] which remained in use until the end of the thirteenth century, when King Dinis insisted on use of the vernacular in official documents. In the early years of the Portuguese nation, there is no evidence of the written use of Galaico-Portuguese, which had evolved from Vulgar Latin and which was spoken throughout the Moorish period. Sancho I (1185–1211), the second King of Portugal, began to write courtly verse in Portuguese, which was by then evolving as a distinct Iberian dialect and also being used as the poetic medium in the Castilian court. As we read on in the archival records, Portuguese begins to appear mingled with Latin, though it is not always correctly written. As early as in 1195, a document relating to land rights in Sintra, written in Latin, nevertheless shows sprinklings of the vernacular. Throughout the following century more and more Portuguese appears in the entries. When we read fourteenth-century documents, Latin has all but disappeared.

The principal beneficiaries under the terms of the *foral* were settlers who lived within the precincts of the castle. This distinction was presumably made on the grounds that the Knights Templar,[2] who played an important role in Portuguese history, lived there. These gentlemen, including one Gualdim Pais, were given possession of thirty houses, including their estates (*fazendas*), in Lisbon from which they would expect to derive a considerable income through rent. The well-being of their families was also protected by rights of inheritance and property transfers could be made between the original householders. Francisco Costa, in his exhaustive monograph on the *foral,* points to the unusual nature of a

---

1   Costa, himself an accomplished Latinist, warns of the dangers of not reading the document in the original. He criticises Viscount Juromenha for relying on a faulty translation. F. Costa, *Foral* p.39.

2   The military order of the Templars (and that of the Hospitallers) played a significant part in the campaign against the Moors. They became considerable landowners. For their role in early Portuguese history, see A. Lorção, *Os Templários na formação de Portugal* (Lisbon, 1999).

provision which grants rights to citizens outwith the territory they inhabited.[1] In the case of the knights of Sintra, the privilege was matched by a duty, namely to defend Lisbon (but nowhere beyond it) in the case of armed conflict. Once a year they had to attend on the monarch in proof of this pledge; it was not a great burden in return for the untaxed revenue on the thirty houses. The King's gesture in giving the houses, although generous, was not entirely disinterested. His intention was to preserve the land around Sintra for his own hunting. By giving the knights of Sintra property in Lisbon, he hoped that they would be less inclined to seek more income by taking land just outside Sintra.

The two categories of citizens who were the beneficiaries of royal generosity were the *milites* and the *pedites*. The *milites* were the knights, the owners of horses, while the *pedites*, as their name implies, were the rank and file foot soldiers. Nevertheless even the latter gained unusual rights under the *foral* and together with the knights, could pass on the benefits, which they had acquired, to their descendants. Widows too, in a strikingly politically correct provision, inherited all the rights and status of their deceased spouses, retaining them until death. Both categories of citizen were exempt from working on Crown lands (a common obligation on all subjects) and, even more importantly, were exempt from a degree of taxation when working on the rich, productive land around the town. This latter exemption was, of course, intended to safeguard the important production of food for Lisbon. A curious exception was the cultivation of wine, which was not exempted. As a result it proved an unattractive option for local landowners, eventually leading to a decline in production. Overall, the various privileges granted by the Crown, as well as the revenues from the thirty houses, made the burghers of Sintra financially very well off, and no doubt stalwart royalists to a man.

---

1   F. Costa, *Foral* p.41.

The Sintra knights were governed by their own leader (*alcaide*). A council of notables (*conselho*) advised the leader. In the nineteenth century, liberal intellectuals like Alexandre Herculano claimed that this self-governing element of the medieval political arrangements were precursors of modern electoral institutions. Indeed, Herculano went even further, tracing links between the royal charters and Roman adminis-trative structures, insisting that the tradition of self-regulation went back to ancient times. His proposition, as H.V. Livermore points out, was rather far fetched.[1] The evidence suggests that the Roman *municipium,* the focus of adminis-tration, had already withered away by the time of the Moorish invasion. During the Suevic period certain rights, including the right to assemble, had become features of political life in the cities. But a direct link between these loose arrangements and self-regulating institutions is difficult to maintain. Nevertheless Herculano's enthusiasm led him to cast the various charters into a typology, ranging from the rudimen-tary, through the complete, to the perfect according to whether genuinely independent councils featured in them or not. Sintra's charter, with provison for an autonomous council, capable of administering law within a defined area, would fall into the most advanced or perfect category.

The judicial arrangements under the *foral* provided for a magistrate (*iudex*) and an executive officer (*saião*) to deal with the various matters that arose from the conferment of rights and privileges. The method of appeal and the type of actions that could be brought are described in the provisions of the charter. The judge and the *saião* were elected from the local authority (*conselho*) though a further layer of authority, headed by the regional governor, was placed above them. The judge heard cases and received a quarter of the fines imposed as penalties; the *saião* executed the decisions of the court and received one tenth of the amount paid to the judge. The rest

---

58 H.V. Livermore, op. cit. p.44.

went to the Crown. The judge was therefore a figure of great power and wealth, wielding considerable influence in the town.

Stiff penalties, some in the form of hefty fines, were laid down for breaches of the regulations. The gravest offences attracted corporal or capital punishment. The harshest sentence of all was for premeditated homicide: a convicted murderer could be buried alive underneath the victim he had killed. Such a provision reminds us that we are considering a society of some primitiveness despite its sophisticated legal framework. Corporal punishment, as well as fines, could be meted out to anyone committing violent acts against the person. The level of fines was often left to the magistrate to determine. He usually took advice from the councillors. Victims of crime were compensated by receiving half the amount of any fine imposed. Penalties attached to men convicted of living in sin – that is living with women to whom they were not married, and there was a particular sanction attaching to the rape of a legal spouse. By taking account of marital status, these regulations were intended to reinforce the institution of marriage, which was regarded as the cement of social life.

Other provisons of the charter protected property, another institution considered vital to maintaining the social fabric. Damage to or destruction of private property was treated as a serious offence, and offenders were punished with heavy fines. To contain the number of incidents leading to damage to property, citizens were not allowed to carry offensive weapons (spears and swords are cited in this category) unless they could show they had good reason to need them. The judge retained the residual power to expel persistent offenders from the precincts of the borough.

The Sintra clergy also benefited under the terms of the charter. They were given the status of gentlemen; so long as they did not commit any crime, they could not be removed from their churches by either the King or the bishop. The clergy had to perform the customary duties of the Church in births, deaths and marriages but tenure meant that local priests had a considerable degree of independence in running their own parishes. This was strengthened by the fact that the priests were recruited mainly from the local community, though occasionally there were exceptions. Once a year, service to the bishop was rewarded. The reward was financial, and expected to be good.

Although the *foral* of 1154 was the main charter of Sintra, other charters were drawn up at later dates. The most notable is one by King Manuel in 1514 which was followed two years later, in 1516, by a *foral* for Colares.[1] Dom Manuel's charter for Sintra acknowledges the rights enshrined in the original *foral* of 1154 but sets out changes that were now to be put in place. In particular it tackles the matter of taxes due from the non-privileged members of the community, who must have greatly outnumbered the descendants of the original benefi- ciaries. Some of the new levies fell to be paid on the feast day of St Martin, a date that Sintra churchgoers, attending services at São Martinho, would not find difficult to remember. Despite these changes, after a period of almost four hundred years, the provisions of the original charter remained largely in operation.

The *foral* of Sintra outlines a legal framework in which the social behaviour of a self-sufficient and at times prosperous community could be accommodated. That community was primarily agricultural though it had, at its centre, an urban nucleus of townsfolk, which included the leaders of the borough. From that political nexus, which operated under the shadow of the Court when the royal family was in residence at Sintra, radiated the legal and administrative regulation of the whole area. Although no other location near Lisbon had the advantages of Sintra as a royal residence, the town still needed to be managed in the Crown's interest. The *foral* ensured that

---

1   For a text of the foral of Colares, see F. Costa, *Foral* pp.117–22.

the King's needs were met whilst at the same time generously compensating the burghers of Sintra.

Sintra's development as a medieval community is well-documented in extensive archives that predate its foundation in 1154. The documents gathered in the *Arquivo Histórico de Sintra* contain copies of legal records – of property ownership, its conferment and the disputes to do with it – as well as occasional reports on commercial, social or topographical matters.[1] The archive is thus a rich source of commentary on Sintra's local history, setting out the detailed workings of administration and law in its domain. One of the most prominent and recurring features of this record is its emphasis on the close connection between the town and the Crown – something that undoubtedly shaped the entire history of Sintra from the point at which it was first incorporated as a borough. The archive paints the picture of a society in which agricultural production is of the utmost importance and is conducted, on the whole, with success. The subject of the granting of rights and the imposition of charges comes up over and over again; Sintra is a society of property owners whose assets are valuable and are, under certain conditions, protected by royal favour. The records also show the establishment of numerous religious societies; the foundation of churches, monasteries and of various charitable institutions where medical treatment was dispensed. In this way they shed a great deal of light on the social history of the town.

The very earliest documentary material in the archive

---

1   Much of the material in this chapter has been derived from the *AHS*. When J.M. da Silva Marques put the archive together in the 1930s, he collated material relevant to Sintra in the national archives at the Torre do Tombo, Lisbon. Although land possession and property deeds figure prominently in the archival record, the papers are also a rich source of material about the social and religious life of Sintra, containing references to the royal connection, agriculture, climate, topography, buildings (both secular and religious) and much else of considerable sociological interest. The archive begins in Latin, evolving gradually into Portuguese during the thirteenth century. I am most grateful to Sintra Council and to Dr Eugénio Montoito, Director of the Historical Archive, for allowing me access to the Archive during my research in Sintra.

suggests that at the time of the so-called re-conquest, a pattern of stability, based on a sound, agricultural economy, was characteristic of Sintra life. The capacity to produce basic goods – fuel from wood as well as cereals and fruit – meant that there was a reasonable level of livelihood for the *saloios,* the name given to the peasants who worked on the land in what is now the greater Lisbon area. An additional source of wealth came from the exploitation of metals – mainly silver and iron – which had been worked in the region since before Roman times. However, though Sintra was airy and umbrageous, it did not, of course, escape some of the disasters that befell medieval society in Portugal and elsewhere in Europe.

The two deadly threats were famine and plague. For an economy based almost entirely on agriculture, any disruption of the production of food meant certain hardship, a crop failure that lasted any length of time was disastrous. The cause of this sort of crisis was usually drought, though from time to time the opposite, inundation by rain, also wiped out an entire year's harvest. The record shows that 1333 and 1334 were particularly bad years, when the entire crop of wheat was destroyed, removing the staple diet, bread, at a stroke. The crisis affected the whole country; people were reduced to eating grass and weeds. Whilst there were years of plentiful harvests, throughout the fourteenth century famine came and went even in Sintra, an area of unusual abundance. The plague also struck periodically, in its various forms. The most severe case recorded was in 1348 when it is possible that as much as fifty per cent of the population of Sintra was wiped out. No doubt the natural advantages of the region made it resilient and ready to rise, phoenix-like, out of each disaster. Nevertheless, each crisis caused immense hardship and suffering.

Questions about the rights to ownership of property, inheritance procedures, and disputes about boundaries and the subject of taxation arise over and over in the long archival record of Sintra through the Middle Ages. Sometimes the documents give planning permission – for example for the rebuilding of houses after the earthquake of 1531. At other times they settle disputes about the exact demarcation of land. As challenges could be made against all landowners, Church possessions are defined as carefully as any others in the deeds setting up religious institutions. Some documents impose restrictions on the use of material, for example of wood. This type of regulation was aimed primarily at preserving royal hunting rather than out of any concern with protecting the environment.

The ownership and sale of vineyards is a subject often mentioned. In 1265 King Afonso III granted certain rights to wine producers in the area but insisted on his usual 'fourth' of profits. By this time profit margins from wine production must have recovered enough to absorb this significant level of taxation. Wine rights often figure in documents relating to Church property, for example in the deeds of the Convent of Trindade, with its estates, in the fifteenth century. A century later, in 1509, when further rights were being granted to them, the citizens of Sintra gratefully acknowledge the royal benefaction, at the same time boasting of their good air, food and wine.

In the reign of King Dinis (1279–1325), Sintra became known as the 'Queen's town'. The King had made over the rights of the town to his wife Isabel, in 1287; its proximity to Lisbon made it a convenient seat of the Court during the hot summer months. The Queen, who was subsequently canonised, was widely admired for her charitable works. A native of Aragon, she introduced the cult of the Holy Ghost into Portugal.

Dinis himself was an artistic man who made a considerable contribution to Portuguese culture, founding the first university in Lisbon in the early 1290s. When the institution was transferred to Coimbra, that town became the centre of Portuguese scholarship. His insistence that Galaico-Portuguese must always be used as the official language gave the vernacular a great boost. The King was inspired by the troubadour tradition, which flourished in Catalonia, his maternal homeland. Troubadour ballad writers were welcomed at court. Dinis' patronage of the arts began a long tradition whereby artists over the ages found a sympathetic audience for their work at the old royal palace. Many important theatrical works were written specially for the royal occasions that took place in its precincts.

The clearest symbol of the relationship between town and Crown was in the very building of the royal palace (Paço Real), whose pepperpot chimneys are silhouetted on the town's outline. Examining the engravings of Duarte d'Armas, which were executed in 1507,[1] the familiar, distinctive chimney pots (echoing similar cone-like structures of buildings in France and Italy) appear more integrated in a range of turrets, towers and etiolated spires. The effect of this precise but rather fantastical representation is to romanticise and idealise the image of the royal palace. There is a clinical symmetry about the houses, which are clustered neatly outside the palace walls, adding to the delicate effect of the whole scene, when it is viewed from the south.[2] The surrounding hills are etched in almost barren relief, and the fairy-tale effect is completed by the conceit of some ducks paddling in the pond in the foreground. In the view from the east, the angle is even sharper so that a tighter, more integrated alignment of all the vertical protrusions is presented. The houses are now all of a piece with the palace, the tower of São Martinho church looms distinctively and the royal standards stick out horizontally in a rather artificial way. In an amusing *trompe l'oeil*, the Castelo dos Mouros seems to be floating on a bank of clouds. In Duarte d'Armas' view from the south-east, the battlements of the ethereal-looking Moorish castle spread out across the moun-

---

1   Duarte d'Armas' views of Sintra, engraved in 1507, were collected in his book *Livro das Fortalezas* (Lisbon, 1510). He is now regarded mainly as an artist of historical interest. See Illustrations 4, 5 and 6.
2.   See Illustration 4.

tains, whilst Pena chapel masses in an almost threatening way.[1]

Several of Duarte d'Armas' towers are not to be found in the existing building; nor, conversely, do his depictions show the subsequent Manueline additions to the palace. What we do see before us is a stylised representation of the palace as it was at the end of the reign of King João I and in the early years of Dom Manuel's reign before his extensive additions were made. We have already noted in the previous chapter that, of the early monarchs, it was King João I who commissioned major work on the palace from the 1390s onwards.

Entering the building through the main courtyard (which has been unenclosed since the outer walls were removed at the time of the Republic in the early twentieth century), the bulk of the palace to the west is Joanine whilst the wing to the east is the addition of King Manuel.[2] This means that the main rooms and internal courtyards – the Sala dos Cisnes, the Central Patio, the Sala das Pegas, the Sala das Sereais, the Council Room, the dining room, the chapel, Afonso V's room (over which King Manuel built the great Sala dos Brasões) and the Patio of Diana – are all part of the Joanine building. The two parts of the building are joined at what is now the Sala dos Archeiros (Hall of the Archers) but which in the original building was an open terrace. In one part of this multi-levelled room is a fountain fed by fresh water from mountain streams that run right through the palace.

The different levels of the two main wings, winding staircases and obscure corridors make it difficult to grasp the layout of the palace at once. Moreover, it is important to appreciate that alterations have been made to many features of the rooms. Doorframes, ceilings and windows, connecting staircases and corridors, have been changed or added to over the ages, until modern times. What we see now is an amalgam of the original designs and the alterations that resulted from royal

1   See Illustration 5.
2   For a plan of the palace, see Plan 1.

demands for a building that was a domestic residence as well as the official seat of the court when the monarch was at Sintra. There have also been attempts at conservation and restoration, though not always with the happiest results.

King João's decision to take up residence in Sintra was, if not prompted by his wife, Philippa of Lancaster, certainly supported by that 'cold, serene and pious' English lady.[1] According to the Count of Sabugosa, Sintra would have reminded the Queen of the damp mists of England; its greenery undoubtedly appealed to her much more than the parched hinterland of Lisbon.[2] The King, and indeed the entire dynasty of Avis, which he founded, was much strengthened by his wife, who proved every bit of a match for the virile, amorous King. She balanced his southern exuberance with a northern sense of discipline.

Philippa brought with her a train of English attendants, who held various positions at Court. The Queen herself, a matriarchal figure, presided over a brilliant family of princes, including Prince Henry the Navigator, whose enthusiastic support for navigational research enabled the Portuguese to take the lead in overseas exploration. The commanding figure of Philippa at court confirmed the status of Sintra as the 'Queen's town'.

One of the more amusing stories about the King and Queen's relationship concerns the theme of the ceiling painting in the Sala das Pegas (Hall of Magpies). This chamber was used for royal audiences when embassies were received at the palace. Like other rooms, it bears the marks of alterations over different periods. Pope Leo X gave the fireplace, a fine piece of Italian marble, to King Manuel in the sixteenth century. It is a strikingly elegant piece of work but looks oddly out of place in the plain room, with its medieval atmosphere. The half-tiled *azulejos* walls of the room are blue and green,

---

1 Conde de Sabugosa, op. cit. p.20.
2 Ibid. p.11.

with elaborate decoration over the doors. The ceiling is divided into 136 triangles in each of which is painted a magpie. Descending from the feet of the bird, but steadied by its beak, flutters a scroll on which are written the words '*Por bem*' (for good). A red rose marks the Lancastrian connection. The decoration, including the partitioning of the whole ceiling, is from a later period.

Legend has it that Philippa surprised the King cavorting with one of her ladies-in-waiting, in this very room. The King's story was that he had plucked a rose from the terrace and, chancing upon one of the young maids of honour, had given it to her in an act of spontaneous gallantry. She curtsied on receiving it, whereupon he kissed her. At that very moment the Queen entered the room. In no time the Palace gossips got to work, noting slanderously that the maid of honour in question was much in their master's good books. To assure the Queen that his intentions had been pure, the King closed the room and had its ceiling repainted with magpies. The number of birds corresponded to the number of ladies-in-waiting, while the label fluttering from the beak of each bird, with the inscription '*Por Bem*' written on it, implied that he meant no harm by the kiss.[1] The Count of Sabugosa, in his account, speculates about which part of the lady's body the King kissed, but comes to no conclusion.[2]

Near to the Hall of Magpies is the dining room which has a distinctly Joanine feeling though it has clearly been altered at various times. There are, indeed, other aspects of the room which predate King João's reign. The impression of his times is given by the windows, which are simple, elegant arches without too much refinement in the finials, resisting the Moorish-style ornamentation we find elsewhere in the

---

1 In a charming recreation of the story in 1891 Henrique Lopes de Mendonça has the maid reassuring the King that no one has seen them while, in a refrain, a painted magpie sings 'It's all for the best'. See J. Rodil, *Serra, Luas e literatura* (Sintra, 1995) pp.110–12.
2 Conde de Sabugosa, op. cit. p.18.

building or the exotic Manueline style which was to follow. The older features appear in the doorframes, particularly in the mouldings and the encaustic tiles (*azulejos*) which may well have been in place when King João began his renovation.

Another story surrounds the paintings on the ceiling of the Sala dos Cisnes (Hall of Swans). The Hall of Swans is the largest in the palace, measuring about twenty-two metres by seven metres. It is long and sweeping, with light coming in from both sides. To the left as one descends into it from the Hall of Magpies, an elegant series of windows look onto the inner courtyard, with a long tank of water just outside. Its ceiling is painted with white swans.

The story about this room is that ambassadors from the Duke of Burgundy were received in the chamber when they came to sue for the hand of King João I's daughter, Dona Isabel. Among the presents brought by the ambassadors were some swans. The delighted Princess had red collars made for them and insisted on their being put in the long, narrow water tank just below the windows of the hall. Stretching her arm out of the window, the Princess could feed her beloved pets without even getting up. When she eventually left for Flanders, the King, afflicted by a feeling of loss (*saudades*) ordered the ceiling of the hall to be painted with images of swans as a reminder of his daughter. The rows of identical swans have not pleased every visitor. In the eighteenth century, Joseph Barretti complained of their monotony, as he did of the rows of magpies in the Hall of Magpies. Nevertheless, the Hall of Swans is an elegant chamber; the large full-length windows, which open out into the patio where the water tank is still in place, enhance its sense of grandeur.

The Sala das Galés tends to be associated with King João's grandson, Afonso V, although alterations to it were made at a much later date. Once again, the most remarkable feature of the room is its ceiling, with maritime views in panels. At the end of the rectangular centre panels are two semi-circular ones. They show Portuguese ships-of-the-line lying off the shore of a distinctly Muslim-looking town, with minarets spiralling on the skyline. In the main panels, a series of different types of Portuguese ships-of-the-line are depicted, emphasising the vital naval element in the colonial expansion eastwards.

The Count of Sabugosa declares that Sintra always attracted monarchs who were huntsmen, poets, artists or sybarites.[1] King Duarte I, brother of Prince Henry the Navigator, who succeeded King João I, was certainly interested in the arts. He was himself the author of a philosophical treatise, the *Loyal Counsellor*. Like other members of his family, Duarte was a dabbler in poetry, earning himself the title of 'the Eloquent'. His Queen, Dona Leonor, is said to have loved the bucolic sadness of the *serra* and seems to have insisted on staying there, particularly during the summer when Lisbon was unbearably hot. Both the King and Queen enjoyed the scenery and cool, clean air of the town, and many documents of their short reign are sealed at Sintra. Their son, Afonso V, had close ties with Sintra: he was born and later died in the royal palace, in a room named after him.

Afonso succeeded to the throne at the age of six in 1438. By this time the overseas expansion of Portugal had begun in earnest. Afonso's uncle, Prince Henry established a centre of nautical and cartographical science in the Algarve. Henry's exact role in these overseas explorations has been seriously challenged by Peter Russell in his recent book, *Prince Henry 'the Navigator': A Life* (2000). Russell paints a rather gloomy picture of the royal Prince, suggesting that his interest was less in science and more in a crusading fervour, the same zeal that undoubtedly spurred on many of the members of the Avis dynasty. Far from being a gracious patron of seafarers, Russell's Henry emerges as a rather grasping, detached character whose motivation is always morally suspect.[2]

---

1   Ibid. p.7.
2   P. Russell, *Prince Henry 'the Navigator': A Life* (Yale, 2000) *passim*.

Whatever Henry's true motivation was, there can be doubt that the royal household was gripped by the fever of discovery. The Atlantic islands were the first to be discovered and annexed. Madeira was reached by the 1420s and was put under the personal authority of Prince Henry, who administered it through chosen appointees. The Azores, where Flemish immigrants joined the original Portuguese settlers, was the next acquisition. The Atlantic islands became an important source of supply of agricultural goods to the mainland, a trade continued to modern times. To-ings and fro-ings from the islands to Portugal meant that captains of the fleet were frequently appearing at the court at Sintra, establishing a long-enduring link between the town and Portuguese territories around the world.[1]

Soon Portuguese interests were extending in North Africa and south along the West African coast. Not all royal forays were successful. In 1437, for instance, Prince Henry tried to capture Tangier, without success. To salvage what he could from the debâcle, Prince Henry arranged for the besieged Portuguese army to leave the city unmolested on the condition that the Portuguese would hand back the much-prized port of Ceuta to the Moors. As a guarantee of this pledge, the Prince's younger brother, Prince Fernando, was given as a hostage until a settlement could be arranged. In fact no such settlement was ever made. Russell suspects that Prince Henry never had any intention of giving up his beloved Ceuta, where he himself lingered for some months after the withdrawal from Tangier. Rather, he was using his brother as a pawn so as to be able to represent the Tangier episode in a more favourable light at home. The affair of the proposed return of the hostage prince dragged on for some years. Dom Fernando wrote piteous letters to his father King Duarte who, unable to resolve the situation, died, grief-stricken, in the following year. Dom

---

1   For an account of these connections, see J.M. da Silva Marques, *Sintra e Sintrenses no Ultramar Português* (Sintra, 1949).

Fernando himself endured six years of squalid captivity, eventually dying of dysentery in Fez.

In the meantime a regency was set up under the eldest prince, the literary-inclined Dom Pedro who corresponded with Juan de Mena and other eminent Iberian men of letters, during the minority of the heir to the throne, Afonso, his nephew. However it was the widowed Queen Leonor who continued to exert the greatest influence at court. She kept such a tight hold over the future King that his supporters eventually removed him from her control. Released from the Queen's influence, the young heir was more susceptible to the seduction of the rising Bragança family although his uncle, Prince Henry, remained as a role model. By the time Prince Henry died in 1460 the Cape Verde Islands had been taken for the Portuguese Crown and the doughty Portuguese caravels had reached as far south as Sierra Leone on the West African coast. Whatever conclusions one might come to about his motives, there is no doubt that Prince Henry's passion for exploration put Portugal foremost among maritime nations and brought it great wealth.

Afonso, spurred on by his young glory-seeking aristocratic friends such as the Falcão brothers, led an expedition to Morocco in person, capturing Alcácer-Céguer and establishing a series of Portuguese fortresses along the North African coast. These exploits earned him the title of the 'African'. They seem glamorous compared to the more domestic practice of keeping a 'Red Book', a manual which identified court etiquette to be observed at Sintra.

Nevertheless, these domestic refinements show that Afonso was far from being a mindless soldier but a King concerned with the proper conduct of behaviour at his court. Like other members of the illustrious Avis dynasty, he was artistic and inclined to music. When he was not pursuing territorial adventures abroad or battling against Spanish incursions, the King enjoyed the crisp airs of Sintra. He also made improvements to the palace, including the installation of a great lamp

at the entrance. On his death, Garcia de Resende describes the
solemn cortège leaving the palace gates, conveying his corpse
to its final resting place in Batalha.

Afonso's successor, João II, was proclaimed King in a stately
ceremony held in the parade ground (Jogo da Pella) within
the palace. The King appeared in full regalia while lords, ladies
and knights attended in court attire. Despite this start and the
reception of embassies at Sintra, the King was often away,
holding court in different parts of his realm. But when he was
in Sintra he followed the family tradition of encouraging the
production of plays and poetry at the palace. João also invited
foreign artists from Italy to work in Portugal, inspiring local
craftsmen to widen their stylistic horizons. In 1498, perhaps
for reasons of pecuniary interest, he received at Sintra an
embassy of Jews who were being expelled from Spain.
Holding back from actually granting them asylum, he nevertheless agreed to allow them safe passage through Portugal to
friendlier countries overseas. The royal coffers benefited
substantially from this decision. The King's tours of the
country were part of a strategy of raising morale in a situation
where there was a constant threat of invasion from Spain.

In 1495 Manuel I, known as 'the Fortunate', succeeded to
the throne, inaugurating the most illustrious reign of the Avis
dynasty. Within three years of his accession Vasco da Gama
had returned from India and in 1500, Pedro Álvares Cabral
discovered Brazil. Plans for overseas enterprises were being
constantly discussed at Sintra; from Cochin, Francisco de
Almeida sent reports comparing Oriental palaces with those
on the *serra* whilst from Malacca, Afonso de Albuquerque
enthused on the supply of gold he had discovered. Wealth
poured into Portugal from overseas, making Manuel one of
the richest and most powerful monarchs in Europe. To match
these imperial pretensions, the Portuguese monarch schemed
to gain control of the whole of Iberia. One way of achieving
his goal was by marriage; he took as his first wife a daughter
of the King and Queen of Castile. In Sintra he set up a grand

court, like his predecessors enjoying the verdure and the cool and well-appointed mountain location.

At Sintra there was also a renaissance of the arts encouraged by the opulent monarch. Among the glittering courtiers who passed their time in the royal palace were writers, musicians, and artists, including practitioners of the popular troubadour tradition. Great literary figures such as Bernadim Ribeiro and Gil Vicente rubbed shoulders with the soldiers and explorers who were extending the King's dominion in all directions overseas. On the death of his first wife, the King soon married another daughter of the Spanish monarchs, by whom he had ten children. With such a large family and considerable means at his disposal, it was natural that he should turn his attention to embellishing and expanding the royal palace.

We have seen, in the previous chapter, that Dom Manuel added substantially to the palace in building his florid looking east wing (see p.59). But he also made considerable alterations to the older part of the palace. His most spectacular addition in that part was the dome of the Sala dos Brasões, which he erected over the chamber of Afonso V, at the eastern edge of the complex. From its large double windows, there are views of the plains and sea in one direction and the *serra* in the other. Like other rooms in the palace, this rectangular hall, which measures about fourteen by thirteen metres, is dominated by the ceiling, itself thirteen metres high. The ceiling is lavishly decorated with the coats of arms of the royal family and the nobility, giving rise to the various names of the room which include the Sala das Armas (Hall of Arms), Sala dos Escudos (Hall of Shields) or the Sala dos Veados (Hall of Deer). It rises steeply into a cupola and is decorated in eight sections, each depicting the coat of arms of one of the royal princes, with pictures of stags below them. All around, in symmetrical order, are the coats of arms of seventy-two noble families. Their names are inscribed on banners that flutter from behind the horns of the stags *couchant* to the back of the shields each one bears. The stags themselves are in various positions; each stag and coat of arms is richly framed in gold so that the effect of the whole ceiling is highly ornate. At the centre of the great octagonal arrangement is the coat of arms of the King of Portugal, splendidly carved on gilded wood.[1]

The heraldic emblems in the arms of the nobility painted on the ceiling panels are highly colourful with representations of both mythological (dragons and unicorns) and real animals and birds (lions and crows). Added to these are crosses, stars, castles and turrets and many other elaborate chivalric features. They are arranged in the order of precedence which the *fidalgo* families enjoyed at the Manueline Court although changes to the order and the actual heraldic depictions were made in the seventeenth century. One of the more curious emblems is the Pacheco family shield, on which cauldrons are depicted. One or two shields fell victim to time or circumstance. After the family's involvement in the so-called Aveiro conspiracy to kill the King, Pombal had the coat of arms of the Tavora family removed from the ceiling. The Count of Sabugosa claims that William Beckford found it lying around when he visited the palace in the summer of 1787. Another shield, that of the Coelhos, seems to have disintegrated and was found in 1842 on a visit of Prince Lichnowsky. According to the Abbade Castro, not always a reliable source, Duarte d'Armas was partially responsible for the paintings in the room. The whole effect of the hall, including its large eighteenth-century *azulejos* covering the walls with hunting or bucolic scenes, is impressively majestic, a shrine to royal despotism and oligarchy in an era which is known to the Portuguese as the 'Age of Gold'.

King João III succeeded Dom Manuel in 1521. The new King's alterations to the palace revived a distinctly Italianate influence on interior design. However, his most significant act was in commissioning Nicolau Chanterene to sculpt the retable for the Monastery of Nossa Senhora da Pena high up

---

1   A detailed examination of the room is given in Anselmo Braamcamp Freire's monumental book, *Brasões na Sala de Sintra*, 1899.

on the mountain peak. That commission set in motion the acceptance of Italianate classicism in the Portuguese plastic arts. Chanterene had come from his native France to Portugal in 1516, steeped in the tradition of Italian Renaissance art at a time when it had barely made an impact in Portugal. The great thrust of the Portuguese Renaissance spirit had been in the direction of science on the one hand, with the nautical achievement of the explorations and in the field of literature on the other hand, with the production of courtly literature. There is little evidence of Renaissance influence on architecture or the decorative arts, which broadly continued medieval design and practice. Even the Manueline style, which was first used in Sintra in the early sixteenth century, has been identified as a continuation of the medieval.[1]

Chanterene had already had a distinguished career by the time he came to Sintra, having worked at the Church of Santa Maria, Belém, in 1517 and at the Church of São Marcos de Tentúgal in 1522. He began work in Sintra in 1529. Determining exactly what he had done at Pena before this is not easy because the building has been damaged by lightning as well as by various earthquakes, including the great earthquake of 1755. There is also evidence of interference with the Manueline features of the cloister and repair work on the altarpiece itself in the nineteenth century. The Pena retable is executed on a grand scale. The whole structure is highly architectonic in form, giving the impression of a multi-storied building with niches, columns and finely chiselled statues at every level. The work is made of two types of alabaster, white and dark blue, brought by Chanterene from Gelsa, near Saragossa in Spain. They are used in a sophisticated pattern of vertical and horizontal movements within the frame, though the overall effect is not entirely harmonious. The columns and cornices are arranged around a series of 'stage sets' in which various passages from the life of Christ and the Virgin Mary

---

1   See V. Serrão, *Sintra* (Lisbon, 1989) p.48.

are dramatised with an almost filigree delicateness. At the very top, in an extravagantly garlanded corona, which is not Renaissance in spirit at all, is a nativity scene. Below it in the aedicular spaces to the right and left are scenes of the Annunciation and the Adoration of the Magi. In the centre, below the nativity scene, the Virgin Mary, patroness of the Convent of Pena, sits comfortably enthroned, teaching the young Jesus to read, a reminder of the didactic duties of the Jeronimite monks.

The main, central scene of the retable depicts the entombment of Christ. Christ's corpse, supported by three angels, manages to appear both stiff and fluid at the same time. The figures in this scene are of a different dimension to the others depicted in the retable, raising a suspicion that it may not have been the original centrepiece in Chanterene's design.[1] An elaborate, decorative arch encases the gleaming white statues. To the right and below are further scenes from the life of Christ, whilst the Last Supper is depicted in bas-relief on the base.

Despite the intense busyness of the retable's design, its overall effect remains ethereal, an impression which is created mainly by the delicacy of the carving. Chanterene's work, which in the opinion of no less distinguished an authority than Robert Chester Smith, would have placed him in the first rank of artists in his native France had he remained there,[2] is particularly strong in point of sculpture, an art form more innovatively developed than architecture in Portuguese classicist art. Numerous local artists reproduced the style in decorative effects in churches around Sintra and Colares; Renaissance features were incorporated in the building of the country villas (*quintas*) of the aristocracy who flocked to live in their sumptuous houses in the hills around the royal town.

---

1   I am indebted to Pedro de Almeida Flor for sharing his detailed knowledge about the retable with me.
2   R. Chester Smith, *The Art of Portugal 1500–1800* (London, 1968) p.159.

Nevertheless, Chanterene's artistic achievement did not prevent his being reported by a disgruntled colleague to the Office of the Holy Inquisition on suspicion of idolatry for possessing objects allegedly of demonic inspiration. They were, in fact, the artist's models.

The Sintra connections of two further monarchs, Sebastião I (1557–1578) the last of the House of Avis and Afonso VI (1656–1668), the second of the Bragança dynasty, lead us to darker, gloomier aspects of the town's artistic connections, which were to be so much savoured by the Romantics. King Sebastião is one of the most romantic figures in Portuguese history. His name is inextricably linked to *sebastianismo,* an ideological concept, which continued to resonate until the end of the Portuguese Empire in Africa in the mid-1970s. Sebastião succeeded to the throne at the age of three, under the regency of his Spanish grandmother, Queen Catarina. When it appeared that her influence was becoming too powerful, the Cortes, called in 1562, declared: 'Let him dress Portuguese, eat Portuguese, ride Portuguese, speak Portuguese, all his acts be Portuguese.'[1] His education had been entrusted to the Jesuits; and when he was not concerned with spiritual contemplation, he was planning military enterprises. The Jesuits did not fail to consolidate their political influence. Luís and Martin Gonçalves da Camara, two priestly brothers, largely controlled the affairs of state from their base in the young King's private office. The King's erstwhile advisers, appointed by his uncle, the Cardinal Henry, were eclipsed.

Sebastião was a crusading king who led his armies in person. In 1574 an expedition to Ceuta failed. Plans were laid for an even greater adventure in Morocco. Some of the scheming took place in the small, dark Sala do Conselho (Council Chamber) in the palace. Its gloomy atmosphere does not recommend it as a good setting for conducting the affairs of state. During one session in the room, King Sebastião's crown

---

1   Quoted by H.V. Livermore, op. cit. p.94.

fell off his head, which was thought to be an alarming omen by those of a superstitious cast of mind. Sebastião was not to be deterred, however, sharing a certain stubbornness common to many members of the Avis dynasty. In 1578 he set off to Africa with a large posse of Portuguese aristocrats, all of whom were spoiling for a crusade against the Moors. The battle at Alcácer-Quibír was disastrous: eight thousand men, including the King, were killed and twice as many were taken prisoner. It was one of the most forlorn episodes in the long history of Portuguese colonial adventures.

The country emerged from the battle severely weakened. After two years interregnum during which Sebastião's uncle, the Cardinal Henry, reigned, Portugal was annexed by the Spanish crown. Despite the protection of the language and local customs and laws, the installation of the Spanish monarchy was deeply unpopular in Portugal. The period from 1580 to 1640, when three Spanish Philips in succession sat on the joint throne, is still known to Portuguese historians as the Spanish 'domination'. King Sebastião became the object of superstitious reverence: a belief that the King would return became widespread among the common people. Several 'Sebastiãos' did appear claiming to be the King – some were hermits from the provinces, but pretenders appeared even from abroad. In time the belief that Sebastião would return became part of a complex myth, a form of national nostalgia with a potent, emotional impact.

Sebastianismo is the term given for this cultural phenomenon. It shares a quality of longing for return (in this case of a person) with the very Lusitanian concept of *saudades,* which is the concern for loss of a person or place. It is at once a yearning that may be spiritual and lyrical as well as materialistic. The dashing figure of King Sebastião represents a romantic moment in the mythology of the kingdom, for he was a Christian prince who had set about the most honourable task of fighting against Islam. Moreover, he was the King of a nation whose fortunes had always been closely associated with the person of the King, and he was one of the first Portuguese Kings to extend his mission abroad, fighting the very enemy who had once occupied the homeland.

The extension of the King's role as saviour and protector of his people was to be hugely expanded as a result of Portugal's new territorial discoveries. New peoples and lands became his personal responsibility. This aspect of *Sebastianismo* persisted until the twentieth century, influencing Portuguese rulers of the Republic to resist the 'wind of change' which marked the end of European colonialism in Africa. Sebastião's conviction that he was right, his reckless quest for glory and the irrational element this becomes in the dogma of *Sebastianismo*, is caught in Fernando Pessoa's chilling lines of his short poem *Dom Sebastian, King of Portugal*:

> Mad, yes, mad, because I sought a greatness
> Not in the gift of Fate.
> I would not contain the certainty I felt;
> Therefore, on the sandy waste
> Remained what my being was, not is.
>
> Let my madness pass to other men
> With all that it implied.
> Without madness, what is man
> More than the healthy beast,
> A postponed and procreating corpse?[1]

The ideology of *Sebastianismo* was linked on the one hand to a materialistic acquisition of land, from which Portugal was to derive great wealth and, on the other, to a spiritual, messianic mission to save a pagan world for Christianity. The figure of the tragic King, planning his crusades, was also seen as the figure of a redeemer who would rejuvenate the nation and spur its sons on to a greater glory, which would be both martial and spiritual. Sebastião's return would, it was thought,

---

1   F. Pessoa, *Selected Poems* (ed. & trans. P. Rickard) (Edinburgh, 1971) p.80.

mark the return of Portugal to a golden age where civic *virtu* would once more reign supreme. Its symbolic significance in Portuguese culture can hardly be overstated.

One of the more sinister chapters in the royal association with Sintra was the incarceration of Afonso VI for nine years in the Royal Palace in the mid-seventeenth century. Afonso had inherited the newly created title of the Prince of Brazil on the death of his elder brother, Teódosio. However, his childhood was marred by illness that may have left him retarded. By the time he ascended the throne in 1656 the threat from Spain had once again become paramount. The Duke of Schomberg who had been put in charge of the Portuguese troops only just held an invasion in check at Borba in 1663. An alliance with England through the marriage of Catherine of Bragança to Charles II provided the possibility of external protection but Afonso's ability to govern was thrown in doubt at a time when Portugal had not long recovered its independence from Spain. His brother Pedro usurped the throne and Afonso was sent in exile to the Azores. He was eventually brought back to Sintra and imprisoned in the palace until his death in 1683. A popular story suggests that the floor near the window of the chamber where he was incarcerated was worn out by his constant pacing. Even now, the room has a sombre atmosphere, with only a bed as decoration and red and black Moorish designs on the wall. The tiled floor, of green, brown and honey ceramics, is a fine example of Moorish work dating from the late fifteenth century.

The royal connection was an important factor in Sintra's wealth, a wealth that was shared by the other commanding institution of Portuguese society, the Roman Catholic Church. Throughout the archival records of Sintra we find deeds relating to the setting-up of religious institutions and communities, as well as the consecration of churches. As we have seen, under the terms of the *foral,* the clergy had been granted the status of gentlemen. Furthermore, the Sintra-born clergy were protected by tenure: they could not be removed from their churches during their lifetime. Challenge to these clerical privileges arose from time to time throughout the Middle Ages but they remained broadly intact.

Only four years after the *foral* had been granted, we read, in 1158, of the granting of rights to establish a monastery at Santa Cruz. By 1220 so many religious institutions existed that it was necessary to hold an inquiry into the various rights and privileges acquired by the clergy in Sintra as well as in the dioceses of Lisbon and Mafra. In Sintra itself the churches of São Martinho, St Peter, two Santa Marias and St John had already been consecrated. In 1318 the Monastery of Chelas springs to life; in 1379 the goats of the Monastery of São Vincente da Fora are mentioned. Convents (in Portuguese the word also applies to monasteries) continue to spring up in the fifteenth century – such as São Domingos and the Convento da Trindade, while any number of hermitages and chapels are scattered about the valley of Colares and in the Sintra hills. A particularly charming example is the small chapel of Nossa Senhora da Piedade, on the road above the Quinta da Capela, which surprises visitors with its rich *azulejo* decoration. Later on, many of the interiors of these small chapels were decorated with the various coloured tiles, *azulejos*, so typical of the interior of Portuguese Baroque churches.

The early parish churches of Sintra were built in the twelfth century at the very dawn of Portuguese nationhood. They exhibit strong elements of the fortified Romanesque style clearly shown in the façade of Lisbon Cathedral, which was built at the same time. The most striking of these features were sturdy towers and thick walls. Their set back portals and a castellated appearance remind us that these buildings were erected in territory recently seized from an enemy, in this case, the Moors. Churches like São Martinho and Santa Maria retain the simple, rectangular shape associated with this style, though many of their features have been added at different periods and both buildings suffered damage from the earthquake of 1755.

The transition from the Romanesque to the Gothic was,

in any case, a protracted business in Portugal, as we have seen in the development of the plastic arts. Although from a very early period – in the middle of the twelfth century – French artisans were working in Portugal, bringing with them new designs, which broadly lightened the heavier, indigenous style, the older Romanesque tradition endured. Romanesque features are still to be found in buildings of the fifteenth century until suddenly the flamboyant Manueline style flourished.

The church of Santa Maria, in its fine location giving panoramic views of the *serra,* is a good illustration of this eclectic history. Situated up above the old town of Sintra on the way to São Pedro, its façade suddenly looms into view on a bend in the road. Although the main portal is arched, its point is not too sharply defined; the three ogival arches, which are highly polished, hark back to a more rounded aesthetic. The classical columns that surround the arch have been added at a later date, as have the Gothic doors, with their anthropomorphic decorations. The interior of the church is divided into three naves, crossed by ogival arches. Despite the accretion of later features, such as the Manueline font, the atmosphere of the space is distinctly medieval, something that may seem particularly striking because the church, unlike other local churches, did not suffer great damage from the earthquake of 1755. The whole building, however, now gives off a sad, abandoned air.

São Martinho, which is located right in the heart of the old town,[1] has always been an important focus for the Sintrense community; its bell tower symbolises the very town in the famous perspectives of Duarte d'Armas. From this church, too, there are fine views of the hills and valleys of Sintra in the direction of Seteais; its vespers have echoed through the streets of the town over the centuries in a regular, unending rhythm. Whilst the medieval origin of São Martinho is not in doubt – in the report of 1758 to Pombal it is described as 'very old, as

---

1   See Illustration 9.

can be seen by its architecture'[1] – it is not easy to establish how much of the church survived the earthquake of 1755. On the fatal day of 1 November of that year, many parishioners, were crushed to death while attending mass, when the church roof caved in and the walls collapsed. According to the records of the time, most of the building seems to have been demolished; it was not fully rebuilt until 1773.

Alves Pereira, in a series of articles later gathered together in his book, *Sintra do Préterito* (1957) explores the question of the exact age of the church. He notes the typical Romanesque use of space – a large *porticus* which is characteristic of early Christian churches – but hesitates over dating different parts of the existing structure. Masonry of hewn or squared stones (ashlars) indicates early work, probably from the thirteenth century. There are marks on the stone, which also suggest this period although later visitors have interpreted them as Masonic signs, which would have come much later. Taking account, one bright April afternoon, of the direction in which the church faces, Alves Pereira concludes that it was probably built at that time of year when the angle of the building allows the sunlight to penetrate to greatest effect. Inside the church, there is a calm air of pious simplicity. The stone slabs on the floor have an ancient, worn look. Simple, stoned arch and plain marble pillars surround the altar, in tiered levels, but it is not greatly adorned. There is little ornamentation throughout the church, apart from a modern Christ draped in purple on the way of the cross in the side chapel.

The appearance of these Sintra churches and chapels and many other religious institutions attest to the consolidation of the power of the Roman Catholic Church in Portugal and its immense influence, both for good and bad, on Portuguese society. Although the Church was an important educational force in the land, and a great patron of the arts, it also became the focus of a growing intolerance that replaced the relatively

---

1   F. Alves Pereira, op. cit. pp.111ff.

liberal tradition of Mozarabic culture. Minority communities
– in particular the Moors and pre-eminently the Jews – became
more and more vulnerable. The Portuguese Crown failed to
protect those of its subjects who belonged to non-Christian
religions, at great social and economic cost to the nation.

Sintra had both a Moorish and Jewish population. It has
been established that the Moorish artisans were responsible for
the building of the royal palace. On the whole they seem to
have been assimilated to Christian society although discrimi-
nation was practised against them. The Jews, as elsewhere in
Portugal, had largely been forced into commerce because of
their general exclusion from the professions. There were
exceptions, however. The Mestre Guedelha, an astrologer and
physicist, was consulted by King Duarte but his advice to delay
the time appointed for Dom Duarte's proclamation as King,
because of bad portents, was brushed aside. The wealth of the
Jews and the tolerance shown to them by the Moorish rulers
is symbolised in the existence of a Jewish synagogue in the old
town. The synagogue is mentioned in a document of 1405,
when planning permission was given for certain alterations to
the building. By the end of that century, the habit of peaceful
co-existence between the different religious communities was
abandoned. Although King João II had offered sanctuary to
refugees fleeing from the Spanish Inquisition out of self-
interest, the climate of opinion within Portugal was becoming
more and more intolerant. The situation had escalated to the
point where Jews would only practise their religion at home,
often under the cover of darkness. Their relative prosperity
did not help – envy stoked the flames of intolerance, as the
churchmen of the Inquisition knew only too well.

Although the Inquisition was not formally set up in
Portugal until the 1530s, persecution of Jews and Muslims had
started in the decades before then. A vivid example of the
atmosphere of suspicion and hatred which now prevailed is
captured in an account set out in the archival records for that
year. Somewhere in the middle of Sintra's old town a young

boy saw four children of 'new Christian' parents carrying a candle through the streets. He followed them into an alleyway. When they entered a house located near the royal palace, he crept in behind them. Somehow he was not noticed and from his vantage point he claimed to have seen a curtain hanging on a wall with the image of a truncated head superimposed on it. All around, tapers burnt eerily. The boy rushed away to report the incident to his father. That bigoted Christian, believing that his son had witnessed some proscribed ceremony, rushed around to tell the local parish priest of the Church of São Pedro do Penaferrim. The priest bore a grudge against people he described as an 'abominable race'. The next day he preached a fiery sermon against the Jews, including details of what the boy is alleged to have witnessed. Needless to say, the story had become further embellished by this time. It was alleged that six or seven 'new Christian' children had paraded through the streets with lit candles.

No doubt the priest's sermon was heard by the worthy, local magistrates attending mass, and in no time charges were made against the Jews who lived in the house. They were accused of taking part in occult and blasphemous ceremonies. On the basis of the boy's flimsy evidence, the Sintra magistrates hastily brought proceedings and the Jews were convicted. As it happened, these Sintra Jews knew their rights and decided to appeal. For once, the justice system worked properly. The higher court not only supported the appeal but also delivered a stinging rebuke to the Sintra magistrates for delivering a verdict based on such dubious evidence. Although the result was a triumph for natural justice, one does not imagine that it did anything to placate the local Christian population. The Jews of Sintra must have realised that their future looked bleak.[1]

The story shows how easy it was to fabricate charges and to persecute Jews on the basis of them. Only six years after this

---

1 *AHS* vol. V pp.9–10.

event in Sintra, in 1506, violent anti-Semitic riots broke out
in Lisbon. The excuse this time was that a 'new Christian' had
blasphemed by doubting a highly improbable event of a
sunbeam shining onto a host, which was interpreted as a
miracle by unquestioning Christian zealots. Mobs roamed the
streets attacking 'new Christians' at will. The fires in Rossio
Square exuded the smell of burning human flesh. It is possible
that a thousand victims met their fate in this manner. The
atmosphere, graphic and terrifying, is well captured in Richard
Zimler's novel, *The Last Kabbalist of Lisbon* (1998). This
chilling story is set in the Alfama, the old Moorish quarter of
Lisbon. It concerns the murder of a prominent Jewish scholar
whose passion is to rescue and safeguard important Hebrew
sacred books. The heroes of the story are the Jewish nephew
and his Arab friend. The hysterical atmosphere of the novel
matches the circumstances in a Sintra where Jews had been
officially condemned on the basis of a child's nonsensical
prattle a few years earlier. By the time King Manuel attempted
to restore order, the fires of racial hatred, stoked up by the
Dominicans, had burnt away any hope of harmony. The
prejudices of Queen Maria, the King's third Spanish wife, led
Portugal down the same damaging path of intolerance that
Spain had already embarked upon.

5

Quintas and Gardens

Sintra had been regarded as a desirable residence for the great and good long before the arrival of the Portuguese kings and queens in the twelfth century. For centuries, the Moors had enthused about the pure waters that streamed down the *serra* and provided a bountiful supply for their fountains which were spiritual, as well as physical, sources of refreshment. The fruit, particularly apples and pears, of Sintra and Colares were already famous during this period and supplied a large part of the region; olive trees, cultivated since Roman times, provided a lucrative export trade through the convenient and well-serviced Tagus estuary. Wine of such quality came from Colares that even the Moorish rulers could not resist it. The excellence of Sintra's produce was matched by a cool, temperate climate which it was thought contributed to the good health and longevity of its inhabitants.

Word of these wonders spread through the medium of poetry, which was always an important vehicle of Arabic culture.

Wild animals such as boar, deer and fowl were an important attraction for the leisured class of noblemen who had gathered around the *walis* or Moorish governor of the garrison at Sintra. These creatures, together with a plentiful variety of birds, made Sintra a hunter's paradise, something the Moors quickly appreciated. Noblemen began hunting the area on horseback, using the falcon and starting a tradition, which was passed through to the Christian inhabitants who followed. In due course the Moorish *almoinha,* or house gave way to the

Portuguese *quinta* or villa as the aristocracy moved into the hills around the town to make the most of their sport.

Almost all the early Portuguese monarchs seemed to enjoy the chase. When the Count of Sabugosa considers what attracted the kings to Sintra, a love of hunting is high on the list. He tells us that King Manuel went riding every day after breakfast.[1] We can imagine the cascade of mounted horseman and barking dogs following the King out of the castle court-yard and through the cobbled streets of the town as the day's hunt began. Even monarchs of an intellectual proclivity (which included most of the Avis dynasty) enjoyed hunting in the Sintra forests. To preserve the stocks for this royal pastime, restrictions were imposed on the number of people permitted to hunt; sometimes only the King himself was allowed to do so. For example, in 1437, in the reign of King Duarte I, there was a prohibition against the hunting of boars and stags on the *serra* or within areas designated as royal parks.[2]

The fashionable aristocracy also shared the royal passion for the hunt. Francisco de Holanda, for instance, spent much of his youth riding in the Sintra hills with the royal princes (see p.11). Mastery of equine sports and etiquette was a prerequi-site for success at court. The Marialva family, for generations Grand Masters of the Horse, enjoyed an intimate relationship with successive monarchs and members of the royal family. As wealth flowed into Portugal from overseas, members of the small upper class became prosperous and began to establish themselves in style in the Sintra area.

This aristocratic society contrasted sharply with the towns-folk of Sintra who were middle-class burghers. The incomers were mainly officers who had served the Crown in some mili-tary capacity and had been accorded special privileges in recognition of those services and to keep them loyal in the event of civil disturbance (see pp.68–9). But the Crown also

---

1   Conde de Sabugosa, op. cit. pp.7 & 93.
2   *AHS* vol. IV p.111.

imposed restrictions on them when it felt its own privileges were threatened. Regulations prohibiting the cutting of trees are recorded from time to time, for instance, there was also the burden of contributions (mainly in kind) from the towns-folk to the royal household when the court was at Sintra.

The gentlemen yeomen had to manage their affairs prudently. Unlike the aristocratic courtiers, they could not adopt a carefree attitude to financial matters or risk incurring debts. Rather, the knights invested their money and effort into businesses, mostly connected with the production of agricul-tural goods for the nearby capital city. Their standard of living depended on successful management of these enterprises as well as on the hard work of the peasants (*saloios*) below them. It is hardly surprising to find in the archival records numerous references to the transfer of property rights and the granting of licences. There are also many references to the property of the Church and to the privileges bestowed on local clergy. Although parish priests might only just qualify for member-ship of the literate classes, bishops of the Church were in a different category. The grandest clergymen, like Dom Dinis de Melo e Castro in Colares, came from aristocratic families; bishops of his ilk were powerful landowners who wielded considerable influence in secular affairs.

We have seen that King João I made great changes to the Paço Real (see p.77). This was partly to accommodate his considerable family but also because he and Queen Philippa were determined to set up the court there on a scale which fitted their concept of a sovereign nation at the forefront of Christendom. Alterations were made to the building so that embassies could be received in appropriately majestic cham-bers. As the palace became the centre of national affairs, increasingly large numbers of people of rank would come and go from Sintra. The holders of high office and the courtiers began to find that it was more convenient to stay in Sintra than to make the daily journey from Lisbon or from their estates in the surrounding areas. They summarily requisitioned rooms, or even whole houses from the local residents; their demands in terms of food and goods and services were considerable. The Count of Barcelos, the Master of Christ, the Master of Santiago, the Master of Avis, Vaz Coutinho, Gomes da Silva and all their families and retinues were just some of the courtiers in attendance at the palace during this time. The seventy-two noble families whose emblems appear on the ceiling of the Sala dos Brasões would have made an appearance at the court at Sintra at various times.

According to Garcia de Resende, in a eulogising verse meant to underline the magnificence of the Crown, the court may have reached five thousand members by the reign of King Manuel at the beginning of the sixteenth century. The poet, himself a constant attendee, assures us that no other court in Christendom could compare to the Portuguese in terms of the honours and distinction poured upon the *fidalgos* by the King.[1] He might have added that there was probably no wealthier court in Europe, for by this time Portugal was enjoying huge financial benefits as a result of its overseas connections. As Duarte d'Armas' engravings show, not only was the Royal Palace itself expanding but the cluster of buildings around it was also increasing.

The gathering of poets and artists, who included foreigners and Portuguese citizens, like Francisco de Holanda who had spent time abroad, brought a cosmopolitan, sophisticated ambience to Sintra. Increasingly, the town was coming to resemble an urbane Italian city-state like Florence. It is not a coincidence that Sintra's links with Italy increased over the same period. King João III had a distinct taste for Italian decoration but he and Manuel, his successor, were beginning to see themselves as powerful Renaissance princes like their Italian counterparts. King João III struck up a friendship with Lorenzo the Magnificent who dispatched the sculptor Andrea Sansovino to work for him in Portugal.

---

1 Count of Sabugosa, op. cit. p.93.

Sansovino came to Portugal in the 1490s and began building in the Renaissance style. However his work (most of which has not in any case survived) did not find immediate favour with the Portuguese *fidalgos*, who were still steeped in medieval taste. According to Robert Chester Smith, Portugal was not yet ready for Renaissance art.[1] Sansovino must have had a frustrating time, never being able to give full flight to his fancy. Vasari says that he was forced to design according to the local style, presumably the Gothic. Only in decorative features could he act a little more freely. It would be some time before Renaissance architecture, based on a Graeco-Roman system of columns, pilasters and entablatures, began to take hold of the Portuguese court. The Italian influence, in the early sixteenth century, remained largely confined to ornamentation. In King Manuel's reign the new architectural style was far from being classical in feeling, as we have seen.

The wealth of the Sintra court was underpinned by the great expansion of Lisbon as a trading centre. Foreigners, whose experience was highly valued by the Crown, played an important part in the financial life of the burgeoning metropolis. Among the foreign community were many Italians, who were pre-eminent because of their specialised knowledge of maritime commerce. One of the prominent Lisbon merchants, for instance, was a Florentine banker, Lucas Giraldes, who became friendly with Dom João de Castro, the ex-Viceroy of India, who was by then settled in retirement in Sintra. The Italian merchants themselves were much attracted to the idyllic surroundings of Sintra, particularly in the summer, when Lisbon became unbearably hot. They noticed that there was a supply of high-quality marble to be quarried in the area, suggesting the possibility of building elegant neo-classical villas, near to the sites where the Romans themselves had built a millennium before. The proximity to the court and

1   R.C. Smith, op. cit. p.56.

to Portuguese *fidalgos* who had influence there was an added attraction for these Italian merchants who, as foreigners, were always conscious of the need to consolidate their own standing in the local community. At the same time, Sintra was close enough to Lisbon for them to return quickly to the city if business affairs required it.

The possibility of a life of bucolic bliss in Sintra suggested something of the idealised world portrayed by Ovid, Virgil and Horace to a man of a cultivated turn of mind, whether he was an Italian merchant prince or a Portuguese *fidalgo*. The quiet moralising of the Ancients on the merits of a calm, reflective pastoral existence had had a great influence on Renaissance culture and art. Virgil's words in the *Georgics* following his praise of apples, might have been written about Sintra:

> All the grove meanwhile no less
> With fruit is swelling, and the wild haunts of birds
> Blush with their blood-red berries. Cytisus
> Is good to browse on, the tall forest yields
> Pine-torches, and the nightly fires are fed
> And shoot forth radiance. And shall man be loathe
> To plant, nor lavish of their pains? Why trace
> Things mightier?[1]

In Horace the human element of the pastoral is more pronounced. Only human cultivation can ensure that the bounties of nature will be most advantageously used. But that very act of cultivation is itself a civilising process; the soldier-statesman, who has retired to his country farm will reflect wisely on the course of public events that he has himself had a hand in shaping. Thus classical writers of the pastoral, though they suggested life away from the city, did not recommend a life severed from it. Interaction with the *res publica* gives sense

---

1   Virgil, *The Aeneid, The Georgics, The Eclogues* (trans. J. Rhoades) (Oxford, 1957) p.347.

and dignity to toils of the retired statesman in his fields. The country idyll is still a social one.

While this classical model had a great impact on figures like Dom João de Castro, it was not the only tradition for inhabitants of the *serra*. Other folk inhabited the hills because they wanted to escape from the world, particularly the world of commercial Lisbon. We have seen that hermitages and retreats were scattered all over the mountains of the area (see pp.15–16). They were occupied by men who believed that wisdom would be found by avoiding, rather than engaging in, social intercourse. The hermitical tradition could and did co-exist with a more communal form of monastic life that was led by members of the religious orders. Although these orders could sometimes practise an ascetic regime, like the monks at Capuchos, they were generally founded first on the idea of a community and then of a connection between that community and the outside world. For this reason they appealed less to the Romantic imagination than did the solitary hermits.

The houses of the noblemen who took up residence in Sintra in the first part of the sixteenth century remained fairly simple in design. They were, for the most part, rectangular structures with plain-fronted walls, suggesting the *villa rustica* or country house rather than something grander. Gradually, the houses were altered and made more elegant, particularly in terms of interior decoration. No doubt a considerable impetus towards making homes statelier came when certain *fidalgo* families decided to make Sintra their principal residence rather than a place to which they repaired only when the court was sitting there. The *villa rustica*, a summer place, was associated with pleasant days outdoors. The names of the early *quintas* often refer to the landscape around, whether rocky or green or near to cascading water. In these aptly named abodes, the newly ensconced *fidalgos*, expected to cultivate the fine arts so favoured at the Court, could also maintain a connection with the land, a bond that tied them to the *res publica* itself.

The *villa rustica*, in its tranquillity, provided respite from the more turbulent life of the city.[1]

The most striking *villa rustica* in Sintra, at least from the point of view of its simplicity and ancient feeling, is Penha Verde. This house was built by Dom João de Castro, 'the terror of Asia', on his return from an illustrious career in the East. Penha Verde (first known as the Quinta da Fonte d'El Rei) was in origin a single storey building, with a rounded solid chapel next to it, dedicated to Our Lady of the Mountain. From the very beginning, Dom João's emphasis was on the building in its surroundings rather than on the building for its own sake. The rustic simplicity of his house was matched by the natural grandeur of the setting; the role of man was effectively placed firmly in the context of a greater nature designed by God. There was no courtly pretension in this pious old soldier's plans; even signs of learning were confined to the chapel, God's home. The structure of the chapel is very solid and ancient in appearance, reminiscent of a Roman mausoleum or family tomb rather than of a Christian church. Indeed, Dom João had intended it as his place of entombment. Whilst its circular shape may mark a Renaissance interest in the heavenly spheres, the inscription in Latin, which gives the foundation date of 1542, once again emphasises its classical spirit. The interior is decorated with unrefined *azulejos*. However, the central tableau of the altar is a finely carved marble representation of the Holy Family, in Italian Renaissance style.

William Beckford was one of the most sensitive visitors to Penha Verde. He appreciated the beauty of its setting but at the same time understood the founder's deliberate avoidance of anything pretentious. By the time he came to Penha Verde in the late eighteenth century, considerable alterations to the

1   For a sensitive account of the evolution of *quintas* and gardens in Sintra during this period, see J.C. da Silva & G. Luckhurst, *Sintra: A Landscape with Villas* (Lisbon, 1989) pp.27ff.

original complex had been made. During the seventeenth century, Bishop Dom Francisco Mello e Castro, the founder's grandson, had placed a fountain in the middle of the patio and had added another three chapels to the house (excessive even for a Grand Inquisitor). He had also altered the gardens, making them more formal and elaborate. Beckford's comments on the bishop's additions are trenchant:

> These scenes, though still enchanting, have most probably undergone great changes since his [Dom João's] days. The deep forests we read of have disappeared, and with them many a spring they fostered. Architectural fountains, gaudy terraces, and regular stripes of orange gardens, have usurped the place of those wild orchards and gushing rivulets he may be supposed to have often visited in his dreams, when removed some thousand leagues from his native country.[1]

Beckford is undoubtedly right in his aesthetic judgement. The fountains, though now mellowed with time, are a long way removed from the simple spirit that Dom João had intended. One, executed in the mannerist style, has a tableau of multi-coloured tiles behind it, depicting scenes from Paradise, with stylised lions peacefully co-existing with domesticated animals such as dogs and horses. Another is placed within an elaborate Oriental pavilion decorated with ornate patterns of peacocks and flowers in a very Eastern manner. Nevertheless, the setting of Penha Verde still evokes a classical image for Beckford, which he compares to the paintings of Gaspar Poussin. The bright green pines, which are said to have been planted by Dom João, and from which the place takes its name, are, according to him, as picturesque and ancient in feeling as any trees in the Negroni gardens in Rome.

Although he does not mention them, Beckford might also have found the Sanskrit inscriptions carved here and there on

---

1 *The Travel Diaries of William Beckford of Fonthill* (ed. G. Chapman) (Cambridge, 1928) 2 vols, vol. II p.127.

stones in the grounds of some fascination. The Viscount Juromenha considers them at some length in *Cintra Pinturesca* (1838), drawing on explanations given to James Murphy by C. Wilkins in the eighteenth century. The inscriptions, which Juromenha lists in detail over seventy-six verses, are devoted to the Hindu god Shiva. They celebrate battles and victories among the gods like Ganesa, God of Prudence. The inscriptions tell stories of the deeds of men and gods interwoven in the grand, heroic manner. Predictions of holocausts and disasters are jumbled into the chronicles.[1]

While Dom João de Castro was performing his heroic deeds abroad, a Sintra family, the Gonçalves, were gradually rising to pre-eminence in the town. André Gonçalves was an official clerk; in 1518, his brother Gaspar became Royal Chamberlain. They acquired property all over the Sintra area, extending as far north as Ericeira. In 1541 the family was ennobled by King João III and took the title of the Lords of Ribafria. Later, Gaspar became the mayor of Sintra. The Gonçalves owned two houses in the area, one an Italianate town house, huddled close to the Royal Palace; the other a country house or *quinta* at Lourel.

The *quinta* at Lourel provides an interesting view of the *villa rustica* in transition. A central tower with crenellated battlements originally dominated the house. The tower was an important symbol of social status for it conferred upon the Gonçalves family a kind of seigniorial distinction associated with those noblemen favoured by the Crown who were allowed to build their estates (*solares*) in the fortified style. The military aspect of older houses also emphasised the responsibility of the lord of the manor to defend his domain and its inhabitants against enemy incursion. As the threat of such attacks diminished, however, the agricultural function of an estate became the most important one. Fruit orchards, vegetable gardens and cultivated fields surrounded the

---

1   Visconde de Juromenha, *Cintra Pinturesca* (Lisbon, 1838) pp.61–72.

Ribafrias' *villa rustica* at Lourel. The principal source of family wealth came from the ownership of land that could be used for agriculture. At a later date, a patio and fountain were built in the middle of the complex, creating a tranquil, domestic feeling throughout the whole estate. Gradually, other features of a more civilised life, in the form of decorations and furniture, would appear in the interior of the house, reflecting the growing prosperity of its owners.

By contrast, the Ribafrias' town house, close to the Royal Palace in the heart of the old town of Sintra, exhibits some of the Italian taste, which was slowly infiltrating the traditional preference for the Gothic style in Portugal. Entering the plain-fronted building from the street, one encounters a large, open space within. The house, which still retains distinctly medieval features, is built around this central patio and features loggias, verandahs and open space. The loggia is particularly Italian in feeling, with its fine columns and the decorations of shells, acanthus leaves and the snouts of lions. Unusual gargoyles of a fantastic type, mixing human, animal and plant forms, which decorate the smaller, upper balcony, indicate a new Renaissance interest in the natural world. The ornamentation throughout the house is a great deal more sophisticated than at the Tower at Lourel. There is a suggestion of the style of Nicolau Chanterene in the medallions and sculptures. Foreign influences were increasingly affecting the design and decoration of Sintra houses.

There is evidence in an inscription that work had been done in the house by Pero Paixão. Since Paixão had been employed at the Royal Palace, it was quite a coup for the *arriviste* Gonçalves to have employed him; their rise to social eminence, though by now assured, had not yet led to their having their arms emblazoned on the ceiling of the Sala dos Brasões. In later years, the Ribafria house acquired many historical associations, for it was the birthplace of the military hero, André de Albuquerque Ribafria, who fought the Spanish at Elvas in 1659. Subsequently, the property passed into the possession of the family of the Marquis of Pombal.

It is not surprising to discover that several of the older *quintas* in Sintra started off as religious institutions, given the valuable concessions made to the clergy under the charter of 1154 and in subsequent years. One of the early ones, the Quinta do Convento da Trindade, situated on the way up to São Pedro just past the Church of Santa Maria, is first mentioned in a document in the archives, dated 25 October 1410.[1] The reference is in a letter from King João I, which grants exclusive privileges to the Convent, including a number of buildings, vineyards and adjacent land. It is a generous gift from the sovereign, which ensured that the order of Trinitarian monks who lived there would be financially protected for a long time.

Although this letter is dated 1410, the appearance of the religious men on the site of the convent took place earlier, around 1374. In that year, several monks from the Trindade Convent in Lisbon decided to migrate to the bucolic surroundings of Sintra, to live as hermits. Among their number were Friar Alvaro de Castro, Friar João of Évora and Friar João of Lisbon, a trio of intellectuals and scholars.

These learned clerics alighted upon the site of Santo Amaro, within the grounds of the present *quinta*, finding it an inspiring place to set up a new community. Some of their followers took to caves in the hillside, in the manner of anchorite occupations in the *serra*. The feeling of these early, ascetic settlements can still be felt at the top of the grounds of the existing *quinta*, where the forest takes over from the cultivated area amid decayed walls and mossy, stone seats. The first building of the Convent itself was constructed at the beginning of the fifteenth century. It was followed by another structure, which was built in the time of King Manuel, a hundred years later. That in turn was replaced by the existing building towards the end of the sixteenth century.

---

1   *AHS* vol. IV p.38.

10. General view of Sintra with Royal Palace (Paço Real), 2000.
Photograph by N. Antunes.

11. Cloister of the Quinta do Covento da Trinidade, 1999. Photograph by Jerry Harpur.

12. Palace of Ramalhão, c.1960.
Photograph. Sintra, Historical Archive, Municipal Archive.

13. Pena Palace in the morning mist, 2000.
Photograph by N. Antunes.

14. The well at the Quinta do Torre da Regaleira, 2000. Photograph by N. Antunes.

15. 'The Eye of God' at the Quinta do Torre da Regaleira, 2000. Photograph by N. Antunes.

16. View from Quinta Mazziotti, Colares, c.1830.
Oil painting attributed to H.L.T. Gurlitt (1812–97), Phillips Auctioneers, London.

OLIVA GUERRA

Roteiro Lírico

de

Sintra

1940

17. Front cover of Oliva Guerra's *Roteiro Lirico de Sintra*
showing the arms of Sintra.
Lisbon, 1940.

18. 'Moorish Castle', 2001. Photograph by N. Antunes.

The monks belonged to the Trinitarian Order, founded in 1198 by St John of Matha with the particular object of freeing Christian slaves who were in Muslim captivity in several different countries, including Spain, North Africa and the Middle East. The Trinitarians' exclusive right to act as inter-locutors in the matter of the Christian slaves was confirmed by a papal bull in the time of Pope Paul V. The Order was an austere one, devoting a third of its income to the cause of emancipation. It is possible that as many as 140,000 slaves were freed as a result of the efforts of the Trinitarians. The dress of the monks was distinctive, comprising a long white habit, with a cross emblazoned on the chest in blue and red and a black shoulder cape. A wide-rimmed black hat completed the outfit. The number of members of the Order had risen to five thousand in the thirteenth century, though it may have started to decline by the time of King João's concessions. In 1597 the order of Barefooted (Discalced) Nuns was formed in Spain and proved the more enduring arm of the Trinitarian Order.[1]

An amusing dispute between the Trinitarian monks and the Prior of the churches of Santa Maria and São Miguel about the ringing of bells is recorded in 1510. Dr João Lobo, formerly Bishop of Tangier and by this time prior of the churches of Santa Maria and São Miguel, tried to prohibit the ringing of bells summoning the faithful to mass at the monastery. He did not want his parishioners to be diverted from attending services at one of his two churches. The Reverend Father Diego, who was in charge of the monastery, refused to comply with the prior's order, continuing to ring his bells when he pleased. The dispute raged on for some time, being heard both in Lisbon by a judge and in Rome by an Apostolic Judge. A compromise was finally worked out whereby the monks retained the right to ring their bells but would refrain from

---

1   I am grateful to Betty Silveira for drawing my attention to this information and I am indebted to Mr Robert Arnold for allowing me to visit the *quinta* during my researches in Sintra.

doing so at times inconvenient for Dr Lobo. As in all sensible settlements, both sides could claim victory.

The convent continued to function as a religious institution until the dissolution of the monasteries in 1834. At that time, when the property was taken over by the state, a considerable number of objects are listed in the various inventories, which were drawn up. They include precious items and sculptures in the chapel, which is of an imposing size. Though some re-appeared in the Quinta da Madre de Deus, a large number disappeared. The favourable location of the land and its fertility made the property a valuable one. It passed into the ownership of various individuals, including the ageing Duke of Saldanha.

The building of the existing *quinta* dates from 1570. It consists of a series of vaulted cloisters with doric arches, fine gardens, fountains, a chapel and various outbuildings including a refectory, which was once a sacristy. The tomb-stones of Tomás Paiva and his wife record their devoted service to the Trinitarian Order. The appearance of the cloisters is Renaissance in feel and style;[1] by the time it was built it is likely that little remained of King Manuel's rebuilding, which, according to Juromenha, had been of poor architectural quality. The best *azulejos* are to be found in the refectory but they also line the main corridors, from which cells give off to a half-level in traditional manner.

The monastery's air of peaceful seclusion has inspired visi-tors. Its generous water supply means that it has always been able to support a lush display of plants and flowers. The French traveller, G. Le Roy Liberge, was captivated by the mystery of the place when he visited Sintra in the last days of the monarchy. He talks of the enchanting mix of the cultivated and the abandoned which gave the Convent its particularly Romantic aspect; he is amazed by the size of the multi-coloured hortensias, which are the tallest he has ever seen.[2]

---

1   See Illustration 11.
2   G. Le Roy Liberge *Trois Mois au Portugal* (Paris, 1910) pp.68 ff. Hortensias still feature in today's garden.

The same tranquil atmosphere captivated the poetess Oliva Guerra on her visit thirty years later. She is inspired by the murmuring sound of the streams running down the hillside in the grounds behind the building.[1] Da Costa Azevedo, writing twenty years after her, in the late 1950s, fondly describes the rustic charm of the long-fronted, single-storeyed building with its wonderful supply of water, which he claims come from fourteen sources. He finds that the old fountain is completely appropriate to the feeling of the *locale*.[2] His enjoyment of the calm ambience of the *quinta* can still be appreciated in the tastefully restored building of today, where the only sounds to be heard on a sunny afternoon are the birds and the breeze rustling in the trees.

During the period of the 'Spanish domination', as it is sometimes known, which lasted from 1580 to 1640, there was a decline in the building and renovation of *quintas* in Sintra. The unification of Spain and Portugal under one crown meant that at this time the Court was based in Madrid, although there is some evidence to suggest that the Spanish kings considered setting up their capital in Lisbon because of its good sea connections. The Great Armada sailed from Lisbon to attack the English fleet in 1588 – something which would have been unlikely to have happened if the two Iberian kingdoms had not been united at the time. However, when it became clear that the Spanish royal family would not come to Lisbon, ambitious Portuguese aristocrats moved to Madrid. Others, giving up politics, retired to their estates in other parts of the country, away from Sintra.

It was left to a man of the cloth to continue with the courtly traditions of Sintra; acquiring the old ruined castle of Colares, Bishop Dom Dinis de Melo e Castro built a grand residence facing east with fine views across the valley. The bishop was an aristocrat who had fought for the Crown in far-away lands.

---

1   O. Guerra, op. cit. pp.41–2.
2   J.A. da Costa Azevedo, op. cit. p.147.

He was a cosmopolitan man of wide culture, who had written a novel as well as poems. His house was decorated in the finest style of its time, with stonework, carvings and multi-coloured *azulejos*. In the grounds was a large, stone water tank, inlaid with frescoes. Appropriately for a land of legend, these represented pagan, mythological scenes. The bishop particularly liked Italian styles in architecture and gardening. With the demise of Sintra during this period, claims have been made that Colares became the true 'court in the village'. If that is an exaggerated claim, still there is no doubt that Colares enjoyed one of its grandest periods during the bishop's 'reign'.[1]

Though he was comfortably ensconced in his palatial mansion, Dom Dinis did not forget his less well-off subjects. Next to his residence he began a foundation to which was attached a hospital for the use of the poor. The foundation is mentioned again in an eighteenth-century portrait of a prosperous and well-ordered parish of Colares.[2] By this time Colares was part of the administrative area of Torres Vedras. It had two hundred and fifty dwellings. The village was largely clustered around the parochial church of Nossa Senhora da Assunção, which has no less than five altars, the best of which are dedicated to the Holy Ghost. Dom Dinis had also paid for the church, which was built by the stonemason André Duarte and the royal architect Pedro Nunes Tincono. By the time of the report the parish income exceeded 6,000 reis. Its wheat and fruit provided a good living for its parishioners. Two local magistrates, who answered to their superiors in Torres Vedras, ran the local council. The bishop's charitable institution was still flourishing.

---

1   See M.T. Caetano, op. cit. p.99. The expression 'Uma corte na aldeia' (a court in the village) was coined by Francisco Rodrigues Lobo during this period.
2   The material is taken from L. Cardoso *Dicionário Geográfico* 2 vols (Lisbon, 1747 & 1752) in *AHS* vol. VIII (pages unnumbered). The remains of the bishop's palace, which was ruined by fire, were eventually demolished in 1903 when the Viscount of Monserrate endowed a primary school on the site. The bishop would have approved of stones from his palace being used to build the school.

It was in the churches too that a great movement in Portuguese art, the Mannnerist, was developing in this supposedly bleak period of Spanish ascendancy. Mannerism is not an easy form of art to define. It was long thought of as a somewhat decadent form of Renaissance art, a falling away from the harmonious ideal epitomised in the works of Raphael. More recently, it has been interpreted as a reaction to the constraints of classicism, influenced by the events of the Counter-Reformation. Deriving its name from the Italian word '*maniera*' (meaning 'style'), the movement was distinguished because it placed a greater emphasis on the ideal beauty in the mind of the artist than on the reproduction of the beauties to be seen in nature. This quest led to a stress on the aesthetic (the 'style'), with a greater value put on subjective powers of the imagination and on originality. It could sometimes lead to an exaggerated manner of painting in which figures are deliberately distorted. Vitor Serrão has identified Francisco de Holanda, the courtier and Sintra artist discussed earlier in this chapter, as the main source of intellectual inspiration for the Portuguese Mannerist style, which flourished in the second half of the sixteenth century.[1] De Holanda expounded a neo-Platonic theory about the idea in the mind of the creative artist and the style (*maniera*) in which it would be represented in art. Although de Holanda could be original in his thinking, however, there is no reason to suppose that he himself saw this new idealism as a violent break with Renaissance classicism.

Mannerist art is found in several Sintra churches. In São Martinho, for instance, there is an altarpiece made up of three panels, which portray St Martin himself, as well as St Anthony preaching to the fish and St Peter. They are represented in a freer, more flowing style than in classical, Renaissance studies. There is a different use of space and the human figures tend

1   See V. Serrão 'A Pintura Maneirista em Portugal', *História da Arte Portuguesa* (ed. P. Pereira) 3 vols (Lisbon, 1999) vol. II pp.429ff. for a comprehensive account of Portuguese Mannerist art.

to be distorted for dramatic effect. There is an intensity of feeling that echoes Portuguese art of a more primitivist type. The works are ascribed to the Master of São Quintinho in the school of Gregório Lopes, a leading Portuguese Mannerist painter whose *Baptism of Christ* hangs in the parochial church of São João das Lampas. Two other Mannerist artists working in the area were Diogo Teixeira, who decorated the chapel in the Paço Real, and Cristovão Vaz, whose pieces for a grand retable can be seen in the Igreja da Misericórdia in Colares.

The decline of Sintra as the centre of courtly life, begun during this Spanish period, was to continue when the Bragança dynasty was installed in 1640. Monarchs preferred to hold court at the Ribeira Palace in Lisbon or at Mafra. When the 1755 earthquake destroyed the Lisbon Palace, Queluz became the favoured royal residence.[1] Despite the less frequent appearance of the monarch at the old palace, Sintra remained popular with *fidalgo* families. A new kind of *quinta*, the pavilion, which boasted of much greater interior sophistication than the old *villa rustica,* made its appearance. Terraces and formal gardens surrounded these more pretentious residences. Unlike the *villa rustica* these newer Sintra houses were no longer working farms; they were built as summer residences for a wealthy upper class which did not depend on agriculture for an income. As the pavilion evolved from the simpler, more rustic style of the earlier villas, it became more influenced by foreign taste, as French and English styles were added to the Italian which, as we have seen, had become popular during the sixteenth century. These refinements are most noticeable inside the houses, although recreational features, in the form of landscaped gardens, begin to feature in the grounds of *quintas* as well.

The Duke of Cadaval's house, the Quinta da Capela, altered in the early decades of the eighteenth century, is a good

---

1   Although Queluz is in the modern borough of Sintra, I have not considered it part of the Sintra story I am relating here.

illustration of the evolving pavilion. While the building still retains something rustic in its simple, one storey elevation, there is an Italianate feeling about it. This is particularly evident in the layout of the gardens, which have a distinctly Roman look. The interiors have a new elegance with their black and white tiled floors and white varnished shutters. In nearby Eugaria, the Quinta da Palma, owned by João Frederico Ludovice, the well-rewarded architect of Mafra, also shows the gradual aggrandisement of the Sintra *quintas* at this time. Two separate wings are linked together by a grand gate, adding a noble aspect to the front of the house. Additions of arches and elaborate gateways to the front of villas show that Sintra was becoming the residence of a more ostentatious set of grandees.

At the Quinta Mazziotti in Colares (originally named the Quinta do José Dias until it was owned by the Italian diplomat, Antonio Mazziotti in the eighteenth century) the terraced gardens also exude an Italian air, although some of its features are French. The French style gained in vogue with the building of the Palace of Queluz, which began in 1746. Although the architect was the Portuguese Mateus Vicente de Oliveira, he was assisted in much of the design work and in laying out the elaborate, formalised gardens by the Frenchman Jean-Baptiste Robillon. Robillon had worked in France with Thomas Germain, the goldsmith who had supplied tableware for King João V. He was extremely versatile: first appointed as royal goldsmith when he reached Lisbon, he also practised architecture and interior design.

Great damage to many Sintra buildings occurred on 1 November 1755, when a severe earthquake struck Lisbon without warning. An eye-witness account of an English resident of the city talks of a fair, clear morning, with the sun shining and 'not the least signal or warning of that approaching event'.[1] A series of tremors, which only lasted minutes, shook

---

1   Anon. An account by an eye-witness of the Lisbon earthquake of 1 November 1755. *British Historical Society of Portugal* (Lisbon, 1985) p.5.

the central area of Lisbon, causing a huge cloud of dust to obscure the entire sky. The earthquake was followed by flooding, caused by a seismic wave, which cascaded onto the foreshore of the city. It swept away a whole area of the lower part of Lisbon, which included the Ribeira Palace, the Patriarchate and important public buildings and storage houses. Later in the day, fires started in various parts of the city. The damage to property and life was considerable. Extensive collections of works of art and books were destroyed, and churches collapsed onto parishioners who were gathered within to celebrate All Saints' Day. It is estimated that several thousand people were killed.

Although Sintra was spared from the effects of flooding because of its altitude, and though some buildings emerged unscathed, the damage to others was not negligible. According to J. de Oliveira Boléo, who was basing his observation on the work of earlier seismologists such as F.L. Pereira de Sousa, the earthquake was 'disastrous' for Sintra.[1] The earlier researchers calculated that the earthquake reached a very high scale on the Mercalli measurement in Sintra itself and in Colares, with a less intense effect in the area of Belas. The royal palace and São Martinho Church were both affected – the church quite extensively. Many other buildings were also damaged and dozens of people were killed in collapsing rubble. In Colares, flashes of fire were reported to come from the open earth, although modern scientists cannot explain what might have caused them.

Although it took decades for repairs to be made, the 1755 earthquake, like all natural disasters, provided opportunities for redevelopment, which would not otherwise have occurred. In Sintra, foreigners, attracted by the perennial charms of its hills and dales, undertook some of this new construction. One of them was Daniel Gildemeester, the Dutch envoy, who had made a fortune from his monopoly of

---

1   J. de O. Boléo, op. cit. p.33.

the diamond export trade, which had been granted to him by the Marquis of Pombal. Gildemeester alighted upon one of the few flat areas of land to the west of the village at Seteais, with fine views across the valley. He bought it from Pombal himself. It was rocky terrain and needed flattening out but Gildemeester had the resources to undertake a large-scale operation. He was granted permission to excavate large amounts of granite in preparation for the erection of his neo-classical mansion, the Quinta da Alegria. The level field he created became a popular place for training soldiers and, at a later date, a favourite picnic spot for the royal family.

Looking head on at the existing building, Gildemeester's pavilion is the one to the left, with its entrance on what is now the left side of the block. The interior layout of the present Seteais Hotel confirms that this was the way the house originally faced. An elaborate balustraded stairway, that breaks into two branches as it goes up, faced the old entrance, which is now positioned on the side of the building. On the first floor a fine, wide gallery runs the length of the house, with rooms coming off it at regular intervals.

The feeling of spaciousness has been enhanced by redecoration after Gildemeester's time. William Beckford (see p.162) gives a very different impression of the house in his description of its opening night on Wednesday 25 July 1787, when Gildemeester gave a party for the Sintra gentry. Arriving through dark and gloomy lanes, Beckford finds the house has 'little more than bare walls and was wretchedly lighted up'.[1] He was, of course, a fastidious aesthete whom no one recently moved into a home would welcome on a tour of inspection. Whatever reservations he had about the décor of the rooms, however, he was nevertheless impressed by Gildemeester's table, which was magnificent even by sumptuous local standards. He records in his diary approvingly:

1 *The Journal of William Beckford in Portugal and Spain 1787–1788* (ed. B. Alexander) (London, 1954) p.145.

There was bright illumination, a profusion of plate, a
striking breadth of table, every delicacy that could be
procured, and a dessert frame fifty or sixty feet in length,
gleaming with burnished figures and vases of silver flowers
of the most exquisite workmanship.[1]

Beckford does not mention the frescoes, which now decorate the walls of Seteais. They are scenes of classical mythology,
which still manage to retain a lightness of touch associated with
the Lyonnais artist, Jean–Baptiste Pillement. Pillement worked
in different parts of the country over a long period in the latter
part of the eighteenth century. His frescoes, which adorn
several Sintra houses, were widely imitated by various local
artists. He was quintessentially a landscape painter who had
taken to decoration. Some of his views are idealised, Claude-
like scenes, but in his decorative pieces he paints flowers and
tropical plants with an exquisite, almost Oriental delicacy. In
the dining room of the Quinta de São Sebastião, light pastoral
scenes, bordered by hanging branches of trees, provide elegant
tableaux around the walls. At Seteais the pictures depict neo-
classical or mythological scenes and show a similar refinement.

The architectural style of Gildmeester's pavilion, with its
broken friezes and lack of symmetry has suggested to some art
historians that the house may have been the work of the
Englishman William Elsden, although there is no clear proof
of his connection with the building. The Quinta da Alegria,
however, certainly looked more like the country seat of an
English gentleman than it did later, when it took on a more
continental appearance after the extensive additions of the
Marquis of Marialva. Marialva, who acquired the house in
1797 after it had been sold by one of the sons of the consul
Gildemeester, also altered the gardens, which were originally
in less formal style than they became.

The fifth Marquis, Beckford's friend Dom Diogo, was a

---

1   Ibid.

grand courtier who intended that the house should be fit for the reception of the royal family. The scale of his ambitions may be gleaned from examining the inventory of bills in the historical archives. There are bills from master carpenters, like Francisco de Paulo de Azevedo and from fine glass-makers like José Joaquim de Torres. There are hefty invoices for bronzes from Bento Martin and for silver and jewellery from Justino Roberto da Silva. Finally there are the accounts of the sculptor and architect Francisco Leal Garcia who was responsible for elaborate work on cornices and decoration of classical busts and fruit on top of them.[1] The Marquis' grandiose plans included the building of another pavilion in a purer, neo-classical style by the architect José da Costa e Silva and the erection of a triumphal arch which connected the new pavilion to the original one. The arch itself, with its Italianate ornamentation, is considered one of the most impressive early examples of the classical revival in Portugal.[2] The entrance to the whole palace was now switched from the side to the front facing the Campo do Alardo where it has remained.

Meanwhile, in Monserrate, down the road, the owner of a ruined *quinta*, Dona Francisca Xavier Marianna de Faro Melo e Castro, was looking for a tenant to rebuild a house which stood in a particularly beautiful spot on a raised mound. She unexpectedly found someone suitable in Gerard de Visme, a wealthy English merchant who had already built an impressive, neo-classical mansion in Benfica, near Lisbon. De Visme came from a French Huguenot family who had settled in London, where he was born. He came to Lisbon at the age of twenty and became a friend of Sebastião Carvalho, later Marquis of Pombal. When Pombal became the *de facto* ruler of the country, he granted De Visme the monopoly for the importation of teak from Brazil. This lucrative concession

---

1   *AHS,* Marialva Papers (Box 1, Item 36).
2   A. Delaforce, *Art and Patronage in Eighteenth-Century Portugal* (Cambridge, 2002) p.333.

turned him into one of the richest members of the English Factory, enabling him to build his palatial home and to become a generous patron of charities. A hospital that he endowed became, in turn, the Anglican Chaplain's home and eventually the British Consulate. C.J. Ruders, a Swedish visitor, describes the dazzlingly magnificent gardens at Benfica; and William Hickey, the traveller and connoisseur, found De Visme living there in princely style.

Monserrate had already had a long history by this time the earliest parts of which Ida Kingsbury says are lost in 'the half-light of legend and tradition'.[1] She relates the story that the original inhabitant of Monserrate, then known as Boa Vista, was a Christian Mozarab. He was eventually challenged to a duel by the governor (*alcaide*) of Sintra and was slain. He was buried by Christians in the hillock where he lived, the site of the present house. Later he was venerated as a martyr and prayers were offered at his burial place for liberation from the Moors. Francisco Costa, taking up the story, relates that by 1540 the land belonged to the All Saints Hospital in Lisbon. Gaspar Preto, a priest who had made a pilgrimage to the Spanish shrine of Our Lady of Monserrat in Catalonia, got permission to build a chapel, which he named after the same image of the Virgin Mary. Henceforth the place was known as Monserrate.[2] In the seventeenth century the house was rented to the Melo e Castro's family, who had connections with Portuguese India. A house which the Melo e Castro descendants built was destroyed in the earthquake of 1755.

De Visme signed the lease in 1790. In the document giving over the house to him, he is described as a well-established Lisbon merchant who had a particular interest in agriculture. The lease was to run for nine years in the first instance; De Visme undertook to restore the fruit orchards and repair build-

---

1   I. Kingsbury, *Castles, Caliphs & Christians: A Landscape with figures. Monserrate* (Lisbon, 1994) p.15.
2   F. Costa, *História da Quinta e Palácio de Monserrate* (Sintra, 1985) pp.9ff.

ings and to construct a new house. Like William Beckford who came to live in Monserrate after him, De Visme was a man of substance who thought nothing of extensively renovating a place without considering how long he intended to stay in it. A few years after signing the lease a house had already been erected and gardens laid out. From contemporary engravings, we see that Monserrate was built in mock-Gothic style, which was then becoming fashionable for country residences in England. The long front façade was interrupted by a central tower, with two turrets at each end embellished with angular, tapering windows and capped by pointed roofs. Its castellated front lent it a feigned medieval appearance, suggesting the retreat of a country gentleman. No doubt De Visme, who was much taken by the seclusion and natural beauty of Monserrate, intended that very effect. He already had a grand, formal mansion near the city. Sintra was to be a simpler, more picturesque rural retreat. Ironically, his friend Gildemeester's house, Seteais, which was situated up the road, was built in the neo-classical style, which was even more conventionally English.[1]

According to Cyrus Redding, Beckford's friend and biographer, Beckford later described the architecture of Monserrate as 'barbarous Gothic built by a carpenter from Falmouth', and was not pleased to be associated with it.[2] His friend, Lady Craven, who visited in 1790, had already condemned the house for its vile appearance. It is quite possible that Beckford made alterations to De Visme's façade in an attempt to improve it aesthetically. Ida Kingsbury speculates on the possibility that Beckford added somewhat flimsily built towers to lighten the heavy neo-Gothic of the original. She rightly says that Beckford had a great taste for towers. It was the flimsy construction of the hastily erected central tower

---

1 See Illustration 21.
2 C. Redding, *Memoirs of William Beckford of Fonthill*, 2 vols (London, 1859) vol. I p.279.

at Fonthill Abbey that in due course led to the collapse of the whole building.[1]

Although Beckford made alterations to De Visme's house, he does not seem to have changed its size. Byron claims it was collapsing by 1809; by 1821 it was a complete ruin. In that year, Mariana Baillie, an English lady, explains that it would originally have been laid out as an English villa with elegant apartments, one in the classical style with fine mirrors and precious, crystal-encased doors. She also notes a large central salon, which opened out onto the lawn, where shrubs and flowerbeds reflected the interior design of the room. That sophistication, together with a rotunda where one could practise echoes, were thoroughly Beckfordian contrivances.[2]

Monserrate may have been the first building in the mock-Gothic style to be erected in Portugal but that was not the only English feature that marked it. The grounds, too, were to be less formally laid out than the gardens at Benfica. Orchards and meadows were left untouched; sheep grazed the grass on the slopes around the house. De Visme's attitude to Monserrate was that of an English gentleman farmer toward his estate: it was a working place to which he retreated from the bustle of life in the city or at court. There was some order to it but it was an order based on the requirements of farming rather than on fussy ornamentation.

Although Beckford professed not to like the style of the house at Monserrate, he did appreciate the benefits of a less formalised style of laying out gardens, though his view of landscaping was more artistic and sophisticated than that of De Visme. As in the case of the house, it is not easy to distinguish between the work of De Visme and Beckford, particularly, as we shall see in Chapter Seven because another English hand was turned to gardening Monserrate in the nineteenth century (see p.187). But for Beckford, at any rate, the real glory of

1   I. Kingsbury, op. cit. p.21.
2   F. Costa *Palácio e Quinta de Monserrate* (Sintra, 1985) p.17.

Monserrate was in its luxuriant woodland and greenery; the gardens needed to be understood in the context of the natural contours and the native trees and shrubs. Vistas of the house were important and are best viewed from chapels or towers, which were built for that purpose in the grounds. Trees and shrubbery native to the area were included in planning the landscape.

Beckford's design of the gardens at Monserrate was influenced by a long tradition that had started in England in the seventeenth century and was in opposition to the excessively formal continental gardens that were much in vogue in France and in Holland. Sir William Temple, writing in the 1690s, had claimed that Chinese gardens incorporated the important principle of randomness or asymmetry. Trees were not planted at regular intervals or in symmetrical patterns as in the West. Yet the Chinese had achieved an order of their own, which was aesthetically pleasing. Temple's views were developed and widely publicised by Joseph Addison in *The Spectator*. Addison objected to the then highly fashionable topiary. Rather, taking a lead from Temple's 'Chinese' style, he wanted garden design to be more subtle. Artfulness had to be applied with a light touch; natural lines and contours should be left alone.

These ideas about landscape gardening continued in circulation throughout the first half of the eighteenth century. They are neatly summarised in Alexander Pope's dictum that gardeners must consult the 'genius of the place'. With growing prosperity and the building of more and more estates, these aesthetic theories began to influence practitioners like 'Capability' Brown, who worked on the gardens at Chatsworth, or Charles Hamilton, Beckford's uncle, at Painshill in Surrey. By now the 'natural' style was somewhat embellished, so that it included the building of temples, Roman arches and grottoes in the grounds. These features were thought to bring a classical feeling to the landscape such as could be admired in the paintings of Claude Lorraine (one of Beckford's favourite artists). There were any number of manuals and guides to help a gentleman who was setting up his country estate. In 1780 Horace Walpole published his *Essay on Modern Gardening*, in which no one before William Kent was credited with any taste in gardening. Kent, he said, leapt over the fence, and saw all nature was a garden.

Beckford was no great admirer of Horace Walpole but he shared his belief that formal terraces, raised canals and parterres had no place in a country setting. Nature could always be improved and guided but should not be overwhelmed. At Monserrate he opened vistas by clearing thickets and brambles but he did so with an eye to preserving what he felt to be the 'Claudian' nature of the place. Sometimes nature had to be improved so that the classical Arcadian beauty of the location was shown up to its full extent. The most spectacular of these artificial embellishments was the creation of a cascading waterfall, which draws water from the many mountain springs and crashes down into the verdant ravine below. Around the waterfall, large boulders were deliberately placed to emphasise the ruggedness of the setting. A rocky arch completed the props of this 'ancient' scenery. Even now, the effect of the falling water and of the densely green woods, which rays of sun occasionally break through, is mysterious and highly satisfying aesthetically. Juromenha, in describing the spot, wryly comments that a great deal of work is required to reproduce the simplicity of nature.

The grounds of Monserrate would not have been so dense with trees and other vegetation in Beckford's time. Nevertheless its sheltered position, in the shadow of the mountain, ensured that it remained humid and half-hidden from the sun. The fact that it faced north-west, with a plentiful supply of water, meant that in later years a wide variety of exotic plants, imported from Brazil and other distant parts of the world, could flourish on the slopes. Beckford himself admired the wild flowers that grew in the dale as well as the luscious camellia and the fragrant jasmine. The possibilities of such exotic cultivation, the intrinsic beauty of the place and its ancient feeling inspired him to recreate the past himself. A large stone cromlech, which still remains in the grounds, is a testimonial to that inspiration; and the ruined chapel, though it was not his creation, must have been a source of great delight. But even more important was the fact that Monserrate provided a place for experimenting with house and grounds, creating landscapes that were as 'natural' as possible. In that way Sintra was the testing ground for his greatest and grandest creation, Fonthill Abbey, in far-away Wiltshire.

6

A Portuguese Paradise

As we have seen, the classical Greek poetic evocation of the contemplative and simple pastoral life (see p.104) had a strong appeal to the Portuguese Renaissance writers who, in the sixteenth century, invented the myth of Sintra as an earthly paradise. The ancient bucolic idyll, transmitted through Virgil, was imbued with nostalgia for a rustic existence, which was stoical and calm and placed above the hurly burly of life in the city.

To the Portuguese humanists, this classical contrast between the city and the countryside could not have been more clearly applicable to their own situation. So long as Lisbon continued to grow as a metropolis, displaying both the wealth and *ennui* of worldly life, Sintra could be represented as a wholesome retreat from it. The ancient mountain was a place where nature, in all her majesty, held sway and where men of noble disposition sought to lead the good life. This artistic and moralistic perception of Sintra as a place of enlightened living was enhanced when it became a royal residence. Sintra, with its high castle ramparts, embodied the image of a fortress protecting the new frontiers of Christendom. As the threat of Muslim attack receded, the defensive role of the fortress declined, becoming more symbolic than real, as Duarte d'Armas' engravings so graphically show.

Intermingled with the classical learning of the Renaissance writers were several strands of Christian thinking which ranged from the ascetic to the redemptive. The ascetic values were most clearly espoused by the hermits and monks eking out a life of solitude on the cool, damp hills. We have found their caves and humble dwellings scattered in the Sintra range. If there were to be rewards for them, they would not come until the next life. Contemplation of that ideal was sufficient compensation for their worldly deprivation. The ascetic life they led was later idealised by the Romantics: Garrett remarks that monasteries in wild places put 'soul and majesty into things, they protected the trees, blessed the springs, filled the land with poetry and solemnity'.[1]

But there was a less arduous Christian option. This was to be found in the theology of salvation, which saw the possibility of redemption on earth itself. On the one hand, the souls of individuals could be saved; on the other a utopian social model became an achievable, social objective. The adherents of this optimistic creed believed that paradise could be regained; that the Garden of Eden could be found again on earth. It only needed a slight stretch of the artistic imagination to locate this Eden in the verdant, mysterious slopes of the *serra*.

Finding the physical location of paradise has been a persistent theme in Western utopian thought as Jean Delumeau shows in his comprehensive account.[2] Whether paradise was represented as a golden age, or an existence in Elysian fields or on blessed islands, it was always described as actual territory with geographical features. These features usually included an abundant supply of clear water, a good climate and fertile lands that supported a productive agriculture and, especially, the cultivation of fruit.

The location of paradise was often protected by a certain inaccessibility, so that mountain settings were much favoured. Vegetation bordered on the lush. Flowers, providing pleasure to the senses, grew in abundance. Paradise was a generous

---

1   Almeida J.B. da Silva Garrett, *Travels in My Homeland* (trans. J.M. Parker) (London, 1987) pp.79–80.
2   See J. Delumeau, *Une Histoire du Paradis* (Paris, 1992).

setting in which man could live off the fruits of the land without too much labour. There was certainly no suffering or hardship to be found within its boundaries. According to authoritative church figures, such as Saint Isidore of Seville or the Venerable Bede, the location of the *hortus deliciarum* was probably in the East, in any case, the direction from which Christianity had come. These teachings led to endless explorations eastwards in search of the fabled lands, which were subsequently associated with the kingdom of Prester John. Gradually, the belief that a terrestrial paradise could actually be achieved was abandoned. There was a gloomy acceptance that original sin was an inescapable aspect of the human condition. The inability of man to rid himself of that burden gave birth to nostalgia for something lost, something no longer obtainable. As paradise itself slipped out of reach, another way of looking at the garden as an idealised space began to take its place.

The Moorish pattern of housing, which was established in the old streets of Sintra, was an urban style that made little concession to nature. Any gardens that existed were small, enclosed and invariably walled. Built to protect its inhabitants from enemies and to keep out the heat, the plan of the urban town house was only gradually modified in the Renaissance by the Italian villa, in which interiors were opened up to allow for loggias, verandahs and patios. Outside the town, fortified country farms gradually gave way to residences designed in classical style.

Across Europe the idea of a space, obviously controlled by man began to dominate the planning of gardens. By the early sixteenth century, gardens with formal avenues, fountains and grottoes were appearing in the Tuscan countryside. The tradition of symmetrical, controlled gardens with features such as fountains and terraces continued to dominate Italian designs and to influence the formal gardens that were later planted in France and in Holland. It was only towards the end of the seventeenth century that this formalistic approach was gradually challenged in England, with the appearance of the Anglo-Chinese garden. As we have seen, a series of English owners, most notably William Beckford, brought this taste to Monserrate, as curves and natural lines began to be considered more important than geometric patterns in landscaping grounds. Although English country gentlemen like Sir William Temple were as steeped in the classics as their continental cousins, they were also looking for new, exotic ways of cultivating the gardens in their grounds. They therefore became experimenters.

Following the irregularities of nature was, of course, ideally suited to the topography of Sintra where there was hardly any flat space to set out formal parterres other than at Seteais, where terraces were introduced in Marialva's time. Nevertheless, throughout the eighteenth century the manmade, neo-classical features − towers, bridges and columns − remained central to the conceptions of the ideal garden. It was only as the Romantic notion of the magnificence of the wild and sublime became dominant that even these features had to be incorporated into dramatic, 'natural' scenery. The garden was now to become the domain of the dreamer, of Rousseau's solitary walker, who communed with nature by submitting himself to her grandeur. If there was a strong spiritual element to this aesthetic it was a pantheistic one: the Christian vision of the garden as paradise had gradually become secularised.

Although the cult of an earthly Eden reached its apogee in the sixteenth century, the influence of the classical pastoral was already apparent in Portuguese poetry in the fifteenth century. Our principal source of knowledge about that tradition of troubadour Galaico-Portuguese verse comes from the anthology of Garcia de Resende, the *Cancioneiro Geral*, which was published in 1516. The collection spanned the previous seventy years of poetry, a period of some cultural unity across the Peninsula. Whilst the Portuguese inherited the troubadour poetry of Provence through the courts of Aragon, León and Castile, Portuguese *fidalgos* also successfully took their language to the Spanish courts where it became the medium for poetic expression. Influenced by Petrarch and Dante, poets in the Galaico-Portuguese tradition wrote heroic and elegiac verse, but also produced the pastoral *cantiga,* which took both a romantic and a satiric form. Side by side with the imported French style was a more local type of verse, the *cançoes paralelísticas* that had been favoured by both King Sancho I and King Dinis. These were rougher, and indeed more rustic, expressions of the pastoral, full of grace and freshness even though, or perhaps because, they lacked sophistication. They were the beginning of a long, populist tradition but were, for the most part, excluded from de Resende's anthology.

Garcia de Resende was, after all, a courtier who remained in charmed, royal circles throughout his life. He was an influential figure over two reigns, enjoying the favours of King João II and King Manuel successively. He was private secretary to the former monarch and travelled with the latter when he visited Toledo and Saragossa. He was therefore in a strong position to influence the tone of court life at Sintra and he encouraged the holding of elegant, cultural evenings when verse was recited or plays enacted. He himself was a contributor to this rich artistic life, writing his moving *trovas* on the death of Inês de Castro. But the more demotic, indigenous verse was hardly likely to appeal to his sophisticated, cosmopolitan taste which showed Italian as well as Castilian influences.

It was somewhat ironic that Garcia de Resende's collaborator in producing the *Cancioneiro Geral* was Gil Vicente (see p.10) whose commitment to the language and manners of rustic life can hardly be questioned. Indeed, had Vicente had the upper hand or collected an anthology of his own, the voice of the mountain villages which he knew so well would have been heard more loudly in it. There would have been more *cançoes,* more of the song which came from oral tradition and which he regarded as the authentic cultural element of Portuguese lyricism. To say that is not to underestimate the sophistication of Vicente's own work, which ranged from comic farces to serious religious works and allegories in the classical style. The diversity of genre is matched by the variety of his characters. From more recognisably human types, who might nevertheless be touched up with some element of caricature, he ranged to personifications of gods or mythological figures in the ancient way. But it was Vicente's artistic intention to bring vernacular Portuguese into his dramatic and lyrical forms since he regarded it as the basis of the national culture. This artistic concern was matched by a political worry that the attraction of the court and the city was depopulating the countryside and undermining the traditional social structures upon which the whole of society was based. There was no radical intention here; rather, a sentimental conservatism which was concerned with the preservation of moral order.

In his *Triunfo do Inverno* (1529) a late work, Vicente employs the powerful image of mythical Sintra to elaborate his themes. But before the mountain makes an appearance in personification, there is oblique criticism of the ways of the court and city in the first part of the work. A pilot who very nearly causes a shipwreck by his incompetence is not censured whilst an ordinary seaman, on account of his own honesty, cannot succeed to the post. Although at times the setting of the court may resemble a beautiful garden, not everything within it blooms healthily. The court is not the only social institution that the poet censures. Although not an Erastian in religious matters, Vicente was unimpressed by what he regarded as the superstitious practices of Rome. Miracles receive short shrift in his writings, and nor does he have much patience with the overblown veneration of saints or Roman practices like the sale of indulgences. When we reach the last part of epic, the 'Triumph of Summer', it is the lush charms of the mountain that prove irresistible to summer, which is also represented as a character taking part in the dialogue. Towards the end of the verse, we learn that the gardens of Sintra are a 'terrestrial paradise' which was bestowed on the King of Portugal by

Solomon himself. The rich, lush green and the mountain air and fresh water are an appropriate setting for the celebration of the summer solstice.

Meanwhile, the Virgilian eclogue, a poem in the form of a dialogue, which would include amorous as well as aesthetic, social and philosophical reflections, was also taking hold.

The master of the eclogue was Francisco de Sá de Miranda (1487–1558). Sá de Miranda, a native of Coimbra, travelled to Spain and to Italy, where he met Sannazaro and other Italian writers before returning to Portugal in 1521. Sannazaro (1458–1530) was a Neapolitan of Spanish descent whose works were translated into Castilian and widely read across the Iberian Peninsula. Inheriting the mantle of Boccaccio, he published the complete edition of his *Arcadia* in 1504. Directly indebted to Virgil, Horace and Ovid, the work was in prose as well as poetry and celebrated the pleasures and moral rectitude of the pastoral life. Sannazaro's shepherds became the heroes of Arcadia and there they lived among the fauns and nymphs of classical creation. Later, in another work, he idealised fishermen, something that would have appealed to his Portuguese readers. From now on romances celebrating the pastoral life were an acceptable art form.

Cosmopolitan, in the way of the Manueline artists, Sá de Miranda spent time at the Sintra court, where he was befriended by the King. He also made the acquaintance of Bernadim Ribeiro in Sintra. But the life of a courtier did not appeal to him. Emulating his classical heroes, he retired to a country manor in the Minho where he pursued his literary work, influenced, but not dominated by, Petrarch and Dante. Indeed his insistence on the use of Portuguese was an important barrier against Castilian dominance at the bilingual court. Cultivated and secure, he was nevertheless disturbed by the treatment of the peasants and complained about local corruption among the magistracy. Like Gil Vicente, he was concerned with securing justice within a traditional social order. There is a strong suggestion in his work that compared to the wholesomeness of life on the land, the city and the court are highly artificial. Sá de Miranda's verse is regarded as among the most significant in Portuguese literature. Highly stylised and refined, it established the importance of the pastoral idyll, though the poet's versatility enabled him to produce verse with religious themes as well as comic drama.

Bernadim Ribeiro, Sá de Miranda's contemporary and acquaintance, was a more dedicated courtier who lived, conveniently, in a tower of the old Moorish castle. He was born in the 1480s, and his first works appeared in the collected *Cancioneiro Geral* (1516). However, his most celebrated work, *Menina e Moça*, did not appear until 1554, when further poems and eclogues were also published. Ribeiro wrote in Latin, Hebrew and Castilian as well as in Portuguese. His interest in Jewish learning was intense, giving rise to the speculation that he was himself of Jewish blood, though he had converted to Christianity. His popularity among Iberian Jews suggests that he might subsequently have converted back to Judaism. With the Inquisition set up in Portugal this was a dangerous faith to hold; he fell out of favour at court, where the Church had strong influence. Whether or not he was himself practising it, his sympathy with Judaism was unfashionable.

Ribeiro joined the other court poets in lamenting the loss of an idealised, rustic existence. There is a deep, Horatian nostalgia in his mood, echoing that of Sá de Miranda. However, it is in his prose romances that he brings a sophisticated twist to the literature of Sintra. Although these pieces are also pervaded by a sense of loss (*saudades*), there is also a deep, philosophical questioning of the meaning of existence in them. The poet is perplexed by his own identity. The many contradictions inherent in his own character suggest the possibility of more than one personality within himself. He begins to distinguish different voices: the 'I' and 'me' offer alternative ways of expressing his lyrical meaning. These preoccupations remind us of Fernando Pessoa and his complex creation of the heteronyms, different characters or voices through whom the poet may speak. Both Pessoa and Mario de Sá Carneiro, who are also obsessed with alienation and futurity, are Ribeiro's twentieth-century heirs. At the centre of Ribeiro's sensibility lies the attempt to understand and express change, a mutability that sweeps everything before it. In *Menina e Moça*, written in the female voice, the complexities of this predicament, the tangle of the emotional, amorous and philosophical reach an existential height. This psychological love story is nevertheless set against a pastoral background; there is a lyricism to the tale that is closer to poetry than prose. The poet of the court is, after all, a brooder as well. Plagued by puzzles about his own existence, he is also influenced by the natural setting. The high, dark mountain, the shadows and mists that form about it, and the sounds of water cascading intrude into the human drama which is already so dense. Bernadim Ribeiro gives more than a hint of the Romanticism that engulfed Portuguese writers and writers about Sintra in the nineteenth century.

The contribution of this quartet of courtly poets was added to, as we have seen, by João de Barros and Luís de Camões on the one hand and Francisco de Holanda and Damião de Góis on the other. Duarte d'Armas' etiolated views of the same period gave visual expression to an ethereal Sintra. Together all these Renaissance Portuguese scholars and artists established Sintra once and for all in the imagination of the nation. This cultural heritage survived even the period of the three Spanish Philips (1580–1640) when the Portuguese courtiers abandoned Sintra for Madrid, the capital of the united kingdom. Throughout this period, works extolling the virtues of the 'sacred mountain' continued to appear.

Francisco Rodrigues Lobo (1573–1621), a new Christian, extols the beauties of an enchanting village, with its ocean views, fresh air and pure running streams. Gabriel Periera de Castro, in his ambitious work, *Ulisseia* (1636) aimed to adapt Homer's original poem to suit the grandiose needs of the Portuguese. The poet is determined to set the seal on a favourite myth, namely that Ulysses himself was the founder of Lisbon. A convenient gap in the Homeric account provides the possibility for this much desired diversion of the hero to Lusitanian shores. And close to where the city was founded is a recognisable garden where orchards of fruit (apples and pomegranates are the most favoured) grow in abundance, where olives ripen all through the year and a sparkling river flows across the plain to the sea.

Weaving Sintra and Colares into the fabric of national mythology is undertaken on a grand scale in the epic poem, *Serra de Sintra*, which was published anonymously. The poem, which has been attributed to João da Cruz, a monk at Pena Monastery, is in six cantos beginning with a rotund verse, which recalls the stately cadences of Camões. The poet announces that Caliope, mother of Orpheus and herself the Muse who guards over epic poetry, has been deified and will preside over the telling of the tale of the valiant Portuguese explorers whose exploits outdo even those of the ancient Greeks and Romans. The centre of this symbolic Lusitanian world is Sintra, the mountain of the moon, where Diana herself was content to pass many days of her existence, bathing occasionally in the clear waters of the Moorish cistern. There is evidence to suggest that the poem may have been written before 1640 but altered to suit the mood of triumphalism which accompanied the accession of the Braganças to the throne in that year. Not only have the Portuguese (always referred to as Lusitanians) conquered their own territory from infidels and latterly from foreigners (Castilians) but they have taken the benefits of their civilization to the far ends of the earth – to Africa, India and the Far East.

Such is the greatness of the nation's achievement that the poet does not need to have recourse to the conceits of poetry. Instead of dabbling in hyperbole or metaphor, he has only to give a straightforward account of the history of his heroic compatriots. There can be only one setting for the tale: Sintra, with its lush vegetation, the majesty of the mountain, the calm silences of the *serra* only interrupted by the sound of water murmuring through rocks or the trill of the nightingale. An impressive range of animals – fox, jennet, bull, wolf and snake – roam the mountain. Colares, too, is painted in Arcadian tints – a place of villas and gardens and orchards, close to the sea, it glows golden in the vision of the seafaring heroes. In fact, so majestic is the region, that the gods themselves would feel as much at home there as in their ancient, mountainous birthplace of Olympus.

The *Serra de Sintra* is replete with references both to the courtly writers of the previous century and to the ancient classics. Pliny and Varro share space with the gods, nymphs, fairies and other spirits, as well as shepherds and earthly folk, that stalk the melodious verses of the poem. There are numerous allusions to classical texts, as well as to Dante, Petrarch, Sannazaro and Boccaccio. Intermingled with pagan and Renaissance philosophy, there is that strand of ascetic Christianity that we have associated with the hermits of Sintra. The poet shows a deep respect for the virtues of monastic life and an admiration for its spiritual achievement. A strong clue to the authorship of the poem arises in the third canto, where we are given a detailed history of Pena monastery. Its association with the Virgin Mary and construction by King Manuel at the time of the great discoveries link it inextricably to the national epic. Perched high up on its peak, with the sublime altarpiece of Chanterene, Pena assumes a commanding symbolic significance; halfway to heaven it shines out as a beacon on a sometimes uncaring nation.

Although the pastoral tradition continued to flourish in the eighteenth century, it was not a period of great additions to the stock of the Sintra legend. In the second part of the century, the prevailing aesthetic philosophy was that of *Arcadismo*, a tightening up of rules to combat what was seen as the excesses of the Baroque. Since this neo-classical movement, influenced by the precepts of Boileau (Nicolas, 1636–1711), played down the metaphorical and the mythological, it did not sit happily with the more fanciful Sintrenese themes of the Renaissance period. Enlightenment ideas of balance and symmetry and a greater use of prose rather than verse diminished the appeal of a place whose legends had inspired poets.

The true heirs to the earlier, Renaissance tradition, were the nineteenth-century Romantics, most prominently Almeida Garrett and Herculano. Garrett came to literary maturity with a knowledge of French writing and English Romantic literature whose exponents had projected their own Edenic vision of Sintra by this time. João Baptista da Silva Leitão (Almeida Garrett) was born in Oporto in 1799. His childhood was partly spent in the Azores, where his uncle was Bishop of Angra. Highly imaginative and studious, Garrett arrived in Coimbra in 1816 with a serious interest in religion. His university days proved formative, for in the heady years that led up to the liberal revolt in Oporto in 1820, radical ideas were in the air and they appealed to the young, budding poet. The fact that the Portuguese liberalism had a distinctly anti-clerical side did not dampen Garrett's enthusiasm for the cause. With the return of a conservative regime in 1832, he went into exile abroad, first to France and then to England. Whilst Garrett's first literary inclination was toward the neo-classicism of *Arcadismo*, his political experience and the influence of French and English letters proved a significant influence in shaping his art. He published two poems in Paris on historical themes – *Camões* (1825) and *Dona Branca* (1826). Both show the effect of Romantic literature on him and both, along with a number of his other works, include references to Sintra.

Garrett's poem *Camões* is regarded as one of the early works of Portuguese Romanticism. The poet uses the bucolic tradition of Sintra to express the emotion of loss (*saudades*) caused by his exile. He mixes the pastoral landscape of the area with his inner thoughts, the 'sentiments of his soul'. Nature presents its most charming and welcoming face in the location of the *serra*; it inspires in the poet a calm that compensates for the turbulence of his life abroad, in the city. However much the poet suffers, memories of nature – the rustling of breezes in the trees, the moss-covered rocks, the greenery of the mountain slopes – never leave him. They inspire him to lyricism, even if their absence lends a delicious sadness to his plight as an exile. The poet asks, rhetorically, whether he will see the sights of Sintra again. The close association of his sentiment and the physical features of nature echo the work of Bernadim Ribeiro, who wrote three hundred years before. Garrett's approach to Sintra inspired numerous nineteenth-century writers who followed him, including Francisco Gomes de Amorim, his disciple and biographer. Amorim revived Gil Vicente's legend of the amorous association of the sun and moon with the *serra* in his poem *A Flor de Marmore ou as Marvilhas da Pena em Cintra* (1878).

Garrett's highly Romantic approach to the Sintra landscape is also present in the work of Alexandre Herculano, his contemporary. Herculano was born in 1810, a bleak time in the affairs of Portugal, which lay devastated after the Peninsular wars. The King and court had gone to Brazil, where they were to remain for another decade. Herculano's personal circumstances were more difficult than Garrett's. Lacking financial backing, he had to forego a university education. Nevertheless, his considerable talent was noticed in Lisbon literary circles when he attended cultural *soirées* at the house of António Feliciano de Castilho, who was himself a notable writer. Like Garrett, Herculano was also taken by foreign literature, and in particular by the poetry of the great German Romantic, Schiller. He, too, leaned to the liberal cause and travelled in England and France, broadening his outlook and making a full conversion to liberalism. It was only when he was appointed librarian at the Ajuda Palace by the Prince Consort in 1839 that he became financially secure.

In verse inspired by the sight of a broken cross near the Convento do Carmo in Colares, Herculano admits to a preference for the night, for the mysterious, dark forces which inspired the Romantics as much as the marvels of a luminous nature. The rustic setting of the ruins is enhanced by moonlight; solitude and darkness encourage the poet to brood on the gloomier aspects of the human situation. The poet's lugubrious thoughts bring to mind Childe Harold's dark musings as he passed through the same mountain and valley.

In linking their Romantic thoughts and feelings to the location of Sintra, Garrett and Herculano were creating an image that may be compared to Wordsworth's creation of 'sacred places' in the Lake District. Both were evocations of a classical mythology common to European culture and known to educated men of the time. The English poet's representation of that ideal can be readily applied to Sintra:

> There is an Eminence, – of these our hills
> The last that parleys with the setting sun;
> We can behold it from our orchard seat;
> And, when at evening we pursue our walk
> Along the public way, this Peak so high
> Above us, and so distant in its height,
> Is visible; and often seems to send
> Its own deep quiet to restore our hearts.[1]

The task of elaborating the Romantic myth of Sintra was left to another writer, this time of aristocratic background, namely João Antonio de Lemos Pereira de Lacerda, Second Viscount Juromenha. Unlike Garrett and Herculano, Juromenha supported the conservative cause of Dom Miguel in the political struggles of the time. Educated in Coimbra, he had to leave the country when the liberals won the civil war in 1834. Juromenha pursued his literary career through the journals of the day, concentrating on the publication of important texts on the history of art.[2] He also edited the works of

---

1   W. Wordsworth, 'Poems on the Naming of Places: III' (1800) from *Poetical Works* (Oxford, 1966) p.117.
2   He wrote in the *Journal de Belas-Artes, A Aurora, O Catolico* among others.

Camões. In 1838 there appeared, anonymously, the work *Cintra Pinturesca*, with a quotation from Garrett's *Camões* in the frontispiece, testimony to the power of literature to cut across political divides. The book begins with a self-conscious intent to link the history of Sintra, mythological and real, with the history of the nation. The author observes that there has been no attempt to set out a full description of the 'enchanted land'.[1] Poets national (Camões) and foreign (Byron) are rapidly called to support; Sintra's glory has been largely conveyed in verse rather than in prose. Whilst he has nothing against this tradition of poetic Sintra, he says, it is time to produce a more factual guide which might also help tourists, including foreigners, who are drawn to the beauty of its woods and its light, fresh, mountain air.

Despite that declaration, Juromenha begins his account by considering the ancient legends handed down by Varro, Strabo and Pliny. He speculates on the etymology of the names of the Cabo da Roca and of Sintra itself, observing that ancient ruins were still to be found on the Cape of the Moon in the time of André de Resende in the sixteenth century. In relaying stories such as Pliny's account of the resistance of the early Lusitanians to Roman rule and in the glories of the reign of King Manuel, Juromenha aims to integrate Sintra's position in the legend of the nation itself.

Although many of these accounts are familiar, Juromenha manages to weave them into a continuous story, which inspired several generations of Portuguese writers and has allowed him to maintain his position as an exponent of legendary Sintra until the present. Nevertheless, he has had his critics. Francisco Costa condemned him for relying on faulty translations of Latin documents rather than going to the originals himself. Failing to read the Latin version led to serious mistakes in Juromenha's account of the provisions of the Charter of 1154; and his flowery style has not found favour

---

1   Visconde de Juromenha, *Cintra Pinturesca* (Lisbon, 1838) p.6.

with the more sober approach of other scholars. Even so, however, Juromenha's book has a sense of historical perspective. If he sweeps rather erratically through the centuries, he still injects a sense of movement into the long chronicle of royal comings and goings from Sintra.

An air of sweet melancholy hangs over Juromenha's Sintra, blessed as it is with chestnut trees, lemon and lime groves, orchards of apple and pear and a generous display of flowers. Monserrate, by now an elegant ruin, still exudes the good taste of its English owners. Its shaded woods encourage a deep nostalgia for what is lost forever; its very dilapidation is thrilling to the Romantic gaze. Anything that is exotic or foreign can only add to the mystery of the place. For this reason, Juromenha is only too keen on what others have regarded as the tenuous Moorish connections of the old, royal palace, the most striking sight in the town and justly described as its heart. He calls it the 'small Alhambra of the Moorish kings of Lisbon',[1] noting that the architecture of the building, particularly its windows and arches, display a chiselled Oriental delicacy and that an Eastern influence is also evident in its water features, from the tanks outside the windows of rooms to the fountains in the courtyards, shaded by sweet smelling orange trees.

However fanciful Juromenha's enthusiasm for the Moorish features of the palace might have been, his observation about the Moorish cultural influence on palace life is noteworthy. He makes the convincing point that at this 'Moorified' (see p.54) Portuguese court, the recital of poetry and the playing of music would have been a perfectly natural continuation of a tradition already settled at the time of the Moorish rulers. The Portuguese kings and queens of the Burgundian and Avis dynasties, so notable for gathering artistic and musical circles around them, were behaving as their Islamic predecessors had done. In another clever association, Juromenha links the heroic legends inscribed in Sanskrit on the rocks of Penha

---

1   Ibid. p.35.

Verde with the classical stories of gods and heroes in ancient Sintra. The Oriental mythology is used to lend support to the rich Greek and Roman imagery of the 'Sacred Mountain' as a home of the gods.

Juromenha is not surprised that men of religious disposition have been attracted to Sintra. He considers that their role is a vital part of the Sintra story. He is fascinated by the way in which Sintra, with its majestic and legendary landscape, has attracted clerical figures of importance from the outside world. One such character was Bishop Bras de Barros, cousin of the great sixteenth-century chronicler and poet, João de Barros, whose work we have considered (see p.10). The bishop was educated abroad, at Louvain, and was involved in the official foundation of the University of Coimbra in the reign of King João III. He was appointed Bishop of Leiria, an important episcopal see, but was prepared to give it up to move to Sintra. No doubt the idea of being near the court attracted him but Juromenha is convinced that the special ambience of Sintra played a part in his decision.

At points in his account, Juromenha makes the effort to abandon the picturesque in favour of the practical and the scientific. A detailed description of the road from Lisbon to Sintra, setting out *quintas* and churches on the way, is intended to entice the cultivated tourist. Roman ruins and the sites of temples and tombs are marked out for the same purpose. However, while distances between monuments are helpfully included, it turns out that they are given in nautical miles. Still in a listing mood, Juromenha gives details of the Latin inscriptions to be read on local stones. In another table, the relative heights of landmarks and buildings are set out, showing that Pena towers over six times the height of Santa Catarina in Lisbon and over four times the height of the Lisbon aqueduct, a graphic enough way of giving an idea of scale. Elsewhere, he adds geological detail; the granite structure that composes the range and its outcroppings are described in the scientific language of the day. In other sections, statistics of agricultural production are listed. Wheat, honey and wine are named as traditional products. A long list of plants is included, with two kinds of 'Moorish' grass and a variety of herbs with medicinal properties. Lastly, in case anyone should doubt the advantages of the environment, a roll call of eminent sons and daughters of Sintra and Colares, including kings, theologians and navigators, proves the excellence of its air for breeding men and women of distinction.

The mixture of the imaginary and real was very much the contribution to the Romantic recreation of Sintra, which Juromenha had so floridly taken forward, of Fernando Augusto Antonio Kohary de Saxe-Coburg-Gotha, the Prince Consort who married Queen Maria II in 1836. Dom Fernando was at that time only nineteen years of age; he was dashing and romantic, with a distinct penchant for the arts, eventually becoming known in Portugal as the 'artist king'. This sobriquet was not meant to be entirely flattering, for there was a lingering suspicion among his subjects that Dom Fernando was a dilettante, devoted to music and fine arts, for whom the affairs of state of his adopted country were of periphery interest. His correspondence with his German relations, which has recently been brought to light, tells a different story revealing that although he was immature and inexperienced, he made a considerable effort to understand the turbulent politics of his adopted country.[1] If his intention was to keep the crown above party politics, that was no bad thing in the plans of a constitutional monarch. Nor was his distaste for military activity a disqualification for the same role. Dom Fernando's loyalty to Portugal was demonstrated when he rejected, in turn, offers of the crowns of Spain and Greece. In the case of the Spanish invitation, he had learnt enough about Iberian politics and culture to realise the disaster that would result from another unification of the two kingdoms.

---

1 See M. Ehrhadt, 'D. Fernando II visto através das suas cartas à família' in *Romantismo Figuras e factos da época de D. Fernando II* (Sintra, 1988).

Sintra captivated Dom Fernando from his earliest days in Portugal. In his letters home, he marvels at the natural setting of the place, describing golden afternoons in the *serra* as especially enchanting. Despite the pressure of royal etiquette, he most liked to wander about the town without an entourage, suntanned and enjoying the outdoor life. He found the Sintra townsfolk more genial company than the courtiers; after the death of Queen Maria in 1853, his retreat to 'the most sacred place in Portugal'[1] was even more complete. Well-read in the history and literature, Dom Fernando was determined to leave a mark on Sintra that would be fitting in terms of Portugal's own history.

At the time he started to make his plans, a new consciousness about the national heritage was taking shape. Dom Fernando himself was to become involved in the restoration of many national monuments around the country, particularly those that were associated with the glories of the past. He was persuaded by a coterie of liberal friends, including Alexandre Herculano (whom, as we have seen, he installed at the Ajuda Palace as librarian) and the art critic, Francisco Adolfo Varnhagen, that the architecture and decoration of the reign of King Manuel was the true national style. Varnhagen, a Luso-Brazilian, coined the adjective *Manuelino* (Manueline style) to describe the elaborate twists and turns of that style, whilst Herculano insisted that it was a continuation of the Gothic and thereby connected to the early growth of constitutionalism in the Middle Ages. Those theories, with their liberal undertones, inspired Dom Fernando to employ Wilhelm Ludwig, Baron von Eschwege, a military engineer who had fought in the Portuguese army for the liberal cause, to undertake the construction of a grandiose palace on the site of Pena Convent. The scale of the undertaking was massive. Given the steepness of the mountain site, the engineering problems were formidable. Tunnels had to be dug at awkward

---

1 Ibid. p.12.

angles to provide access to the summit. The baron knew what he was doing; he had already written a detailed, geological treatise about the granite structure of the mountain.

The original plans of the building reveal that Baron von Eschwege intended to build a Germanic-looking medieval castle, with towers, battlements and rampart fortifications. He was familiar with buildings of this type in Germany; the castle of Rheinstein (1824) and Schinkel's Stolzenfelds (1834) have been singled out as influences on him.[1] The original drawings of the new palace immediately remind us of Duarte d'Armas' engravings of the old royal palace, except that the new structure is more massive and solid in feel. This impression is confirmed by the huge, cylindrical tower and the polygonal entrance towers. Dom Fernando added the drawbridge and other mock medieval features. To the other end of the main façade is the familiar clock-tower, which does not appear on the first sketches.

Building began in the early 1840s and proceeded apace so that by the end of that decade, the main features of the new palace as we now see it were already in place. Throughout the project, which continued until his death in 1885, Dom Fernando took a personal interest in the work, adding ideas of his own to the design. The King's additions were very often those neo-Manueline features that were now considered to be the 'national' style and which featured in many other buildings he was having restored in different parts of the country. The two ornamental turrets of the main gateway at Pena Palace imitate the Tower of Belém, on the Tagus estuary. Serpents, a symbol long associated with Portugal, are carved onto the entrance arch. Other parts of the façade remind us of the royal palace, nestling far below in the town. Many of the elaborate, ornamental features appealed to Dom Fernando's sense of chivalry and legend. The most dramatic external design is the

---

1   See P. Pereira & J.M. Carneiro, op. cit. p.38. This is an excellent, learned account of the building and contents of Pena Palace.

Triton portico.[1] Here the myth of the Triton, which we have seen was reported to Emperor Tiberius in Rome, is immortalised in a large sculpture that hangs down rather menacingly over the entrance. The Triton sits on a conch, which he was supposed to have blown from time to time. On his shoulders he supports an intricately carved corbel, above which rests a bay window. The Triton's expression on this occasion is grim; he is, after all, carrying the whole weight of the world. The style of this impressive piece of masonry is said to reflect the influence of the Manueline window at Tomar, with its intricate twists of rope and seafaring images; the Triton also reminds us of Camões' monster, Adamastor, in the *Lusiads*.

Dom Fernando's taste is evident within Pena Palace as well as in the architectural features of the exterior. More obvious Germanic influences can be seen in the Stag Room, with its Bavarian themes or in the chapel where a medieval atmosphere is created by the use of stained glass, depicting both the royal arms of Portugal and those of the Saxe-Coburg-Gothas, Dom Fernando's own family. Although the King was attached to these European features and designed others himself, his taste was not restricted to Western decoration. He enjoyed the mock-Moorish features of Pena as well. Gothic and Moorish styles are jumbled together against a backcloth of interiors that had the typically heavy draping of curtains and carpets of the period. Large pieces of furniture appear alongside occasional pieces of elegant French porcelain, or Chinese Ming bowls; heavy silverware and great ostrich feathers add a domestic, if rather grand, touch. The private dining room, which is of a modest proportion, most captures this mixture of styles; it strikes the viewer as a setting for informal, and perhaps even jocular, family occasions.

If the castle itself, which was perched on the mountain, became the symbol of a new Gothic Sintra, 'romantic and solitary,'[2] the grounds of the Pena Palace also came to reflect the

1   See Illustration 23.
2   J. Rodil *Sintra na Obra de Eça de Queirós* (Sintra, 2000) p.60.

King's taste. Eighteenth- and early nineteenth-century descriptions, including Byron's, of the way up to Pena tend to
emphasise the cragginess of the slopes, and the huge bare faces
of granite exposed to the sky that anyone looking upwards
would see.[1] The terrain inspired Childe Harold because of its
bleakness; but there was a need to convert those barren slopes
to something more Edenic and lush if the Romantic wanderer,
following Rousseau's solitary dreamer, or reading Almeida
Garrett's evocation of an earthly paradise, was to be enthralled.
Dom Fernando set about doing just that. He converted Pena's
grounds into an abundant forest, as Sir Francis Cook (who we
shall see in Chapter 7) was doing at Monserrate, by importing
large numbers of trees and plants from abroad to add to the
indigenous stock. Dom Fernando actually visited his English
neighbour's estate to see what tips he could glean from Burt,
the head gardener. Supplies for the Pena Park came from
Australia, North America and the Far East as well as from
England and France. Palms and cedars were added to chestnut
and fruit trees; ferns flourished amid the native grasses.[2]

Like his English neigbours at Monserrate, Dom Fernando
was also trying to create a 'natural' setting, wanting to give the
impression that the exotic, imported species had grown up by
themselves at Pena. The forest was to be a primitive cloak
around the castle; in its shades their Oriental but equally spiritual cousins, peris and afrits would join classical creatures, such
as nymphs and fauns. Here and there, fountains and clearings
would be made to add to the magical setting. Bridges and grottoes, pergolas and cascading streams were all part of the effect.
An occasional building could be allowed. One was the *Templo
das Colunas*, a curious, mock-Renaissance pavilion, topped by
a Moorish crescent on its roof. Elsewhere a cottage *orné*, which
became known as the *Chalet da Condessa*, was a curious mix
of an English cottage and a North American ranch, with

---

1   See Illustration 22.
2   His efforts were much appreciated by Lady Jackson, op. cit. p.186.

incongruous Gothic arched windows. It was named after the Condessa d'Edla, the King's second wife, and was designed as a retreat in the woods where the royal party could picnic in complete privacy.[1] The courtiers did not share the King's enthusiasm for these outdoor events. Nor did they by any means approve of the Condessa who, as Elisa Federica Hensler, had been a mere singer, though one of international repute, before being swept away from the São Carlos theatre in Lisbon to join the royal entourage in Sintra.

The pursuit of romance was the very motive of Carlos de Maia, the dark hero of Eça de Queirós' novel *Os Maias* (1888) for going to Sintra. The aristocratic and restless Carlos undertakes the journey just on the off chance that he may capture a glimpse of an English lady with whom he has become infatuated. The fact that she is married to another man, a worthy member of the Lisbon bourgeoisie, adds a racy element to the story. Henceforth, Sintra may also be thought of as a place for secret trysts; somewhere for the enjoyment of illicit passion as well as for the more mundane pleasures of the day-tripper. In the *Tragedy of the Street of Flowers*, the dandified Damaso is reported by the Lisbon gossips as having been caught *in flagrante delicto* with the Countess of Aguiar in the Capuchan monastery.

Eça's imaginative projections were influenced by the years he spent abroad in the diplomatic service. In England, he admired the bustling Victorian society which he encountered. He was convinced that the energy of the upper classes meant not only that England was a well-governed country but that its rulers were able to direct the affairs of a significant portion of mankind effortlessly. At the same time, Eça was much taken by the refined politeness and dandified dress of the typical English gentleman.

In France, where he was also posted, Eça admired another kind of effortlessness, that of intellectual sophistication, which was also associated with an advanced technological society.

---

1   The chalet, made of wood, survived intact until 1999, when it was burned down in a fire.

The state of France contrasted vividly with his own backward, semi-feudal Portugal; Paris, with all its metropolitan glitter made Lisbon seem dowdy and provincial. Above all, Paris was the place for intellectuals; its cafés were packed with artists and writers from every corner of the world. An ironic and ambiguous contrast between life in a smart *quartier* of Paris and the calm but wholesome existence in a rustic province of Portugal is the theme of his last work, *The City and the Mountains,* published posthumously in 1901.

Despite his suave cosmopolitanism, Eça's contacts with English and French society did not make him any the less patriotic. Rather, they increased his sense of frustration with his own country and fuelled his satirical tirade against the languid and supine Portuguese upper crust. English and French experiences inspired a radicalism in Eça, a desire for social change, but they did not preclude an aesthetic enjoyment of decadence and even decay. Eça's *saudades,* his nostalgia for things lost, is evident throughout his writing, as much in the earlier novels which critics have labelled as works of realism as in his later, more languid excursions into pastoralism.

The complexity of Eça's moods is captured vividly in *Os Maias* where the treatment of Sintra as a bucolic paradise is compromised by considerations about the innate greed and corruption of mankind. Carlos de Maia and his friend Ega arrive, full of enthusiasm for the delights of the clean mountain air and the wholesome atmosphere of the town. The butter of Seteais seems an innocent enough pleasure to covet. Their first decision, to stay at the Hotel Neto, rather than at the Lawrence, is made on the seemingly reasonable ground of the superior food of the first establishment. The Lawrence, though comfortable, is rather dull for this lively metropolitan pair. It would also have been inconvenient to be quite so near their prey for Eduarda, the married lady Carlos is stalking, was already installed there.[1]

---

1   J. Rodil, in his informative and subtle account, says that the Hotels Neto,

Before long the two friends pick up a pair of Spanish prostitutes. The tawdry scenes with the Spanish courtesans jar against the noble backcloth of the sacred mountain. Nevertheless, the two Lisbon gentlemen do not miss out on touring the usual sites. They trek up to Pena and admire the tranquil setting of Seteais. Gazing with interest at the old royal palace, their thoughts are somewhat disturbed by the notion that its huge kitchen chimneys suggest that it may have been built 'on a scale to suit the gluttony of a king who daily devours his kingdom'.[1] Even so, the pastoral beauty of the landscape cannot fail to move them. The soothing rustle of leaves, the murmuring waters and the velvety air soothe their troubled, city brows.

Looking down from a vantage point, perhaps from Pena peak or in the Volta do Duche, they admire the dense growth of trees covering the sides of the mountains and the peaceful idyllic valley below; the *quintas* scattered here and there and the old stone walls covered in lichen. Hidden in overgrown gardens are streams and ponds with water lilies and flowering plants perfuming the air. In his exhilaration at being in the bosom of nature itself, Carlos roundly declares that Sintra is 'neither old stones or Gothic ruins. This is Cintra – water, a bit of moss'. The calmness and simplicity of those primeval things reminds him of man's blissful existence in the Garden of Eden.

Nevertheless, as the night descends and at a time of day in Lisbon when the prospect of a lively evening would lie ahead, the tourists find something sad and remote in the air. If Sintra has inspired its fictional visitors with an awe of nature, it has also made them feel insignificant, valueless, and slothful. They begin to realise that there may be no place for them in this all

---

Lawrence and Vitor form a triangle in Eça's novel, reflecting the emotional tangle of the plot. *Sintra na Obra de Eça de Queirós* (Sintra, 2000) p.49.

1 J. Eça de Quierós, *The Maias* (trans. P.M. Pinheiro & A. Stevens) (London, 1998) p.199.

too beautiful setting. Despite its inconveniences, life in the city is morally and aesthetically less demanding. When Carlos and Ega do take their leave of Sintra, it is not the wonders of nature they remember but, absurdly, the fact that they have forgotten to sample the famous, local cheesecakes.

However much Eça teases his characters as well as his readers with these touches of bathos, his evocation of Sintra as a romantic destination, just within reach and somehow just beyond the grasp of city devotees, added profoundly to its image and symbolism. If the behaviour of his characters can be downright coarse, the mountain setting remains noble and romantic. Ramalhão is given his floweriest treatment:

> I saw her one sweet night
> When the nightingale was singing,
> The sky was filled with stars,
> A brightly lit pavilion:
> Ah Sintra! I can still hear
> The sweet babbling of your fountains,
> Feel the shadows cast on our faces
> By the trees of Ramalhão.[1]

At other times Eça's characters are gripped by the delicious melancholy of Sintra. In *The Tragedy of the Street of Flowers*, when Vitor finds his beloved Genoveva and Damaso at the Hotel Lawrence, the three go for a walk in the damp, cool evening. While Damaso complains that Sintra is dull and dreary in winter and makes him sad, the secret lovers are enthralled by its romantic atmosphere and cling to one another unnoticed as the three figures stroll through the evening mist.

Even travelling to Sintra brought one into contact with the mysterious. In *O Mistério da Estrada de Sintra* (1884),[2] which Eça wrote with Ramalho Ortigão, there is talk of passengers,

---

1   J. Eça de Queirós, *The Tragedy of the Street of Flowers* (trans. M.J. Costa) (Sawtry, Cambridge, 2000) pp.92–3.
2   It was written much earlier, probably in 1870.

whose personal writing paper is embossed with a crown, travelling incognito on the road from Lisbon to Sintra. The prospect of meeting such people en route adds excitement to the journey. Indeed, so important is the element of suspense that there is no need for fulfillment: the travellers on the road never actually reach Sintra. By his suggestion of mystery and high drama, Eça added significantly to the legendary power of the place.

7

An English Eden

Writing in the first decade of the twentieth century, A.C. Inchbold notes that 'upon English minds Cintra seems to have exercised an extraordinary and attractive influence'.[1] His opinion is borne out by the enthusiastic and at times effusive, accounts of English visitors to Sintra from the late eighteenth century onwards. In the 1780s, James Murphy toured Portugal to survey buildings of architectural interest. He produced a book of detailed illustrations, which took in most of the important monuments at Sintra and was dedicated to the Prince of Brazil. Other English visitors included clerics who were accompanying troops or based as chaplains at the factories in Oporto or Lisbon. William Bradford, for instance, was an army chaplain during the Peninsular wars. He left engravings of Sintra and other topographical landmarks such as the Lisbon aquaduct. William Kinsey, another cleric, made a record of a later visit, illustrating his book with engravings of Lisbon and Sintra. He added dire warnings about the dangers of food and of catching disease.[2]

However, the most flamboyant and discerning Englishman to visit Sintra during this period was William Beckford, who set up residence in Ramalhão in 1787. On two subsequent visits, in 1794 and 1798, he lived at Monserrate (his influence on the building is discussed on pp.123–7). Beckford left an

---

1   A.C. Inchbold (illus. S. Inchbold), *Lisbon and Cintra* (London, 1907) p.146.
2   See J. Murphy, *Travels in Portugal* (London, 1795), William Bradford, *Sketches of the Country, Character and Costume in Portugal and Spain* (London, 1809) and William Kinsey, *Portugal Illustrated in a series of Letters* (London, 1828).

entertaining account of his sojourns, which was very much directed to a middle-class reading public in England. He also left a less sunny, private diary recording his anxiety and frustration. Of all the English visitors to the area, it is Beckford's ghost that seems to haunt it most.[1]

Beckford first came to Sintra in July 1787 to visit the villa being built for his friends, the aristocratic Marialvas, in São Pedro. He had been in Lisbon for several months by this time, having disembarked from a ship that was taking him to visit family sugar plantations in Jamaica, from which he derived his enormous wealth. Beckford was young and dashing, as well as rich, but his alleged involvement in a homosexual incident with his younger kinsman, William Courtenay, had created a scandal (the 'Powderham affair') which had forced him into exile from England. As if that misfortune were not enough, other misadventures dogged the Wiltshire grandee. His young wife had died in childbirth, leaving him with two infant daughters. His great Oriental tale, *Vathek*, the most exciting thing he had written, had been published without his permission.

Thus the rather haughty and grand young man who affected to despise the English merchant community in Lisbon (folk who, unlike him, had to make a living) had already been scarred by bitter experiences. His arrival in Portugal, with a bevy of household servants, furniture, silver and books, caused a great stir. The French envoy, the Marquis de Bombelles, observes in his diary that the Lisbon public was much taken by the arrival of a young man who, apart from owning superb possessions in England and in Jamaica, had a disposable net income of 30,000 louis a year.[2] Soon after his arrival, Beckford met the Marialva family. In particular, he was befriended by

---

1   For an account of Beckford's time in Portugal, see Malcolm Jack, *William Beckford: An English Fidalgo* (New York, 1996) and 'Beckford's Portuguese Palaces' in *William Beckford, 1760–1844: An Eye for the Magnificent*. Catalogue of an exhibition at the Bard Graduate Center, New York, 2001 (New Haven, 2001).
2   Marquis de Bombelles, *Journal d'un Ambassadeur de France au Portugal 1786–1788*, (ed. R. Kann) (Paris, 1979) p.117.

Dom Diogo, the fifth Marquis, an influential courtier who was Master of the Horse. The connection with the Marialvas would prove decisive in Beckford's stays in Portugal.

The one Englishman in Lisbon whom Beckford did not despise was his agent Thomas Horne, a long-time resident who dabbled in a number of different businesses. It was Horne who found Beckford the *quinta* at Ramalhão, on the foothills of the *serra*.[1] Ramalhão was at that time owned by José Street Arriaga Brum da Silveira, a rich merchant of Luso-Irish extraction. The site of Ramalhão had had a long history by the eighteenth century, as Francisco Costa has shown.[2] In 1470, King Afonso V granted land to one Diogo Gomes, a courtier, at a spot where the road from Lisbon meets the road from the coast, exactly on the site of the modern Ramalhão. Some fifty years later, royal permission was given for the building of a house, which was already to be named Ramalhão, to one Fernando Eanes Canaval. For many years a hospice and charitable institution co-existed with the main house.

The mansion, which Beckford rented, was built in the early eighteenth century. In 1707 the owners were consulting lawyers about renovation and rebuilding. By 1748 the house had the characteristic longitudinal dimensions which Beckford described. Its owner was now Francisco Garcia de Bivar, something of a colonial hero, who fought against the Spanish in South America, a continent which would figure again in the history of the house after Beckford's time. The house suffered damage in the earthquake of 1755, for there is evidence showing that after that time Bivar's widow was again involved in rebuilding. Despite her husband's standing, the widow Bivar must have found herself in financial difficulties, for Ramalhão was later sold fairly cheaply to a rich Lisbon lady, Dona Maria da Encarnação Correia. During her time, consid-

---

1   See Malcolm Jack, 'Ramalhão: Beckford's First Sintra House' *Beckford Journal*, Vol. 3 1997, pp.20–4. Also see Illustration 12.
2   See F. Costa, *Beckford em Sintra no Verão de 1787* (Sintra, 1982).

erable additions were made, including the eastern wing of spacious apartments which Beckford so much admired. An archway was erected over the Lisbon road, linking the gardens of the house to an extended area of orchards and fields, which Dona Maria must have added to the estate.

By now, the mansion itself was of considerable proportions. It formed a long rectangle, falling in a south to north direction with a central patio on the western side, facing the range of Sintra hills. On the eastern side, where the wing of apartments had been added, there was a long terrace, supported by colonnades, with a view to the coast in the far distance. Gardens sloped down in front of the terrace, providing a pleasing prospect. The house was set on raised ground, which made it visible as one approached the foothills of Sintra. As Beckford was to discover, however, Ramalhão's exposed position meant that it could be blasted by winds, which, even in the height of summer, would suddenly roll across from the littoral. He noted with alarm that there were no fireplaces or chimneys in any room, something that boded badly for winter days. The air that swept about Ramalhão was alternately bracing or balsamic; the changes in climate seemed to match Beckford's own volatile moods as he described them in his private diary, part of which was written in the house.

Nevertheless, Ramalhão's salons were spacious enough for Beckfordian whimsy to operate on its usual grand scale. Beckford decorated the main room, which boasted eleven glazed doors and windows of large dimensions, in what he called an 'Asiatic' style. His description of the room is exotic and mysterious, a veritable Aladdin's cave:

An agreeable variety prevails in my Asiatic salon; half its curtains admit no light, and display the richest folds; the other half are transparent, and cast a mild glow on the mat and sofas. Large clear mirrors multiply this profusion of drapery, and several of my guests seemed never tired of running from corner to corner, to view the different groups of objects reflected on all sides in the most unexpected directions, as if they fancied themselves admitted by enchantment to peep into a labyrinth of magic chambers.[1]

The decoration of the rooms reminded one of Beckford's Portuguese friends of apartments furnished for King João V when he secretly visited the Convent of Odivelas on his amorous adventures. Great entertainment was arranged at Ramalhão (at a cost, which was later to shock Beckford) by Jerónimo Francisco de Lima, a leading Portuguese composer of the day in these 'magic chambers', who produced music for all occasions. He was flattered by Beckford's patronage and was no doubt well aware of the rumours circulating in Lisbon that the English visitor was one of the richest men in the world. A band of six musicians, who wore brightly coloured costumes and donned straw hats, gave off a languid, Eastern air. Standing near the gilt trellis work of the windows, with the fish and lily tanks below, they languorously strummed away their *modinhas* (the Brazilian love songs much in vogue in Lisbon of that time) for hours on end.[2]

But not everything about Beckford's stay at Ramalhão was so ephemeral. The house also acquired an important sentimental association for him. During his stay in Lisbon he had been introduced to the teenage student Gregorio Franchi, whose family was of Italian origin, at the Patriarchal Seminary. Franchi's good looks, musical talents and high spirits made him highly attractive to Beckford. Nevertheless, Beckford's experience in England had left him wary of getting involved with a younger man again. He therefore kept a certain distance between himself and the lively and amorous Franchi. But this

---

1   *The Travel Diaries of William Beckford of Fonthill* (ed. G. Chapman) (Cambridge, 1928) 2 vols, vol. II p.99.

2   For an account of the music of the time, see M.C. de Brito, 'A Música em Portugal no tempo de William Beckford' in *William Beckford and Portugal: An Impassioned Journey*, Catalogue Raisonné of an exhibition at the Palace of Queluz, 1987 (Lisbon, 1987) pp.51–62.

display of English *sang froid* did not convince the impetuous young seminarian, who turned up unannounced at Ramalhão. Installed in the great salon so lavishly decorated by his English hero, he dashed off Haydn motets on the pianoforte, music which we must imagine pouring onto the terrace and the lawns below. The whole house came to life and Beckford was enthralled by Franchi's presence. Later, when Franchi had left, Beckford found the house silent and depressing.

Beckford's life in Sintra was a highly social one. The Marialvas' house in São Pedro was only a short horse ride from Ramalhão. If Beckford was not dining with them in their home, he was often entertaining them at his own. When the others were out, he enjoyed the company of the old Abbade, a nonagenarian friend of the family, with whom he spent hours chatting. At no great distance, on the other side of the village, was the Dutch Consul Gildemeester's Quinta da Alegria (Hotel Seteais) where Beckford attended the opening dinner (see p.119). Mrs. Gildemeester, in particular, seems to have amused Beckford by her somewhat caustic wit and pampered him with her milk and cheese, which was produced to exacting Dutch standards. On the way to the Gildemeester's, Beckford would have passed the house of Thomas Horne, his agent, and would probably have called in for a glass of port and a biscuit. Horne and his family (including his cousin Sill, whom Beckford called the 'turkey-poult', and Sill's daughters) became regular companions, if not close friends. The terrace at Horne's house, which was overhung by a vast cork tree, which is still in place today, delighted Beckford. It had a sheltered position that contrasted favourably with windswept Ramalhão.

Although Horne sometimes expressed anti-Portuguese sentiments common to the expatriate English community, he was well-received in Portuguese, as well as in English, circles. He therefore acted as an important link between the two communities, moving freely between them in a way not common to members of the English Factory, who tended to stick to themselves. His advice on property matters was usually sound and Beckford, who always respected practical men, tended to accept it. Clearly, Sill did not command the same respect but Beckford enjoyed the company of Sill's eldest daughter, Betty, who became something of a favourite. He describes her as of good nature and sensible judgement and, significantly for an aesthete, of more taste and imagination than is generally found in members of her class. Betty Sill was courting another of Beckford's Sintra set, João Paolo Bezerra de Seixas. Bezerra was, in every sense, a vivid character. He was of striking appearance, with lively, dark eyes and a spirited manner. Convivial in company, Bezerra was a man of intellectual and aesthetic tastes. He became one of the earliest Portuguese readers of *Vathek,* something that must have flattered its author. In later years he enjoyed a successful diplomatic career, visiting Beckford when he had returned to building Fonthill Abbey in Wiltshire. Eventually, Bezerra became a minister in the Portuguese administration.

Two other members of the Sintra clique were clerics – Henrique de Aguilar e Menezes, a prelate at the Patriarchate and Octavino Acciaoli. Aguilar had fiercely independent views, which, ironically, included strong feelings against the Church. Acciaoli (of Italian extraction) was a more jovial character whose sociable good humour made him a welcome guest at any gathering. Sometimes Dom José de Mateus, a wealthy landowner from the north of Portugal, would join the friends. He, like Bezerra, had serious literary interests and Beckford admired his good taste and discernment. While each of the Sintra group appealed to Beckford for different reasons, they were all men of the world who understood the provincialism of Portuguese society. Although they had much to teach a foreigner, their jaundiced view, along with Horne's carping, made Beckford too critical of Portuguese society, as well as encouraging him to sneer at the local English community. But they did provide an escape from the cloyingly familial atmosphere at the Marialvas'.

There was always a great deal of excitement and bustle

when the Queen was in residence at the royal palace. Following hallowed custom, the citizens of Sintra were expected to provide food and lodgings for the numerous hangers-on at court. Beckford was anxious for an audience with the Queen, believing that it would help him in his quest for re-establishment at home in England. Despite the strenuous efforts of the Marquis of Marialva, however, he failed to be formally presented to her because of the objection of the British envoy, the Hon. Robert Walpole. The prevailing convention was that foreigners could only be presented to the monarch by the envoy of their own country. Walpole, who had been posted to Lisbon for a long time, may have been acting on orders from the British Government. It is also likely that he despised the effete young millionaire who, unlike the envoy, was never required to be polite to anyone he didn't like.

The result of Walpole's obstreperousness meant that on the evening when the Queen visited the Marialvas' villa in São Pedro, Beckford had to watch proceedings from behind a latticed window. He describes the Queen as maintaining a dignified air throughout the rather overblown courtly etiquette that surrounded her reception in the house. To amuse and entertain his monarch, the Marquis laid on a huge firework display, which must have lit the skies all over the *serra*. A distinctly bathetic tone is struck in Beckford's description of the scene:

> Presently the Queen and Princess of Brazil came forth from their *merenda* [light meal] and seated themselves directly under the window behind which I had placed myself. A mournful silence prevailed. The Count de Sampaio and the Viscount Ponte de Lima knelt by the royal personages with as much abject devotion as Mussulmans before the tomb of their prophet or Tartars in the presence of the Dalai Lama. My friend alone [Marialva], who stood right opposite Her Majesty seemed to preserve his ease and cheerfulness. The

Prince of Brazil and D. João stalked about with their hands in their pockets, their mouths in a perpetual yawn, and their eyes wandering from object to object with a stare of royal vacancy. Few princes are more to be pitied than these. Condemned by a ridiculous etiquette to strict confinement within the walls of their palaces, and never allowed to mix incognito with the crowd, they experience all the gêne of sultans, without their power or their luxuries.[1]

From time to time there was an incident in the town to divert everyone. Beckford tells the amusing story of an old English lady, staying at the Sintra Inn (Lawrence Inn) who converted to Catholicism on her deathbed. The priests, including Acciaoli, and Mascarenhas, a fellow prelate from the Patriarchate, together with the devout old uncle of the Marialvas, the Count of São Lourenço, rushed to her side to administer baptism in the 'nick of time' before the 'feeble old creature [was] despatched to Paradise'. The rumour spread through Sintra that a miracle had occurred. A large crowd gathered outside the Inn where the corpse was ready to be taken for burial. A great procession, composed of local men and women who would not have known the dead woman, formed in the street. A cross was held up and tapers lit as the cortège made its way to São Martinho amid a general bustle. Peeling church bells and clouds of dust, raised by the mourners, completed the commotion in the middle of the old quarter.

However sociable Beckford was, he was also a man of solitary pursuits. His favourite way of spending a morning was to ride out on his own into the countryside, where he would ramble for hours on end. Beckford was enchanted by Sintra and Colares. He was the first Englishman of real literary sensibility to succumb to Sintra's natural splendour. He enthuses

---

1   *The Journal of William Beckford in Spain and Portugal 1787–88* (ed. B. Alexander) (London, 1954) p.233.

about paths, which lead through 'chestnut copses and orchards to irregular green spots, where self-sown bays and citron bushes hang wild over the rocky margin of a little river, and drop their fruit and blossoms into the stream'.[1] The Sintra cliffs, with their green blanket, capped by the ramparts of the old Moorish Castle, stirred his Romantic imagination, as did the leafy lanes, with their moss-coloured walls leading down to hidden spots like Horne's terrace at the Quinta do Relógio or to the lush gardens at Monserrate. Sometimes, in a gloomier, melancholic mood, he rode up to Cork Convent, high up in the misty hills, surrounded by rocks and thickets that bear the grim signs of the devoutly ascetic life. When the mountains closed in too tightly, there was always the vista of the boundless ocean that could be glimpsed from promontories and cliff tops. In the valley of Colares, Beckford rode through chestnut copses and citrus orchards, surrounded by green meadows amply supplied from cool, mountain streams. An exotic note is often sounded:

> These level paths wind amongst a labyrinth of light and elegant fruit-trees; almond, plum, and cherry, something like the groves of Tonga-taboo, as represented in Cook's voyages; and to increase the resemblance, neat cane fences and low open sheds, thatched with reeds, appear at intervals, breaking the horizontal lines of the perspective.

He rhapsodised about the cool, translucent streams, overhung by cork trees and lemons, just as Robert Southey was to do when he stayed at his uncle's lonely cottage in the same hills. The Arcadian landscape reminded Beckford of Savoy and of Switzerland, though the blooming orange and fragrant myrtle added an exotic touch not found in the northern climes. His delight with the bucolic charms of Sintra is a northerner's delight with the south; and he describes life in the open air on

---

1   *The Travel Diaries of William Beckford of Fonthill* (ed. G. Chapman) (Cambridge, 1928) 2 vols, vol. II p.140.

the terraces, with the perfumed scents of flowers in the air, the sun-drenched woods in the afternoons and the lightly falling mist in the evenings.

Beckford's recreation of these idealised scenes smacks of artfulness. He explains how one day, rambling in the valley of Colares, he gets lost. While trying to decide which way to go, he is surprised by the appearance of a stout, ruddy-faced peasant, dressed in brown and scarlet, driving a mule before her, laden with two enormous panniers of grapes. The girl tells Beckford which direction to take and then disappears. She is one of those mythological creatures that we have seen populating Sintra since earliest times. When Beckford finally finds the farm she has directed him toward, an idyllic, Claudian scene is painted. There are droves of cows and goats milking; the smell of freshly baked cakes emerges from huge, old ovens; sheds are crammed full of yellow, muscat grapes hanging to dry. In this blissful setting Beckford is given a warm welcome by the farm steward, offered good country cheese and surrounded by curly-haired, chubby-faced children.

Beckford's creation of an exotic and romanticised Sintra had a lasting effect on the imagination of the Portuguese. Indeed, his own role as a lordly and dashing figure became an important part of the modern Sintra legend. It was Beckford's association with the *ancien régime* that added lustre to his reputation. Not only was his wealth reputed to be fabulous but the air of mystery and hint of personal scandal which surrounded his arrival in Portugal added spice to the story. Most nineteenth-century Portuguese came to know about Beckford through periodicals that enjoyed a wide middle-class readership. Like readers of Beckford's own travel accounts in England, these bourgeois Portuguese hankered after tales of a more spacious era. The aristocratic circles in which Beckford moved seemed fascinatingly decadent to them, while their association with the royal family appealed to their snobbishness. In 1863, Rebelo da Silva, who was both a novelist and historian, introduced a Beckfordian hero into his story,

Lágrimas e Tesouros, portraying him as a man of mystery and imagination. Da Silva's creation is, according to João de Almeida Flor, 'one of the most complex literary figures and cultural prototypes of European Romanticism, together with Prometheus, Werther or Byron'.[1]

The literature of nostalgia continued into the twentieth century. In 1906 D. Luís de Castro ran a series of articles in *Ilustração Portugueza* on the lost summer of 1787.[2] His intention is to associate Beckford with the glamorous life of the old noble families. De Castro emphasises Beckford's links with the aristocratic Marialvas, whose title became extinct on the death of Dom Pedro, the fifth Marquis' son. Dom Pedro was Beckford's favourite until he was supplanted in the Englishman's affections by the altogether livelier Gregorio Franchi. De Castro dwells on the glamorous life led in the *quintas* of Seteais and Ramalhão. Portuguese readers would have known that, after Beckford's time, Seteais was bought and made grander by the Marquis of Marialva. During the same period, Ramalhão became the home of Queen Carlotta Joaquina when they returned from Brazil, when she became estranged from the King, João VI. Tropical motifs, painted on the walls of the refectory, are said to be a testimony to her *saudades* or nostalgia for the better days she had passed abroad.

Before these changes were made to the Sintra palaces, however, another Englishman of literary taste had arrived on the scene. Robert Southey's infatuation with the country and its culture had been slow to develop. When, at the age of twenty-one, he first learnt that he was to go to Iberia, he told his friend Grosvenor Charles Bedford that he would go with a heavy heart and only to please his mother. Despite his gloomy pronouncement, Portugal and things Portuguese had figured in Southey's imagination long before his departure for

---

1   J. de Almeida Flor, 'Portuguese Tears and Treasures: On Beckford's Literary Fortune', *The Annual Lectures of the Beckford Society 1996–1999* (2000) p.30.
2   *Illustração Portugueza*: 29 October, 5 November, 12 November, 1906. Also see below p.190.

the Peninsula in 1795. As a boy, he had spent a considerable amount of time at his aunt's house in Bath. She, a Miss Tyler, had visited Portugal where Southey's uncle, the Reverend Herbert Hill had been chaplain to the English Factory from the 1770s. There were mementoes of the Portuguese visit all over the family home, as well as books about the great Lusitanian seafaring explorations in the age of discoveries. Southey's aunt must have talked to him a great deal about his uncle's life. Being a cultured woman, she also took Southey to the theatre in Bath where he saw a number of plays with Portuguese themes including *Braganza*, which dealt with the restoration of a Portuguese royal dynasty in 1640. The adolescent Southey, who was still to go to Oxford, meet Coleridge and dabble in the radical politics of pantisocracy (their utopian, communist political theory), was already becoming familiar with the history and literature of the Peninsula.

Despite this background, when Southey first arrived in Madrid, his reaction to Spain sounded much the same as that of many English tourists of the time. He complains of the unbearable heat, the lack of hygiene, and insects. He finds the inns squalid and the food greasy. As for the inhabitants they appear easy-going to the point of slothfulness. That, of course, is due to their adherence to the pernicious creed of Catholicism, which deeply offended his Puritan sensibility. Not all of his comment is to be taken seriously. He observes, dryly, that the foolish Spanish dogs cannot respond to English. Even so, he has been disappointed; the country has not lived up to the image of grandeur and chivalry inspired by his reading of its literature and history.

The fifteen-day journey from Spain to Portugal, across the scorching central plain and over very bad roads, may have made Southey more receptive to a change that he notices on crossing the border at Elvas. Suddenly, there were houses with tolerably well-kept gardens that might even compare to English ones; the Portuguese inns were more comfortable and cleaner than their Spanish equivalents, while the country seemed less arid and more welcoming. Arriving at his uncle's house in Lisbon, though, Southey's good humour dissolved, for there was no mail from England waiting for him – something that particularly disappointed an ambitious budding young author. Despite the comfortable domesticity of his uncle's home in the Buenos Ayres district on the river, he, like Beckford, was also appalled by the filth of a city where piles of rat-infested refuge lay in the streets and deformed, bedraggled beggars roamed at large. A particularly unpleasant local habit he noted was the practice of emptying rubbish out of windows into the street, hitting any luckless passer-by who happened to be in the way. It was a far cry from the gentility of his childhood Bath.

Nor did the Portuguese themselves impress the stern young critic. The lower classes were filthy and idle, unwilling to work for more than the barest subsistence. At the other end of the social scale, the aristocrats or *fidalgos* could be identified by their feeble and blighted bodies, which resulted from the 'vice of their ancestors'.[1] The vice he refers to is sexual promiscuity, encouraged in the decadent atmosphere of a Catholic country where immoral priests wielded immense power. Unlike Beckford, the Puritanical Southey was not attracted to the pageant of Catholicism, a religion he considered to be based entirely on superstition. Whenever he wished to condemn the Portuguese, something he did often and roundly, he dragged up the matter of the Inquisition and the barbaric practice of public burnings (*auto-da-fé*) which was its most sinister aspect. Southey knew and approved of Pombal's attack upon the Church and his expulsion of the Jesuits. He regretted the fact that with the death of King José in 1777 and the accession of Queen Maria, the clergy were reinstated in their position of power and the various Pombalese reforms, which may have modernised Portugal, were put to one side.

Southey's criticism of Lisbon society included the English

---

1   A. Cabral, *Southey e Portugal 1774–1800* (Lisbon, 1959) p.408.

as much as the Portuguese. He found the expatriates a vacuous lot who were as lazy as the locals, frittering away their time at tedious dances or at the card tables. Like Beckford, he noticed that no one ever seemed to read a book or to have made any study of the country or culture in which they were living. The future Laureate's boredom was only contained by the fact that his uncle, a well-read man, had a good library of books. Browsing among them, he found plenty of literature on Portugal and its history. His uncle also encouraged him to improve his Portuguese. Occasionally the daily tedium was relieved by the appearance of someone of note, such as the Italian poet Angelo Talassi, with whom he could discuss literature and more elevated matters than were the subject of conversations at the English Factory.

Although Southey enjoyed some aspects of the city of Lisbon on this first visit of 1796, notably the exotic atmosphere of the old Arab quarter, the Alfama, it was only when he reached Sintra that his enthusiasm was really evident. At last something significant has affected his spirit:

> I know not how to describe to you the strange beauties of Cintra; it is, perhaps, more beautiful than sublime, more grotesque than beautiful, yet I never beheld scenery more calculated to fill the beholder with admiration and delight. This immense rock or mountain is in part covered with scanty herbage, in part it rises into conical hills, formed of such immense stones, and piled so strangely, that all the machinery of deluges and volcanos [sic] must fail to satisfy the inquiry of their origin.[1]

Southey's description evokes all the quality of scenery so much admired by the Romantics – the beautiful and sublime landscape with a hint of the grotesque lurking mysteriously below the surface. The only surprise is his reference to 'scanty herbage', until we remember that there was a great deal more

---

1 Ibid. p.163.

exposed rock before the massive plantings of the nineteenth century.[1] After describing the 'glass house' chimneys of the 'old irregular pile', the royal palace, he goes on to emphasise the wooded slopes of the *serra*:

> But the abundance of wood forms the most striking feature of this retreat from the Portuguese summer. The houses of the English are scattered on the ascent half hid among the cork trees, elms, oaks, hazels, walnuts, the tall canes, and the rich green of the lemon gardens. On one side of the mountain eminence stands the Penha convent, visible from the hills near Lisbon. On another are the ruins of the Moorish castle, and a cistern, within its boundaries, kept always full by a spring of purest water that rises in it.[2]

Southey's picture of Sintra is a landscape in which the beauty of nature is locked in by the manmade – in this case the two ancient structures on the summit ridges. It is an enclosed, idyllic space, an idealised world of Rousseau-like ambience, only appreciated by men of sensibility and artists. The physical boundaries of this paradise are clearly drawn: Southey observes the 'dreary wilderness', which lies north-ward towards Mafra. It is a flat, dull plain that no Sintra man of sense would ever want to cross. If this is the macrocosm of Southey's Sintra (which did influence the Portuguese Arcadian views of the nineteenth century) the microcosm centres on his uncle's cottage, tucked away in the hills. There, amid an ever-varying sky, were little green lanes with lemon gardens where a cool breeze would blow refreshingly in the evening. There are no sounds except the sounds of nature; we are in a Wordsworthian space of tranquillity, far away from the heat and dust of the city. In a bucolic flourish, in which Southey expresses the Portuguese sentiment of *saudades* or a sense of nostalgic loss, he adds:

---

1   See Illustration 22.
2   A. Cabral, op. cit. p.163.

26. King Carlos, c.1890.
Photograph by A. Bobonne. Sintra, Historical Archive,
Municipal Archive.

25. Quinta do Torre da Regealeira, c.1960.
Photograph. Sintra, Historical Archive, Municipal Archive.

24. Dom Fernando de Saxe Coburg-Gotha, c.1850.
Lithograph. Sintra, Historical Archive, Municipal Archive.

23. The Triton Gate, Pena Palace, c.1960.
Photograph. Sintra, Historical Archive, Municipal Archive.

22. Pena Monastery, c.1840.
Lithograph by M. Luiz. Sintra, Historical Archive, Municipal Archive.

21. Palace of Seteais, 1860.
Lithograph by M. Luiz after C. Brélaz. Sintra, Historical Archive, Municipal Archive.

I shall always love to think of the lonely house, and the stream that runs beside it, whose murmurs were the last sounds I heard at night, and the first that awoke my attention in the morning.[1]

Southey did not return to his beloved Sintra for another four years. During that time he lived with his wife Edith in Bristol and poured out plays, ballads and reviews. His capacity for work was always prodigious. Inspired by his visit to Portugal, he began to plan an exhaustive work about the Lusitanian world. It would run to many volumes and would cover the history of Portugal itself, as well as Brazil and the Portuguese Empire in Asia. There would be an accompanying volume on literature. Southey's plan shows the influence of Edward Gibbon's *Decline and Fall*, a work he knew well. Portugal would provide a modern example of an imperial power that flourished and declined as ancient Rome had done. In the event, Southey only produced a voluminous *History of Brazil*, which was lukewarmly received a decade later.

Nevertheless, Southey's growing expertise in matters Portuguese made him critical of the work of his fellow countrymen. He found W.J. Mickle's translation of Camões' *Lusiads* (1776) heavy in style and showing signs of too much interference with the original text. Not only was the rhythm of Camões' verse entirely lost by this treatment but, even worse from the scholarly point of view, whole episodes which did not appear in the Portuguese version found their way into Mickle's translation. Another work that displeased Southey was James Murphy's account of his travels in Portugal, which appeared in 1795. Although Southey recognised that Murphy's book contained much useful information, he, like Beckford, found the account dull and commonplace. He complained of its arrangement as well as its style. Clearly, Murphy had not been writing for aesthetes.

---

1   Ibid. p.164.

These critical projects were only part of Southey's self-imposed punishing programme of literary work. He was determined to make a name for himself as a scholar as well as a poet and critic. He took on as much as he could and more. Not surprisingly for one who was never robust, his health collapsed under the strain and he began to suffer from insomnia, loss of appetite and palpitations in the chest. The doctors suggested he go abroad, and so in the spring of 1800 the Southeys set off for Lisbon.

Southey's second visit to Portugal lasted a year and a half and it confirmed his Lusophilia. There is a palpable excitement in his description of the first sight of Lisbon with its churches and convents silhouetted on a blue sky and its harbour crammed full with all types of vessels. Before long he and Edith (who had suffered badly from seasickness on the voyage) were ensconced in a house near his uncle's house in Buenos Ayres. From the very desk where he wrote, he had a fine view of the bustling estuary of the Tagus. It was an auspicious vista for an historian of empire. In this setting Southey was reinvigorated; his lassitude passed. His days were spent arranging his papers and planning his research, while evenings were given over to intelligent conversation with his uncle, one of the well-read clerical fraternity. Southey was a good deal more relaxed than on his first visit, especially in his attitude to the Church. He even befriended various priests, coming to realise that they were the most cultured people in the local community. Having learnt his lesson on the first visit, he kept away from the English community, annoyed by the philistinism of the merchants on the one hand and the frivolity of the *beau monde*, who came to have fun in Lisbon, on the other. But his peace of mind was soon disturbed. Working daily in his uncle's well-stocked library, he was plagued by the constant ringing of bells, sometimes from chapels in nearby private houses. As summer approached, it became uncomfortably hot and sticky. Edith was as carping and dreary as ever. He needed inspiration. It was time to return to Sintra, a place he regarded as being fit

19. Hotel Lawrence, c.1850.
Photograph. Sintra, Historical Archive, Municipal Archive.

20. Ruinous condition of the 'castle' of Monserrate in 1859. Engraving. Sintra, Historical Archive, Municipal Archive.

only for Goths, whether of the German or English variety.[1]

Once back in his uncle's solitary cottage, with its running brook and lemon trees, Southey was happy. The scenery was magnificent, there were no noisy neighbours or bothersome English visitors; his compatriots found the cottage too far out of the way to visit. If he was not writing at home, then he was exploring Sintra on a donkey, accompanied by a local guide. The picture he paints of this existence is that of a cultured sybarite:

> I eat oranges, figs, and delicious pears, drink Colares wine, a sort of half way excellence between port and claret, dream of poem after poem and play after play, take a siesta of two hours, and am as happy as if life were but one everlasting today; and tomorrow not to be provided for.[2]

If Edith was as dull as ever, there was the company of a Miss Barker, who was happy to accompany him on his donkey rides and share picnics in the pretty hills around. When the amiable Miss Barker had to leave, Southey complained bitterly of her departure in letters home. Had they fallen in love? It seems possible suddenly, for the first time, he felt isolated and cut off in Sintra. His 'mental famine' is matched by a growing craving for fresh bread and butter, which apparently could not be found. Beckford, before him, had already remarked on the same deficiency, finding the only good dairy products at the Dutch Consul Gildemeester's table.[3] Southey did not have such practical and hospitable friends.

---

1   Those who may have qualified as Southey's 'Goths' were the naturalist Heinrich Link whose writing on flowers and plants was published at the time of Southey's first visit; Johann Strauss, who came to see Pena Palace being built in 1845; and later, Hans Christian Andersen who visited Sintra in 1866. Andersen enthused on the verdure of Monserrate and the romantic, Moorish feeling of Sintra. See H.C. Andersen, *A Visit to Portugal 1866* (trans. G. Thornton) (London, 1972) pp.68 & 89.

2   Rose Macaulay, *They Went to Portugal* (London, 1946) p.157.

3   Costa records Gildemeester saying that a whole family was brought over from Holland to make the butter. F. Costa, *Estudos Sintrenses* 3 vols, vol. II p.83.

These inconveniences and the fretting after Miss Barker's departure made him cantankerous. He began to rail against the wealthy Portuguese who never read a book and, if they came to Sintra, spent the entire day playing cards at an inn. They were not much better than the English philistines who lived in their villas around the *serra* with no idea about the country or its culture. Always sensitive to Sintra's natural beauty, Southey had nevertheless lost all sense of inner calm. A true Romantic, he had worn himself out with emotion. The Southeys left Sintra in the autumn. They toured Portugal extensively before returning to England the following year.

Southey's interest in Portugal did not diminish after he had left it for the last time. Nor did his longing to return. He schemed, unsuccessfully like so many others, to get the British consulship in Lisbon. Like Beckford, he dreamed of happiness in a blissful, southern clime, with blue skies and mountains and cool sea breezes. Above all, Sintra was the place he most longed to be. Far away and having long forgotten its irritations, his vivid descriptions of the misty *serra* contributed to the legend that held such a sway on English minds and brought Lord Byron, the most celebrated English visitor of all, to sample a little of paradise for himself.

Unlike Beckford and Southey, Byron arrived in Portugal with little knowledge of the country and even less of the language. He boasted, with characteristic swagger, that his Portuguese was confined to swear words, which he used to startle the locals into compliance with his wishes. In fact, the poet's first impression of Lisbon was very favourable:

> What beauties does Lisboa first unfold
> Her image floating on that noble tide
> Which poets vainly pave with sands of gold.[1]

On the point of departure, a mere two weeks later, his opinion does not seem to have changed, for he writes cheerily

---

1   Lord George Byron, op. cit. p.183.

to Frances Hodgson that he has been happy eating oranges, talking to the monks in bad Latin, swimming across the Tagus and enjoying many other touristic pleasures. Certainly Byron and John Cam Hobhouse, his travelling companion and Cambridge friend, covered a lot of ground in their short stay, getting to the theatre, visiting churches and monasteries, making the trip to Sintra, and no doubt imbibing their fair share of Portuguese wine. Even so, they were shocked by the griminess of Lisbon. The wild dogs mentioned by every English traveller of the time were nasty enough, but tourists wandering about on their own also faced the prospect of being attacked by gangs of youths armed with knives. The mendicant clergy who thronged the streets of the city particularly affronted Hobhouse, with his keen Protestant sensibility. Unlike Byron he was not amused by their poor command of Latin. Byron's reaction to Portugal seems to have been mixed. In his letters home, his tone is quite positive but when *Childe Harold's Pilgrimage* appeared, three years later, in 1812, there is a distinctly Lusophobic tenor in what he writes.

Byron and Hobhouse had come to Portugal at a bad time: the country lay under the threat of French invasion. A survey undertaken in 1807 by three Portuguese officers had suggested that Sintra itself would be the target for the invaders after they had landed on the nearby coast.[1] In 1807, General Junot did invade but he did so overland from Spain. The Portuguese royal family and most of the court fled to Brazil on British ships and Rio de Janeiro became the capital of the united kingdom of Portugal and Brazil in 1807, and this remained the case until 1821. During the years of war that followed the invasion, there was considerable physical destruction to buildings and land in Portugal. Houses were burnt down and churches pillaged; many of the country's art treasures

---

1   The officers identify the Praia das Maçãs as the likely point of landing for a French force, which they thought would sweep across the valley of Colares and take Sintra, thereby being in a strong position to threaten Lisbon itself. *AHS* vol. VII p.92.

disappeared. The French were eventually driven out of Portugal because of British intervention, but once Portugal was liberated, the British exacted a price for their support.

Portuguese troops were put under the command of an English general, William Beresford. He became the *de facto* ruler of the country. At the time of Byron's visit, Lisbon was full of British officers whose prejudice against the Portuguese was shared by most of the British community. Their patron-ising, even colonial, attitude found its way into the verses of *Childe Harold*.

Nevertheless, Byron was impressed by the grand scale of the buildings he visited in Portugal. He particularly liked the polychromal interior of Mafra chapel, as Beckford had done before him. But it was Sintra, with its natural splendour and cliff-top dwellings, that most enthralled him. It was in Sintra, too, that he found religious men whom he could respect. As the Englishmen clamber up to the monastery at Pena[1] the tone of his verse is serene:

> Then slowly climb the many-winding way
> And frequent turn to linger as you go
> From loftier rocks new lovliness survey.
> And rest ye at 'Our Lady's house of woe';
> Where frugal monks their little relics show
> And sundry legends to the stranger tell
> How impious men have punished been...[2]

The obvious sincerity of the Sintra monks made up for the disillusion that Byron and Hobhouse had felt on seeing the dissolute bands of Lisbon clergymen idly hanging about the streets of the city. Although Byron's own style of living could hardly be further removed from the ascetic, he was deeply affected by the piety of the Jeronomite brothers, who received

---

1 Byron mistook the meaning of the word 'pena' for 'woe'. It is in fact a corrup-tion of 'penha' meaning 'rock' or 'cliff'. (See above p.17 n.1.)
2 Lord George Byron, op. cit. p.184.

their English visitors cordially. By now, the towering landscape was also having an effect on him. Surveying the
panorama from the summit of the mountain, he enthuses:

> Lo! Cintra's glorious Eden intervenes
> In variegated maze of mount and glen.
> Ah me! what hand can pencil, guide or pen,
> To follow half on which the eye dilates
> Through views more dazzling unto mortal ken
> Than those whereof such things the bard relates
> Who to the awe-struck world unlock'd
> Elysium's gates?[1]

Byron is carried away, as Southey was, by the craggy cliffs,
the cork trees and damp mossy glades, the green vales touched
with orange from the fruit, and the streams cascading down
the rocks. He tells Hodgson, in a letter sent home to England,
that he has come to the most beautiful village in the world.[2]

Byron put up at the Lawrence Inn, set in a dip surrounded
by thick woods, a short walk from São Martinho church in
the middle of Sintra. The inn had become a favourite English
haven by the 1780s. From the room Byron stayed in, on the
first floor, there is a sweeping view across the hilltops into the
vales. It is lush and extended, giving the impression of an
enclosed garden on a grand scale. The landlady, Mrs Dyson,
was to make much of the fact that Byron had stayed at her inn,
and saw no reason to deny the rumour that he had composed
Childe Harold there.

In the direction away from the village, the road sweeps
round toward the Quinta do Relógio, before sloping down,
in stages, towards Monserrate. Byron walked along here, ever
curious to discover the 'fairy dwelling' of Beckford, whose
Vathek he admired and whose unpublished, heterodox tales,
The Episodes of Vathek, he had heard about and wanted to read.

---

1   Ibid. pp.183–4
2   Lord Byron, *Selected Letters and Journals* (ed. P. Gunn) (London, 1984) p.45.

By the time Byron was in Sintra, Monserrate was already in a bad state of repair and the gardens, it seems, had become wild and overgrown, though we must allow for poetic licence in his description of it:

> On sloping mounds, or in the vale beneath
> Are domes where whilome kings did make repair;
> But now the wild flowers round them only breathe;
> Yet ruined splendour still is lingering there.
> And yonder towers the Prince's palace fair:
> There thou too, Vathek! England's wealthiest son,
> Once form'd thy Paradise, as not aware
> When wanton wealth her mightiest deeds hath done,
> Meek peace voluptuous lures were ever wont to shun.
>
> Here didst thou dwell, here schemes of pleasure plan,
> Beneath yon mountain's ever beauteous brow,
> But now as if a thing unblest by Man,
> Thy fairy dwelling is as lone as thou!
> Here giant weeds a passage scarce allow
> To halls deserted, portals gaping wide;
> Fresh lessons to the thinking bosom how
> Vain are the pleasuances on earth supplied;
> Swept into wrecks anon by Time's ungentle tide![1]

This is chilling stuff indeed. However much Beckford may have appreciated the cadence of the verse, he could hardly have been pleased with its sentiment. Hearing that his beloved Monserrate was a ruin must have been distressing enough, but to read Byron's attack on his shallow, hedonistic life there must have been deeply wounding. Apparently he was spared something even worse, however, for Byron had prepared another stanza alluding to an unnamed crime, doubtless sodomy, which was never published. It is hardly surprising that Beckford refused to meet Byron, despite the poet's declared

---

1   Ibid. p.184.

admiration for *Vathek* and his interest (conveyed to Samuel Rogers, who had heard them read aloud on a visit to Fonthill) in Beckford's tales, the *Episodes*.[1]

The references to Beckford are not the only sinister note in Childe Harold's comments on Sintra. On his way up to the summit of the *serra,* he notices small crosses which he assumes mark the spots where victims have been killed in a lawless society. In fact, the crosses were put down to remind the passer-by of the Passion of Christ. Byron's railings against the Portuguese reach a crescendo when Childe Harold passes Seteais, believing that the Convention of Cintra was signed there in 1808, the year before his visit. The armistice had, in fact, been drawn up in Lisbon and was ratified by the British Commander-in-Chief, Sir Hew Dalrymple, at his headquarters in Torres Vedras. By the terms of the Convention the French armies were allowed to withdraw from Portugal with their booty intact. No reparations were sought for the extensive damage that they had caused in Portugal. The French negotiator, Marshall Kellerman, must have been delighted by the Convention's terms. Although the British officers may have negotiated what they thought was a practical solution that achieved victory without further loss of British lives, the Convention was a bad settlement for Portugal, leaving her entirely dependent on British military support. That may have been exactly what the British Government wanted.

Byron did not seem to accept that the Convention had been foistered unfairly on the Portuguese. Although he blames the British for their part in it; he seems to believe that the Portuguese had been craven to accept its terms without a struggle. The terms of the armistice raised a storm of protest in England. The press, who up to that point had been emphasising the strength of the French bargaining position, now declared that the settlement was 'scandalously disgraceful'. Wordsworth wrote a tract and a sonnet on the subject and

---

1   See B. Fothergill, *Beckford of Fonthill* (London, 1979) pp.303ff.

spoke out publicly against the settlement. Beckford and Southey were appalled. While some people like Sir Walter Scott wished that Sir Arthur Wellesley had been at the head of the army in the Peninsula instead of Sir Hew Dalrymple, others blamed the whole outcome on the great man himself. No true friend of Portugal could believe that she had been well served by her oldest ally.

Childe Harold continues to ponder morosely on such matters whilst still beholding the splendour of Sintra's land-scape. His gloom turns into a typically Romantic introspection, lamenting his own misspent youth. Gradually he leaves the pastoral beauty of the mountains and heads off toward the expanses of Spain. It is the beginning of his long wanderings in Europe and his eventual death, a hundred and eighty-six stanzas later, at the edge of the deep, blue Mediter-ranean Sea.

Although Byron denied that *Childe Harold* was in any way autobiographical, the travel accounts of the brooding pilgrim make him the prototype of the Byronic hero. He is a defiant, melancholy outcast whose reflections of history inspire no great love of the human race. Liberty is Harold's political clarion call, whilst a love of nature, in the Rousseauist style, make him spiritually a pantheist.

Harold's love of nature explains his great fondness for Sintra, where the pilgrimage begins. The terrain of the *serra,* rugged and majestic, exactly meets the poet's need to create a huge canvas on which the drama of Harold's pilgrimage will be painted in glowing verse. But not all of nature's effects are benign. There are primeval and even demonic forces associ-ated with Sintra's wind-battered peaks and isolated location. Its majestic scenery, which was welcoming at the beginning of the journey, becomes sinister and alienating. The lonely pilgrim, already racked by internal anxieties and doubts, now faces a threatening environment, cut off from all civilised amenity. In the distance swirls an ocean of utmost ferocity and unfathomable depths. Childe Harold's gloom is deepened by his belief that the Portuguese are an apathetic people who do not care about their own freedom.

Byron's violently expressed Lusophobia has been the object of much comment by Portuguese critics. Francisco Costa ascribed it to malevolence in Byron's character. A more fanciful explanation is that Byron was enraged at being publicly castigated by a cuckolded husband outside the theatre in Lisbon and exercised a terrible revenge. A great deal of energy has been spent on *chercher la femme* with no tangible result. Byron himself comments in a footnote to *Childe Harold*, in the following way:

> As I have found the Portuguese, so I have characterised them. That they are since improved, at least in courage, is evident. The late exploits of Lord Wellington have effaced the follies of Cintra, changed the character of a nation, reconciled rival superstitions, and baffled an enemy, who never retreated before his predecessors.[1]

The poet's comment makes it clear that he took against the Portuguese because of what he perceived to be their lack of martial spirit. It had only been with the arrival of an English commander that they began to show more inclination to stand their ground against the French. Although this is a harsh judgement against a small nation attacked by the strongest European power at a time when its ablest leaders had fled abroad, it would have been an opinion shared by many Englishmen who were involved in the Peninsular wars. What is more, Byron was a young man imbued with ideas of military glory, which gained a particular glamour when they could be linked to the cause of national freedom or liberty. Such clashes were the stuff of heroic legend. For all his gloomy musings, there is in Childe Harold a ruthless streak, excited by the call to arms, albeit in good causes.

Byron's attitude towards the Portuguese is therefore a

---

1   Lord George Byron, op. cit. p.874.

complex one. His outbursts seem unreasonable and petulant.
Having made up his mind that they are a servile race, he is
very reluctant to consider them in any other light. Even the
Spanish, against whom he might also have had a prejudice,
shine out in comparison. On the other hand, his evocation of
Sintra as a terrestrial paradise is enthusiastic and lush. Childe
Harold cannot sing the praises of the *serra* more highly than he
does, nor can he present it in more Romantic and glowing
tones. Byron's evocation of this mysterious and magical Sintra
had a profound influence on both the English and the Portuguese, guaranteeing that Childe Harold would be only the first
of many pilgrims to seek out the mountain range. Byron's
vivid verses raised Sintra to the status of an idealised locale,
making up for what Rose Macaulay has described as 'the
callow prejudice of a vulgar adolescent in a temper with life'.[1]

No one could accuse Sir Francis Cook of being a petulant
youth. As another English millionaire owner of Monserrate,
he was to leave his mark not only on that estate but also on
the whole of Sintra. Cook came from solid Norfolk stock but
had chosen to make his career in the City of London, where
his family was in the textile business. When the business
moved location, James Knowles, a self-taught architect, who
was to play a significant part in Cook's Sintra story, designed
the new premises. Cook travelled widely and eventually came
to Lisbon in 1841, somewhat on the make. He joined the firm
of Gonne, Lucas and Gribble, which was by this time well
established in the English Factory at Lisbon. The ambitious
new boy consolidated his position by marrying the boss's
daughter, Emily Lucas, within weeks of his arrival. From his
father-in-law, Cook acquired various habits, including the
collecting of paintings and *objets d'art*. But the greatest influence that Lucas had on him was to imbue him with his own
love of Sintra and, particularly, of Monserrate. The older man,
like so many other English residents of Lisbon, loved to escape

---

1   Rose Macaulay, op. cit. p.174.

to the shady tranquillity of the *serra* during the hottest summer months. He and Emily and young Cook would go on picnics in the grounds of Monserrate. Already, in 1821, Mariana Baillie, whose attribution of the house to Beckford has been noted (see p.124), described Monserrate as a ruin, albeit a charming one:

> Here [in Portugal] such a structure really appears as if raised by fairy hands... but how this enchanted palace has been neglected! And how has the beautiful house been suffered to fall into decay, now to become the property of a Portuguese family. They have evinced the most deplorable want of taste and feeling in regard to it, for at this moment it is completely a ruin; a fit residence only for the bat and owl or to serve as casual shelter for the wandering goatherd and his shaggy flock... I never beheld so striking an image of desolate loneliness, and could have spent hours here in the indulgence of a reverie, mournful yet fraught with a nameless charm that can only be comprehended by the veritable children of romance.[1]

The Cooks proved to be those children of romance, committed to restoring Monserrate to its former glory. Cook had ambitious plans for the whole estate. He began by rebuilding the house in 1858. From the outset, the project was undertaken on a grand scale, with the object of creating a mansion fit for a millionaire to live and entertain in. Cook employed James Knowles, his London acquaintance, to draw up plans for the house. Knowles' experience was mainly as an architect of urban buildings; his most notable design was the Grosvenor Hotel in Victoria, London. At the time the exotic Oriental style was all the rage in England: Brighton Pavilion

---

1   I. Kingsbury, op. cit. p.47. Lady Jackson makes the interesting observation that one reason for the collapse of the house was Beckford's impatience in altering it quickly without using proper materials. The same accusation was made against him when the central tower of Fonthill Abbey, his Wiltshire house, collapsed in 1825 after he had sold it. Catherine Charlotte, Lady Jackson, op. cit. p.199.

was widely admired. Knowles, who probably never visited Portugal, began designing a building on an Oriental/Moghul model for his wealthy client. The new house was built on de Visme's original foundations and followed the plan of his building. The earlier house had been of very solid construction, with three feet thick walls. Knowles planned a long gallery, which would run right through the building in an east-west direction. The central rotunda, a feature that would have appealed to Beckford, was retained.

The central section of the new house is over eighty metres long, with a width of about a third of that length. A massive dome cupola dominates the centre. Looked at from the outside, there is something colossal and a bit overbearing about the structure; inside it is ornate to the point of being fantastic. Elaborate tracery and geometric patterns abound. Entering through a pillared portico, there are eight columns with foliate spandrels and elaborate Moorish arches, trebled to give a more louche, Eastern effect. The long gallery, which runs through the whole length of the house, has rows of marble columns, arches and filigree tracery, making it the interior with the most obvious Moorish influence in Sintra, as has been already discussed. Ida Kingsbury, who lived at Monserrate, counted over five thousand arches and as many as six hundred columns.[1]

At the western end of the house is a circular room of great ornateness. Sixteen marble columns, crowned with gilded capitals and supporting Gothic arches are exotic enough, but they are capped by classical medallions in high relief, representing among other classical figures, Cecilia and the Muses since this was to be the music room. The frieze and cornices are elaborately carved and there is Moorish-style tracery in the arches. Decorated with palms and Chinese porcelain in their heyday, the room must have appeared very extravagant. Beckford would have been amused by it, even if he might have found the taste bordering on the vulgar. It would have made

---

1   Ibid. p.57.

an appropriate setting for the Eastern dress parties he gave at
Ramalhão in 1787. However, he may have found the room
at the other end of the house, a solemn, sombre library lined
with old books and benefiting from an open fireplace, more
snug. He would certainly have been touched to find his statue
of St Anthony of Padua by Rossi, which had been bought by
Sir Francis and shipped to Portugal, in the house.

A more sturdy English presence is in evidence in the
grounds. A green sloping lawn, said by some to be the first in
Portugal, runs down steeply from the house into the vale, with
mourning cypresses draping the middle. Although its effect is
so English, the lawn follows the natural relief of the land,
which is convex rather than concave. It is watered from the
centre instead of the sides. De Visme's more formal arrangements of orchards and thickets, which had already been
tampered with by Beckford, were now completely planted
over with a huge variety of trees and plants. William Neville,
who advised Cook on botanical matters, worked closely with
William Stockdale, an artist and Fellow at Kew, to create a
'natural' Victorian garden landscape.

Like Beckford, these garden designers were concerned to
make use of the natural contours of the place and to allow a
certain freedom to the trees to grow without excessive cultivation. So cork trees were left gnarled and twisted. The plan
was also to create a landscape in which wild and cultivated
plants and flowers could be mixed together. In some cases this
meant adding to species already found in the grounds. This
was done on a spectacular scale with the planting of palms
(some of which now tower near to the house). As many as
forty species of palm, growing outdoors, provide an unusual
feature in a European garden.

However, Cook's team was not shy of introducing entirely
new species to Monserrate. Trees and plants from every corner
of the world were brought to the gardens to grow next to the
indigenous varieties. From Mexico came the white pine, with
its elongated cones as well as the fan-like yucca with its long,

spiky leaves and the strangely drooping elephant's foot. From China and Japan came the bright red persimmon and the delicate maidenhead. The grislena tree came from New Zealand and the eugenia from Australia, whilst the Atlantic islands were represented by a number of species, including the stink laurel. A fig tree was brought from as far away as Fiji, despite the existence of local varieties. Several of these trees were the only species to be found in the country.

The introduction of these species, together with the climate and abundant water at Monserrate, gradually created a new atmosphere of immense complexity and sophistication, which nevertheless did not entirely displace the old. Camellia, magnolia and honeysuckle added colour and scents and the absence of frosts ensured some flowering the whole year long. Ida Kingsbury distils the exotic essence of the new Monserrate in rather purple prose:

> What was it here in Cintra that haunted and sometimes ruffled the peace? Something primal perhaps, about this garden of ferns and bells, bells of blood and fire, glowing trumpets, ramping to the tops of trees and producing combinations of leaf and flower that were purely fantastic. Trees united in strange marriages, spouting one from the other as if law and order were lost and then found again as the plants processed before Adam to be named. This Eden of dews and sunshine brought forth crystal waters and bubbling springs to fertilise it as if from the beginning of things. Those old Victorians, Francis Cook and Burt, a Fellow from Kew and an Academy artist, had woven an enchantment with their palms and daturas and sheets of agapanthus catching the sunset in a purple glow. Hoary cork trees spouted ferns from every branch and camellias of every hue bejeweled the sky as you looked upwards. Secret glades and shadowy ponds were fringed with delicate mosses and maidenhair. These gardens were a paradise of every growing thing and the mists which often cloak the

shoulders of the *serras* hardly seemed to dull but enhanced the scene suddenly brushed as if an antechamber of the sun.[1]

In this glowing paradise Francis Cook lived the life of a benevolent English country landowner. He spent a great deal of time inspecting his trees and plants, riding about on a donkey as Southey had done before him. When he was not consulting Burt, the gardener, about estate matters, he was tending to charitable works, endowing a number of institutions, which included a school for the children of his workforce. For these contributions to the community he was eventually given a Portuguese title, becoming known as the Visconde de Monserrate. His appetite for acquisition did not diminish as the years went by and he was always looking out for land to add to the Monserrate estate. His acquisitions included one of the nearby properties, the Quinta de São Tiago. The house had already been in English hands. It was owned by Admiral Sir George Sartorius, a veteran of the battle of Trafalgar, who had been well rewarded for his services to the cause of Dom Pedro in the Miguelist wars.[2] The estate was accompanied by a title. Later, a daughter of the family married into the Cooks, creating an English Sintra aristocracy. There was even connection with the English royal family, for it was alleged that one local resident, Major Astley Campbell Smith, was a grandson of William IV through an illegitimate line. The family property, the Quinta do Pombal, was also bought by Cook.

Social life at Monserrate flourished on a grand scale. There were endless parties and *soirées* for the well-established English community at Sintra. In a season that lasted for three months, house guests arrived from England and stayed for weeks. The lifestyle of the Cooks was a grander version of that of members

---

1 I. Kingsbury, op. cit. p.60.
2 The civil war was fought between Dom Miguel, representing the Absolutists, and his brother Dom Pedro, supporting Liberal Constitutionalism. The war lasted from 1828 to 1834 and led to Dom Miguel's defeat and exile.

of the English Factory, whose addiction to balls, card playing and gossip had attracted Southey's scorn. It was an expatriate life that excluded most Portuguese, except for a few chosen favourites and for that reason alone would have caused considerable resentment, had not Cook's philanthropy stifled any criticism. In 1884 Cook's first wife, Emily, died. After only a year he married again, this time to the vivacious Tennessee Claflin, an American lady who had moved in aristocratic circles in England. She proved to be an even greater socialite than the first Lady Cook, so that functions of even greater extravagance took place and continued long after Sir Francis Cook's death in 1901.

The glitter of the Cook's Monserrate is captured in an issue of *Illustração Portugueza* of 26 September 1904. Appealing to its middle-class readers, the front cover of the journal displays a full-length portrait of Frederick William, heir to the German throne, and his Danish bride. On the next page, the Cooks appear more modestly displayed in medallion-style portraits and later a large family group is seen on the steps of the verandah, in royal style. The journalist is enthralled by the sumptuous opulence of the house. He describes the wonders of velvet and carving, the *objets d'art* and rare books, the grand furniture from the East, the blazing light of innumerable chandeliers and the richly worked mosaics and friezes. There are photos of the grand staircase, the dining room with table fully laid, the music room and library, the billiard room where the visitor notices a chair used by the Doge of Venice.

In the library a group of elegantly dressed aristocrats are cavorting, and a smiling Viscount Cook admits that many of the Oriental features of the house were made in Bombay. This group is speaking in English, the language of De Visme, whose alterations to the estate are also mentioned. But more than anyone, it is the ghost of 'Lord' Beckford, 'full of spirit and literature' who hangs over the place.[1] His connection with St

---

1   *Illustração Portugueza*, 26 September 1904.

Anthony, the patron saint of the house (whose family home was in nearby Colares), was happily re-established when Sir Francis Cook bought the Rossi statue. It is the 'gallant Lord' Beckford's cascade that adorns the garden; it seems that even his interest in Oriental interiors has inspired the décor chosen by the Cooks. Despite all this dazzling opulence, the journalist notices with approval that there is a box for the collection of alms for the local poor prominently placed at the entrance.

The reputation of an Arcadian Sintra, added to by the grand projects of Sir Francis Cook, brought English visitors to the *serra* throughout the nineteenth century. Most fell to eulogising its charms. One of the earliest, J. Moyle Sherer, who must have been a practical man since he was a sea captain, nevertheless shows this typical effusiveness. He says rather breathlessly:

> The scenery, as you approach the town, is truly enchanting. The rich and variegated wood, which clothes the side of the mountain rising above Cintra, the sunny brown or rather the golden tinge of the mossy sward towards the crest of it, and, the bare, grey, and rude-shaped rock, which crowns its lofty summit, form a picture, such as only the pencil of a master, or the pen of a poet, could attempt to sketch with fidelity.[1]

The everyday, matter-of-fact language of eighteenth-century visitors like James Murphy, was henceforth completely thrown over in favour of the hyperbolic. Not a poet herself, but the daughter of one, Dora Quillinan (née Wordsworth) takes up Sherer's challenge a generation later, in the 1840s. By this time Beckford's *Sketches*, with its nostalgic picture of a long lost Sintra summer, had been published (1834) and was enjoying a wide readership. Dora is categorical: no one who has sampled Sintra's charms can ever forget them:

---

1   Quoted in J. de Almeida Flor, *Sintra na Literatura Romántica Inglesa* (Sintra, 1978) p.24.

Enchanting is the sudden transition from a comparatively barren and treeless waste to the richest verdure and most beautiful garden land, woodland and finest forest scenery, with those fine mountain peaks rising out of the mass of foliage, where the nightingales in this season sing rapturously, and whence at all seasons comes other way-laying music, that of the streams and rivulets, which come dancing and leaping and rushing down the steep hillside, over huge greasy stones, or amongst stones clothed with the greenest moss and overshadowed by the noble trunks and branches of secular – twice, thrice, secular trees...[1]

In 1874 Catherine Charlotte Lady Jackson published a considerable volume of memoirs of Portugal with the title *Fair Lusitania*. In her preface to the book, the fair-minded Lady Jackson makes it clear that she is intent on counterbalancing the bad opinion that the English have of Portugal and the Portuguese. The somewhat colonial attitude of the English had been encouraged by Byron's descriptions of a people lacking martial spirit and by the belief that only British intervention in the Peninsular wars had saved Portugal. It was also, as Southey had remarked, an attitude held in a largely philistine community whose interests were almost exclusively commercial and who stood to benefit by Portugal's dependence on Britain.

Despite her surprising intention to correct her compatriots' arrogance, Lady Jackson's reasons for going to Sintra were not unconventional. She wanted, like so many English visitors to Lisbon, to breathe a cooler, fresher air and take in the beauties of nature. Unlike those who had gone before her, she had the convenience of going by train, for the new Larmanjat line had just opened. But Lady Jackson was not impressed by the service. The journey lasted over two hours, and was jolty and dusty, as the train churned up the debris of sands and stones on the track. The murky atmosphere blocked out the view.

---

1   Ibid. p.26.

Choking with dust and thoroughly jolted, she and her fellow passengers arrived hot and bothered in Sintra, to be assailed by a crowd of beggars waiting for victims at the station. Nor did the Hotel Lawrence at first seem enchanting:

> A more bare and comfortless one [establishment] could scarcely be found. Some of the sleeping rooms are on the lower ground floor. One of the adjoining sitting rooms, looking on nothing at all, was furnished with three or four small oblong tables, full dressed in white muslin petticoats and dimity covers, after the fashion of toilette-tables; a long, deep seated straight and high-backed sofa, with round bolsters, the whole covered with dimity; and three or four armchairs, high and deep seated, straight backed and covered *en suite*. A few staring old prints, and a little crockery and glass, made up the ornamentation.[1]

Nevertheless the linen was clean and white and after some initial awkwardness, Mrs Lawrence seemed to become friendly and helpful. What is more, despite her moderate prices, the breakfasts and dinners at the hotel proved to be excellent. There was no shortage of fresh butter, the absence of which had so upset Southey.

Not that concern with these domestic trifles for a moment dimmed Lady Jackson's enthusiasm for Sintra. The sight of Estefânia with its pretty villas, streamlets and groves, lifted her spirits. Waking up next day in Sintra, she noticed the mist capping the mountain peaks, shrouding the Moorish castle and only gradually clearing up, as the morning sun grew hotter. Then there were the delights of Colares with its plentiful fruit orchards, Ramalhão with its orange and citron trees and always behind, the 'lofty and jagged mountain peaks, that wondrous mélange of massive grey stone, clusters of pine, hanging shrubs, sparkling waterfalls and luxuriant vegetation'.[2] Lady

---

1   Catherine Charlotte, Lady Jackson, op. cit. p.174.
2   Ibid. p.178.

Jackson has joined the lyrical enthusiasts. Although many writers before have described this enchanting region, it is Beckford she singles out for the highest accolade:

> Many pens have attempted to describe Cintra – I know of none but Beckford's that has succeeded in making its beauty *felt*, and he does not so much attempt to describe the place as the effect of its spell-like loveliness on his sensitive and poetic temperament.[1]

By the time she left Sintra, Lady Jackson was totally converted. Sintra is the 'portal of paradise', where every bucolic pleasure is to be found. Broad walks, cloistered avenues of foliage, picturesque kiosks and fine views of the sea are all delightful.

Not every English visitor to Sintra, even those of poetic temperament, was spellbound, however. Lord Alfred Tennyson, Poet Laureate and F.T. Palgrave came at the height of summer in 1859. Tennyson found Sintra suburban whilst Palgrave thought that a place praised by Beckford and Byron should be more wild and rich in nature. Neither could deal with the intense heat or the flies and mosquitoes. The Poet Laureate had toothache and the sun burnt them both. Bitten and exhausted, they rushed back to England without discovering Elysium or learning about the Portuguese Golden Age. Minor irritations had made them blind to Sintra's charms. 'The Iberian Peninsula in summer,' observed Rose Macaulay wryly, 'was too much: they could not take it. The New Forest was safer.'[2]

Not that the threat perceived by Tennyson was so far-fetched. As the century wore on, the proximity of Sintra to Lisbon began to impinge upon the natural feeling of the place. The setting up of the rail link between the town and the city was a significant development, which made Sintra accessible for the day-tripper who had neither a commitment to poetry nor an interest in Elysian Fields.

---

1   Ibid. p.180.
2   Rose Macaulay, op. cit. p.189.

8

Sintra Eterna

Despite the rail link established in the mid-1870s, the rich, upper-class inhabitants of the metropolis continued to regard Sintra as a desirable place of residence, particularly in the hot summer months. No doubt the town's *fidalgo* connections, to say nothing of its links to the royal family, encouraged the ambition of the new rich to live there, as it had done over the ages. One wealthy entrepreneur, who was familiar with the literary and artistic associations of Sintra as well as being attracted by its royal connections, was António Augusto de Carvalho Monteiro.[1] In 1893, Carvalho Monteiro acquired the Quinta da Torre de Regaleira, which is half hidden in the road that winds up past the Quinta do Relógio to Seteais.

Like so many other Sintra *quintas*, Regaleira had a long history, with early clerical connections. It first belonged to the Franciscans; by the fifteenth century the Capuchans, so much associated with Cork Convent high up in the *serra*, owned the site. By the early eighteenth century the house was connected to the parish church of Santa Maria, being registered in the name of Francisco Alberto Guimarães e Castro, the prior. During the nineteenth century it passed through the hands of various families, several of which had Masonic connections. Eventually, it became the property of the widow of a rich Brazilian, who took up the title of the Baroness of Regaleira.

---

1 Although their fortune was made in Brazil, the Monteiros were an old *fidalgo* family who could trace their lineage back to the founding of the nation under Afonso Henriques. See V.M. Adrião, *Regaleira de Sintra (Uma Comenda Lusignan)* (Sintra, 1997) p.49.

The Baroness was Ermelinda Allen Monteiro d'Almeida, the daughter of Edward Allen, British Consul. Her husband, José Monteiro d'Almeida had been a port-wine merchant with close business connections to the English Factory in Oporto. The Baroness's family had Masonic links. Because the Freemasons in Portugal were associated with the Liberal cause (and later with republicanism), the family had to go into exile on the return of the Miguelites in 1831. They went first to Paris and then to London, joining the liberal émigrés, who effectively formed an official opposition. After the accession of Queen Maria II in 1834, Ermelinda decided to return to Portugal. She was granted her title in recognition of her and her family's loyalty to the liberal cause. The Baroness first set up home in Lisbon, entertaining on a grand scale in a house crammed full with *objets d'art* and paintings. She also maintained a villa, the *Beau Sejour* in fashionable Benfica. However, being close to royal circles, she soon felt the need for a Sintra home. Regaleira, so near to Seteais where the royal family went to listen to outdoor concerts, was the ideal place. She bought it in 1840. Her house, situated on the site of the present building, was in traditional style, extending over two floors, with a turret-like tower. It was surrounded by rustic gardens, shady chestnut trees and fruit orchards. There had always been an abundant supply of water in the grounds.

Whilst the Baroness was setting herself up in Regaleira in some style, Carvalho Monteiro, heir to a fortune made from coffee and precious stones, was born in far-off Rio de Janeiro in 1849. Despite these overseas beginnings, or perhaps because of them, Carvalho Monteiro's attachment to Portugal was strong. His family, which was part of the old aristocracy, was connected to the Lusignan Portuguese and to the romantic myths that surround the legend of the nymph Melusina. No wonder the ten-year-old boy arriving in Lisbon was precocious, with a sense of historical destiny. Still in his teens he went to study at Coimbra and, after a further five years' residence in Brazil, returned to live permanently in Portugal in the 1870s.

Carvalho Monteiro was a cultivated, religious man who had a passion for the writing of Camões, the tercentenary of whose death was widely celebrated in 1880. Carvalho Monteiro amassed a significant collection of the poet's work, as well as other books, paintings and precious objects. A naturalist as well as a connoisseur of the arts, he had one of the best collections of butterfly specimens in the world. He was interested in fauna and flora, particularly exotic species, which would have reminded him of his native Brazil.

When Carvalho Monteiro acquired Regaleira in the 1890s Portugal was going through a difficult period in terms of national identity. Her imperial ambitions in Africa had been dealt a summary blow by the British ultimatum of 1890, which made it clear that Britain would not tolerate a territorial link across the continent joining Angola and Mozambique. The Portuguese, who had harboured ambitions of uniting their two vast colonies, were forced to back down. This national humiliation contributed to an already widespread feeling of despondency and decline, but it also spurred on a revivalist, ultra-patriotic movement. The new ideology drew on myths of the Golden Age of Discoveries, though it was tinged by a touch of the mournful *Sebastianismo* that had always been present in Portuguese imperial policy (see p.91). The two different reactions to the crisis were expressed, on the one hand, by Guerra Junqueiro (a contemporary of Carvalho Monteiro's at Coimbra) who lamented the 'funeral' of the nation and, on the other, by those who insisted on the need for regeneration.[1] This ambiguous mix is eloquently expressed in the novels of Eça de Queirós, which are imbued both with a wish for change and a nostalgia for the past.

Carvalho Monteiro, a patriot and a monarchist,[2] decided

---

1   Abilio Manuel Guerra Junqueiro (1850–1923). Poet, satirist and philosopher.
2   Adrião traces the Monteiro's connections with the royal family. Carvalho Monteiro's father knew Dom Fernando well, since they were both Directors of the Zoological Gardens. Carvalho Monteiro himself was an intimate of King Carlos, something that made him an object of suspicion once the Republic had been established. See V.M. Adrião, op. cit. pp.38–9 & p.51.

that one way of counteracting public gloom would be to build a spectacular house, which would be a symbol of national revival. The only truly patriotic style to use was extravagant Manueline, which was deliberately used to evoke the period of successful Portuguese explorations and national glory. Other buildings in Lisbon, such as Rossio Station, were also being constructed in this revivalist style. For Carvalho Monteiro, Sintra, which was closely associated with the early days of the nation, was the only place to build his monument. But the fact that he chose the traditional Manueline style to build in did not mean that he was prevented from adding his own, esoteric signature to the appearance of the new Regaleira.

He appointed as his architect the Italian Luigi Manini, who had had considerable experience in recreating Manueline features at the Grande Hotel de Buçaco, a town which had been described by the Queen, Maria Pia, wife of King Luís, as the 'Sintra of the North'.[1] At Buçaco, Manini erected a building that included a tower reminiscent of the Tower of Belém. Other Manueline features made up its elaborate façade. Terraces and cascading staircases added to the dramatic effect. In the grounds of the house there were charming garden houses, bridges and Chinese pagodas, which enhanced the exotic style of the whole complex. When Manini came to Sintra, he brought with him a talented team of stonemasons and sculptors, some of whom had worked with him at Buçaco. Among them was António Gonçalves, who was known to be a Mason and a republican.

Manini worked on and off at Regaleira for eight years from 1904. The exterior of his building is in florid neo-Manueline style, with turrets, pinnacles and elaborate stone carving covering its entire surface. The effect is to combine different features of Batalha, Tomar and the Tower of Belém at the

---

1   *O Neomanuelino ou a Reinvenção da Arquitectura Dos Descobrimentos*, Catalogue of an Exhibition at Galeria de Pintura do Rei. D. Luís (Lisbon, 1994) p.227.

same time, mixing and adding to them just as Dom Fernando had done at Pena Palace. Levels are used to emphasise different perspectives; and octagons, terraces, and ornate window frames give an ecclesiastical feel to the whole structure. Elaborate finials and spires enhance that effect.[1]

The inside of the house also has ornate features, although the dark, tropical wood used in the hall is sombre. The most elaborate Manueline piece, a huge, baroque fireplace, is in the dining room, (also known as the Hunting Room). This edifice has an elaborate frieze, with twin towers at both ends and a knight standing upright in a niche in the middle. Its medieval insignia is mixed in a design suggestive of a Masonic temple. Elsewhere in the house, the sculptured friezes – attributed to Rodrigo de Castro – imitate Renaissance motifs. Templar crosses, reminders of knightly gallantry, are found throughout the interior.

Wooden ceilings, in the old Moorish style add to the closed-in feeling of the rooms, despite their views of the open courtyard and the trees. In one room a gallery of Portuguese monarchs hangs proudly. Those monarchs such as King José or King João VI, who displeased Carvalho Monteiro or who he may have considered less than full-blooded patriots, are left out. Queens with special qualities of sanctity, such as Queen Isabel, are included. There is, of course, no sign of the three Spanish Philips. Carvalho Monteiro's own study is largely undecorated except for the Manueline portal that leads into it, and a painting of three buxom Graces, according to one inter-pretation a Masonic echo but considered to be merely of classical inspiration by another.[2] Carvalho Monteiro's austerity reminds us of William Beckford, who slept in a small cell-like

---

1   See Illustration 25.
2   See D. Pereira, P. Pereira & J. Anes, *Quinta da Regaleira, história, símbolo e mito* (Mem Martins, 1998) p. 96 for a Masonic interpretation but V.M. Adrião, op. cit., p.61 for a denial. A detailed exploration of the house's esoteric symbolism is given in an interview of José Manuel Anes by Victor Mendanha published as *O Esoterismo da Quinta da Regaleira* (Lisbon, 2000).

room in the vast vaults of Fonthill Abbey. Both lovers of outward grandeur and effect, they also share an ascetic quality which gave them an air of detachment from their fellow men.

If the inside of Regaleira expresses Carvalho Monteiro's romantic attachment to Portuguese mythology, the grounds outside are equally imaginative. While the terrace, cloaked in camellia and decorated with classical statues, gives a respite from the highly elaborate stonework of the house, many features in the grounds return to the owner's preoccupation with the exotic. The tower has a sturdy, castle-like appearance, as have the battlement walls. There is an area that resembles a mausoleum in an English Victorian cemetery. Scattered throughout the grounds are statues of nymphs and goddesses (Venus, goddess of the moon, who was closely associated with Sintra, naturally features prominently); there are twists and turns, circular and labyrinthine features throughout the stonework.

One of the most striking features is a deep well of some five storeys, each with niches and columns which are visible as one looks down from the top.[1] Curiously there is no water in it; the whole structure is more like an inverted tower than a simple hole in the ground. There has been much speculation about the symbolic meaning of the well, which has been linked to Dante's rings of hell on the one hand and on the other to contemporary ideas, like Jules Verne's, of travelling to the centre of the earth. Elsewhere in the grounds, dragons and other mythological creatures guard grottoes as well as obscure passages with spiral staircases, and caverns with hidden pools. These details evoke a sense of mystery. The grounds of Regaleira would have appealed immensely to the young William Beckford.

The chapel, which is dedicated to Our Lady of the Trinity and connected to the house by a secret passage, is in elaborate Manueline style, with elegant fan-vaulted plaster ceilings.

---

1   See Illustration 14 (showing view from the bottom).

Manini brought materials for the mosaics and the stain-glass windows from Italy. At the entrance to the crypt of the chapel is a striking piece of Masonic imagery in the form of a triangle with the eye of God in the middle, irradiating light. This is God represented as the master builder of the universe, the supreme architect of nature.[1] The criss-cross mosaic on the floor of the crypt replicates similar features of Masonic temples. Carvalho Monteiro's interest in Masonic matters is also evident from the considerable collection of histories of Freemasonry in different parts of Europe which were found in his library. Despite all this evidence, however, some historians have been keen to deny that Carvalho Monteiro was a Freemason lest it damage his ultra-Catholic, patriotic credentials.[2]

Retreating into past glories as Carvalho Monteiro did at Regaleira was one reaction to the British ultimatum of 1890 but another was to look at the way the country was governed and to seek change. A serious challenge to the monarchy had been building up for some decades. Without realising it and despite his good intentions, Dom Fernando contributed to the growth of Portuguese republicanism. In the first place he was a foreigner, which no amount of adaptation could disguise. Even more puzzling for the Portuguese, he was a self-disciplined constitutional monarch who kept his distance from party politics. In a country used to strong, absolutist rule, this role was not clearly understood or appreciated. To make matters worse, it seemed that the King was more committed to frivolities, such as the arts, than to the serious affairs of state. He surrounded himself with artists and musicians, who had always been regarded as outcasts in bourgeois society. He even

---

1 See Illustration 15.
2 Carvalho Monteiro's library is now at the United State Congress in Washinton DC. For a history of the Freemasons in Portugal, who are alleged to include the Marquis of Pombal in the eighteenth century and the Cardinal Patriarch Saraiva in the nineteenth, see A.H. de Oliveira Marques, *História da Maçonaria em Portugal* 2 vols (Lisbon, 1996).

took a singer as his second wife. His artistic leanings were passed down to the last Bragança kings – Luís enjoyed literature and translated Shakespeare into Portuguese, while Carlos painted watercolours. The withdrawal of a succession of monarchs from the political arena left a vacuum, which was filled by middle-class politicians. Some of these public figures were democrats who looked toward France, where the Third Republic was in place, as a model for the future of their own country. At the other end of the scale, revolutionary groups not opposed to employing violence to gain political ends, were being formed in Lisbon and Oporto.

Despite these developments the twilight of the Portuguese monarchy drew out into the twentieth century. One member of the royal family who played a significant role in its survival was the last Queen of Portugal, Amélia, who came to the country as the bride of Dom Carlos. She was the daughter of the Count of Paris, and had spent part of her childhood in England. No doubt her first impression of Sintra was a vivid one as she and the Prince chose to spend their honeymoon in the exotic Quinta do Relógio. In her private diary she refers to a 'savage luxuriance, too reminiscent of Africa'[1] for the delicate palate of someone brought up in the wholesome greenery of the Normandy countryside. Pena Palace, with its jumble of styles reminded her of something from the *Arabian Nights* – a fact she did not find reassuring. However, a few years later, when she was raising her own family, her attitude had changed. She writes enthusiastically:

> We are at Cintra which I used not to love but which I find delightful this year. Everything is exquisitely green. We go for long walks along the mountains, which are a little like the Esterel. I ride on horseback, a great deal. On Sunday we gave a little dance or rather a *cotillon* which brought back many memories to my mind.[2]

1   L. Corprechot, *Queen Amélie of Portugal* (London, 1915) p.94.
2   Ibid.

Sintra now appeared a haven of bliss compared to the frenetic atmosphere of the Lisbon court. The Queen took to drawing whilst the King painted watercolours. They both admired the sweeping prospects of the countryside from their terrace at Pena.[1] Amélia brought a northern commonsense to the bringing up of the royal family, discarding a great deal of the pomp and ceremony of her predecessor Queen Maria Pia (wife of King Luís), whose insistence on rigid etiquette at court was notorious. The domestic ambience Amélia created was in keeping with Dom Fernando's original intention to keep Pena as a retreat where the younger members of the royal family could grow up in a more natural environment than in the palaces of Lisbon.

Nevertheless, the prospect of a peaceful life was rapidly disappearing. Amélia's diary is full of foreboding about the growing unrest in the early years of the new century. Matters reached a bloody climax in 1908. The King and Queen, accompanied by their two sons, were being driven through central Lisbon in an open landau when republican extremists fired on them. The King was killed at once, while Dom Luís, the Crown Prince, was mortally wounded, but the Queen and Dom Manuel, her younger son, escaped unharmed.[2] The youthful Dom Manuel ascended the throne in these inauspicious circumstances but two years later his short reign was over. It is poignant that it was in the silence of the Sintra hills that the Queen heard the rumbling of distant guns, which signalled the revolution that ended the Bragança dynasty.

The end of the monarchy, with which Sintra had been so closely associated throughout the history of the nation, was bound to have an effect on the town. Kings and queens had come and gone from Sintra for more than seven hundred and fifty years. Suddenly the royal palace was no longer inhabited;

---

1   S. Bern, *Eu, Amélia, Ultima Rainha de Portugal* trans. D.C. Garcia (Barcelos, 1999) pp.100–1.
2   Ibid. pp.15–20 for a moving account of the assassination scene in a street leading off the Terreiro do Paço (now Praça do Comércio) in Lisbon.

the bustle that accompanied the royal presence in the town abruptly ended. The *quintas* of the *fidalgo* families, on whose terraces and in whose gardens the affairs of state would once have been routinely discussed, became mere summer residences of families who had no great influence in the affairs of the Republic. Even in local politics their influence waned, with the result that it was not until 1922, a decade later, that the Democrats, the party they supported, was able to take control of the town hall.[1]

Although Sintra had become a popular tourist destination for the bourgeoisie of Lisbon by the end of the nineteenth century, rival centres of attraction were growing up in Estoril and Cascais. In an effort to keep their clients, Sintra hotels, like the Grand Hotel Costa (now the regional museum) put out advertisements, which boasted of their French cuisine and the fact that English was spoken in their establishments. But it was difficult to stem the tide: more and more visitors chose the sea over the mountains as their holiday destination. As tourism increased on the coast there was a marked decline in the population of Sintra as young people went looking for work elsewhere.

The eclipse of royal Sintra can also be traced in its historiography, a useful barometer for measuring social changes in local history. Nineteenth-century writing on Sintra is dominated by the great Romantics – Juromenha, Braamcamp Freire and Sabugosa – who were themselves part of the aristocracy or privileged classes. These authors were devoted to promoting the colourful aspects of Sintra's history – its ancient legends, its heraldry and its intimate connection with the royal family. Sabugosa, writing at the end of the monarchical period, is *par excellence* the historian of the kings and queens of Portugal. He portrays them as the great landlords of Sintra,

---

1   See M.C. Proença, *Eleicões Municipais em Sintra* 1910–1926 (Sintra, 1987) p.39. This is an interesting account of the first decades of Republican political life in the town.

surrounded by courtiers who had taken up residence in the hills around the old town. Although Sabugosa's book is ostensibly about a single building, the old royal palace, it is in fact a chronicle of national history because he was keenly aware of the important historical associations of the town.[1] An endless succession of soldier-statesmen, writers, artists and court officials people his pages, bringing the whole story of the palace to life. When the book was finally published, in 1903, it was dedicated to Queen Amélia, who ironically was to be the last Queen of Portugal.

The so-called 'first generation' of aristocratic, Sintra writers was followed by a more sober set of scholars whose intentions were to trace in detail particular aspects of local history.[2] Félix Alves Pereira, prominent in this group, began a long series of investigations into archaeological sites at Sintra, considerably advancing knowledge of the ancientness of human habitation of the *serra*. His studies of prehistoric rock formations and tumuli laid the foundation for serious fieldwork on local sites. He drew attention to the wealth of Roman remains, particularly in the form of funerary monuments, now housed in the considerable collection at the Museum of Odrinhas. His work also extended to careful inspection of medieval aspects of Sintra churches, particularly of São Martinho and Santa Maria. Significant work in another area of scientific study, the geographical and geological, was done by J. de Oliveira Boléo. His survey of the different land formation of the *serra* and the earthquake fault lines that run through it, make us feel that this is indeed *terra firma*. Sintra may be a place of legend and history but it is also a real place, with specific topographical features. It is this insistence on making real the location of Sintra, usually by examining one particular aspect of its character, that marks

---

1 Sabugosa was not much concerned with Pena Palace which, by comparison with the old palace, is historically uninteresting.
2 F. Oliveira & L. Martin have identified three generations of Sintra scholars. See *Jornal de Sintra* (Sintra, 23 April, 1999).

a change of emphasis in the second generation of Sintra scholars.

Two of the most eminent local historians of this group were J.M. da Silva Marques and Francisco Costa, who were successive heads of the municipal archive. Da Silva Marques began the historical archive, cross-referencing material held locally with material in the national collection. His work was invaluable in setting the context of Sintra's history over the centuries. Francisco Costa's contribution was of diverse but equally scholarly quality. He produced an authoritative text of the charter of 1154 in Portuguese, publishing it alongside the original Latin one. He went on to catalogue the extensive literature already written on Sintra as well as writing a series of elegant and informative monographs on particular buildings, including the Paço Real, Ramalhão and Monserrate.[1] To the work of these scholars was added the important sociological and partially anecdotal record of the town brought together in the scattered writings of J.A. da Costa Azevedo.

A third generation of Sintra scholars has been identified among those students who were at university at the time of the Revolution of 25 April 1974.[2] That event, which was brought to a head by the prospect of endless colonial wars in Africa, brought Portugal's imperial role to an end and launched the country into the modern era. The academics in the new régime tended to become narrower specialists than their predecessors, but their writing is nevertheless informed by the stock of knowledge handed down from the preceding two generations. New techniques, for example in the study of art history, have led to interesting revelations about hitherto unseen connections in the development of taste and style.[3]

---

1   In a new, three-volume edition of the works of Francisco Costa there is also an essay on the Palace of Seteais which he had been working on but had not been previously published. See F. Costa, *Estudos Sintrenses* (Sintra, 2000) 3 vols, vol. 3 pp.75–154. Costa was a poet and literary man as well as a local historian, at one stage editing the journal *Athena* with Fernando Pessoa.
2   F. Oliveira & L. Martin, loc. cit.
3   The work of Vitor Serrão is particularly noteworthy in this field.

Some of this work has continued in scientific areas, particularly in the fields of archaeology and geology. A great deal more is now known about the prehistoric and Roman origins of the area, as the impressive tome *Sintria* demonstrates.[1]

Progress has been made in other areas of study. Modern scientific methods have been applied to examining the granite structure of the mountain, showing that rare rocks, millions of years old, are encrusted in the range. It is now possible to reconstruct a landscape of Sintra predating the earthquake period; the complex structure of the region can be seen in a different topographical context as it becomes clear that large areas situated off the coast, and now submerged in the ocean, were originally part of the landmass. Ironically, the emergence of this scientific data strengthens the hitherto fantastic notion of dinosaurs wondering on the *planalto*, where some have claimed to find their footprints.

Despite the attempts of modern scholars to pinpoint and explain features of the Sintra landscape, something elusive and undefinable has remained in its air to inspire poets and dreamers. Even the scholarly community contains a faction driven by the need to ascribe spiritual meaning to rocks and brickwork; and arguments about the symbolism of Regaleira rage on. The expansive lyricism of the nineteenth century has never disappeared from writings about Sintra. Only two years after the founding of the Republic, in 1912, Mario Beirão is still describing Pena as an altar under the heavenly clouds. No less an eminence than Manuel Teixeira Gomes, who was President of the Republic from 1923 to 1925, remained convinced of the balsamic effects of Sintra's airs on a visitor's spiritual, as well as physical, well-being. The lyrical tradition continued in the works of writers as varied as Fernando Pessoa, António Quadros and José Saramago.

Pessoa, of course, despite his modernism, indulged in nostalgia for Portugal's imperial past and maritime glory. The

---

1   See *Sintria I:II, tomo 1 1982–83* (Mem Martins, 1884–7).

poem he wrote about King Sebastião, in which he hints that the vivid glory-seeking of the past is more admirable than the grey of the present, has been quoted (see p.91). As an urban poet – of the pavement, tramlines and seedy bars of Lisbon – Pessoa is a universalist not given to clear localisation. His approach is ever paradoxical: one wants to be in Sintra to escape Lisbon, while simultaneously wanting to be in Lisbon to escape Sintra. In his *Book of Disquiet*, the poet and his soul-mate (himself or no one) wander through forests thick with undergrowth. Here and there, in the openings between copses of trees, the flowers of the *serra* – the lily, the poppy and the camellia – grow wild. There is a

> freshness of the mosses, and we had passing by the palm trees, the faint intuition of other lands... Oak trees of knotty centuries caused us to stumble over the dead tentacles of their roots... Plane trees unexpectedly sprang to view... And through the nearby trees, you could see hanging in the distance, in the silence of the trellises, the blue-black reflection of bunches of grapes...[1]

Pessoa's landscape is part of his escapist metaphysics, an extreme subjectivism that casts doubt on the very notion of reality itself. The description of the Sintra-like landscape takes on the form of an inverted dream. Informed by foreign (French) Futurist and Modernist ideas, his view is nevertheless essentially linked to a nostalgia that is thoroughly Portuguese. Sintra is part of the nation's symbolic past but it can only be perceived through the refracted lens of the present.

António Quadros' mystical feelings for Sintra are no less ethereal than Pessoa's. He reflects on the oral tradition of Sintra, dwelling with an almost sensual pleasure on its ancient Greek connections, its legendary status as Diana's moonlit hunting ground. For Quadros, any scientific explanation palls against a tradition which transcends the physical nature of the

---

1   F. Pessoa, *The Book of Disquiet* (trans. Ian Watson) (London, 1991) pp.78–9.

place itself. Trying to explain the unique quality of Sintra by reference to climate or geology is utterly futile; Sintra is a place where beauty is in the very air, waiting for poets to breathe it. The buildings of the town – the Moorish castle and the Paço Real, 'heavy with history'[1] – add to its sense of unreality; they are set in an exotic landscape of running streams and semi-tropical vegetation which suggests a work of art or imagination rather than a real place. The natural and the manmade are exactly complementary. When there has been rainfall, the clouds swirl over the range, creating a different, more remote landscape. 'But of a sudden,' A. Quadros has written,

> the mood changes again when the clouds lift. The castle and the palace, which had seemed so sombre, become lighter and clearer, as if they have forgotten the past and come back to life. From the valley the voices of labourers and the sounds of their toils grow louder and echo [in the hills].[2]

José Saramago's treatment of Sintra is less mystical but distinctly philosophical.[3] He advises the traveller to choose his own way of getting to the town although all roads lead to it. The idyllic charms of Sintra are most evident in Monserrate, with its dense greenery, clear-flowing streams and a silence only interrupted by the sounds of birds and bumble bees. The manmade elements, buildings and fountains, blend smoothly into this heavenly terrain. The sinuous road which leads up to Seteais from Monserrate and the vistas across from the terrace add to the ethereal atmosphere of the place. Even Pena Palace, with its curious mixture of architectural styles, appears perfectly placed, adding a harmonious crown to the mountain cliff. This odd jumble of stones and the Moorish castle on the other ridge enhance the unreal effect of the Sintra landscape.

---

1   A. Quadros, 'A Estranha Aventura de Sintra' *Panorama* nos. 36 & 37 (Lisbon, 1948).
2   Ibid.
3   See J. Saramago, *Viagem a Portugal* (Lisbon, 1981).

For Saramago, as for Byron, the humble monks and hermits, long since gone, are the true guardians of the place.

If the gods have left Sintra for man to enjoy, a man of philosophical inclination enjoys it best. Saramago is such a man. He considers the different modes of time in Sintra, a place where relativity may be clearly demonstrated. In Pena time is petrified; in Cork Convent it is suspended in questioning, while in Monserrate it is entirely lost. Only in the Paço Real do we find traces of the passing of time, the footsteps of history, marked on its worn-out stones. The relics of the ages, no longer possessed, are left to be admired by posterity. Elsewhere Saramago is equally lyrical. Let us leave Sintra with the Laureate talking about the 'justly renowned Serra de Sintra, the pride of the nation and the envy of foreigners... an admirable paradise if God had decided to have another go...'[1]

---

1   J. Saramago, *Baltasar and Blimunda* (English translation of *Memorial do Convento* by G. Pontiero) (London, 1998) p.28.

Chronological Table

BC

1m to 200,000	*Homo Erectus* comes to the Iberian Peninsula from Africa
20,000	Paleolithic remains: Coa Valley; Escoural, Alentejo
3,500	Neolithic remains in Sintra area: Santa Eufémia
1,000	Phoenicians reach southern Portugal
700	Celtic tribes invade northern Portugal
600	Greek traders in Portugal
535	Carthaginian occupation of Portugal
218	Roman invasion of the Iberian Peninsula: resistance of Lusitani
139	Death of Viriatus
	Romanisation of Sintra area: *planalto*

AD

25	Roman province of Lusitania
410	Alaric the Visigoth sacks Rome
	Suevi in Portugal
	Visigoths in Spain
475	Extinction of Western Roman Empire
711	Moorish invasion of Iberian Peninsula
	Moorish castle at Sintra being built
	Moorish palace in old town being built
833	Reconquest of northern Portugal by

	Christians: Portucale established
1147	Capture of Lisbon and Sintra by Afonso Henriques.
1154	Charter of Sintra
1287	Sintra styled the 'Queen's town' by Royal Letters
1333–34	Famine caused by crop failure
1348	Plague kills 50 per cent of Sintra population
1410	Convento da Trindade mentioned in Royal Letters.
	King João's building of the Royal Palace
1470	Ramalhão mentioned in Royal Letters
1497–98	Vasco da Gama discovers the sea route to India
1500	Pedro Alvarez Cabral discovers Brazil
1507	Duarte d'Armas' engravings of Royal Palace
	King Manuel's additions to Royal Palace
1514	Manueline Charter of Sintra
1516	Garcia de Resende's *Cancioneiro Geral* Charter of Colares
1521	João de Barros' *Crónica do Imperador Clarimundo*
1529	Gil Vicente's *Triunfo do Inverno*
1540	Chapel dedicated to Our Lady of Monserrat (Catalonia) at Monserrate
1544	Bernadim Ribeiro's *Menina e Moça*
1560	Capuchos Monastery founded
1572	Luís Vaz de Camões' *Lusiads*
1578	King Sebastião's war council at Sintra and defeat at Alcácer-Quibir in Morocco
1580–1640	United kingdom of Spain and Portugal Bishop Dinis de Melo e Castro at Colares
1640	João da Cruz's poem *Serra de Sintra*
1755	Lisbon earthquake affects Sintra area

1780s	Lawrence Inn opens
1787	William Beckford's first visit to Sintra
	Gildemeester's Palace of Seteais built
1796	Robert Southey's first visit to Sintra
1803	Marialva additions to Palace of Seteais
1807	French invasion; royal family go to Brazil
1809	Byron's visit to Sintra
1810	Battle of Buçaco; Wellington's Torres Vedras lines
1812	Byron's *Childe Harold*
1821	Royal family return to Portugal
1825	Almeida Garrett's poem *Camões*
1828–34	Civil war in Portugal
1834	Expulsion of religious orders; closing of monasteries
1838	Dom Fernando buys Pena monastery
	Juromenha's *Cintra Pinturesca*
1840	Pena Palace started
1856	Cook buys Monserrate
1874	Larmanjat rail link from Sintra to Lisbon
	Lady Jackson's *Fair Lusitania*
1888	Eça de Quierós' *Maias*
1890	British ultimatum on Africa
1903	Sabugosa's *Paço de Sintra*
1904	Quinta de Regaleira started
1908	Assassination of King Carlos and Crown Prince Luís
1910	Revolution marks end of monarchy
1930s–1960s	'Second' generation of Sintra scholars including J.M. da Silva Marques, Francisco Costa and F. Alves Pereira
1971	José Saramago's *Viagem a Portugal*
1995	Sintra declared a world heritage site

The Kings and Queens of Portugal

Afonsin (Burgundian) Dynasty

Afonso Henriques m. Mafalda of Maurienne and Savoy	1128–1185
Sancho I m. Dulce of Aragon	1185–1211
Afonso II m. Urraca of Aragon	1211–1223
Sancho II m. Mécia Lópes de Haro	1223–1248
Afonso III m. 1) Matilde, Countess of Boulogne 2) Beatriz de Guillén	1248–1279
Dinis (the Husbandman) m. Isabel of Aragon	1279–1325
Afonso IV m. Beatriz of Castile	1325–1357
Pedro I (the Cruel) m. 1) Bianca of Castile 2) Constanza of Castile 3) Inêz de Castro	1357–1367
Fernando I m. Leónor Teles	1367–1383

Avis Dynasty

João I m. Philippa of Lancaster	1385–1433
Duarte I m. Leónor of Aragon	1433–1438
Afonso V (the African) m. Isabel of Portugal	1438–1481
João II m. Leónor of Portugal	1481–1495
Manuel I (the Fortunate) m. 1) Isabel of Castile 2) Maria of Castile 3) Leónor of Spain	1495–1521
João III m. Catarina of Spain	1521–1557
Sebastião (the Regretted)	1557–1578
Henrique (the Cardinal-King)	1578–1580
Antonio, Prior of Crato	1580

Austrian Dynasty (Spanish Kings)

Felipe I (Felipe II of Spain)	1580–1598
Felipe II (Felipe III of Spain)	1598–1621
Felipe III (Felipe IV of Spain)	1621–1640

Bragança Dynasty

João IV m. Louisa de Gusmán	1640–1656
Afonso V m. Maria-Francisca-Isabel d'Aumale of Savoy	1656–1683
Pedro II (Regent from 1668) m. 1) Isabel d'Aumale 2) Maria-Sofia-Isabel of Neuberg	1683–1706
João V (the Magnificent) m. Maria-Ana of Austria	1706–1750
José m. Mariana-Victoria of Spain	1750–1777
Maria I m. Pedro de Bragança	1777–1816
João VI (Regent from 1792) m. Carlota-Joaquina of Spain	1816–1826
Pedro IV (abdicated) m. 1) Maria Leopoldina of Austria 2) Maria-Amelia of Leuchtenberg	1826–1828
Miguel m. Adelaide-Sofia of Loewenstein-Rosenberg	1828–1834
Maria II (da Glória) m. 1) August of Leuchtenberg 2) Ferdinand of Saxe-Coburg-Gotha	1834–1853
Pedro V m. Stéphanie of Hohenzollern Sigmaringen	1853–1861
Luís m. Maria-Pia of Savoy	1861–1889
Carlos m. Marie-Amelie of Orléans	1889–1908
Manuel II (the Unfortunate) m. Augusta-Victoria of Sigmaringen	1908–1910

Bragança Dynasty in Brazil

Emperor Pedro I	1822–1831
Emperor Pedro II	1831–1889

Bibliography

Archives

Arquivo Histórico, 34 vols, (ed. J.M. da Silva Marques) and manuscript boxes, Arquivo Municipal, Sintra.

Secondary Sources

Adrião, V.M. *Regaleira de Sintra* (Uma Comenda Lusignan). Sintra, 1997.

Alexander, B. 'Beckford's Debt to Portugal' *British Historical Society of Portugal*. 5th Annual Report and Review. Lisbon, 1978.

Alves, A. (et al.). *Sintra: Uma Janela Atlântica com vista para o Universo*. Mem Martins, 1997.

Amarante, E. *Portugal Simbólico, Origens sagradas dos Lusitanos*. Lisbon, 1999.

Andersen, H.C. *A Visit to Portugal 1866* (trans. G. Thornton) London, 1972.

Anderson, B. & E. *Landscapes of Portugal. Sintra. Cascais. Estoril.* London, 1995.

Afonso. S.L. & Delaforce, A. *A Palácio de Queluz: Jardins.* Lisbon, 1989.

Anon. 'Letter from an eye-witness of the Lisbon earthquake' *British Historical Society of Portugal*. Lisbon, 1985.

Atanazio, M. *A arte do Manuelino* Lisbon, 1984.

Atkinson, W.C. *A History of Spain and Portugal*. London 1960.

Azevedo, J.A. da Costa. *Velharias de Sintra*. 6 vols Sintra, 1957.

Barretti, J. *A Journal from London to Genoa* (intro. I. Robertson) London, 1970.

Barros, C.V. da Silva *Four Altars to the Virgin.* Lisbon, 1978.

Beckford, W. *Recollections of an Excursion to the Monasteries of Alcobaça and Batalha* (ed. B. Alexander) Sussex, 1972.

—— *Sketches of Spain and Portugal in the Travel Diaries of William Beckford of Fonthill* (ed. G. Chapman) Cambridge, 1928.

—— *The Journal of William Beckford in Spain and Portugal 1787–88* (ed. B. Alexander). London, 1954.

Bern, S. *Eu, Amélia, Última Rainha de Portugal* (trans. D.C. Garcia) Porto, 1993.

Boléo, J. de Oliveira *Sintra e Seu Termo.* Sintra, 1975.

Bombelles, Marquis de *Journal d'un Ambassadeur de France au Portugal 1786–1788* (ed. R. Kann) Paris, 1979.

Borges Coelho, A. *Portugal na Espanha Arabe.* 2 vols Lisbon, 1989.

Bottineau, Y. *Portugal.* Norwich, 1957.

Boxer, C.R. *The Portuguese Seaborne Empire.* Manchester, 1991.

Bradford, W. *Sketches of the Country, Character and Costume in Portugal and Spain.* London, 1809.

Breyner, S. de Melo, *Log Book: Selected Poems.* Manchester, 1997.

Bridges, A. & Lowndes, S. *A Selective Traveller in Portugal.* London, 1949.

Brito, M.C. de 'A Música no tempo de William Beckford' in *William Beckford and Portugal: An Impassioned Journey.* Catalogue Raisonné of an exhibition at the Palace of Queluz, Portugal. Lisbon, 1987.

Byron, Lord George *Poetical Works.* Oxford, 1967.

—— *Selected Letters and Journals* (ed. P. Gunn) London, 1984.

Cabral, A. *Southey e Portugal 1774–1800.* Lisbon, 1959.

Caetano, M.T. *Colares.* Sintra, 2000.

Campos, Correia de *Monumentos de Antiguidade em Portugal.* Lisbon, 1970.

Camões, Luís Vaz de *Lusiads.* (trans. L.V. White) Oxford, 1997.

Candeias, A. *Portugal em Alguns Escritores Ingleses.* Lisbon, 1946.

Cardoso, L.P. 'D. Francisco Manuel de Melo "As Vistas das Fontes" e a Ermida de São Mamede de Janas' in *Sintria I–II, tomo I 1982–83*. Mem Martins, 1984–7 pp.1029–65.

Carneiro, J.M.M. et al. *Palácio Nacional da Pena*. Lisbon, 1987.

Carvalho, S.L. de *História de Sintra*. Sintra, 1992.

Carvalho, M. de *A God Strolling in the Cool of the Evening*. London, 1997.

Castro, D. Luís de 'Beckford em Cintra' *Illustração Portugueza*. Lisbon, 1906.

Castro, G. de *Ulisseia ou Lisboa Edificada* (1636) (ed. J.A. Segurado e Campos) Lisbon, 2000.

Catálogo das Inscrições Lapidares do Museu de São Miguel de Odrinhas. Sintra, 1956

Centano, Y.K. (ed.) *Portugal: Mítos Revistados*. Lisbon, 1993.

Corprechot, L. *Memories of Queen Amélie of Portugal*. London, 1915.

Correia, A.M. de Arez Romão e Brito *Palácio Nacional de Sintra*. Lisbon 1993.

Costa, F. *Beckford em Sintra no verão de 1787*. Sintra, 1972.

—— *Bibliografia Sintrense*. Sintra, 1940.

—— *Estudos Sintrenses*. 3 vols Sintra, 2000

—— *História da Quinta e Palácio de Monserrate*. Sintra, 1985.

—— *O Foral de Sintra*. Sintra 1976.

—— *O Paço Real de Sintra*. Sintra, 1980.

Delaforce, A. *Art and Patronage in Eighteenth-Century Portugal*. Cambridge, 2002.

Delumeau, J. *Une histoire du paradis*. Paris, 1992.

Domingues, G. *História Luso-Arabe*. Lisbon, 1945.

Ehrhadt, M. 'D. Fernando II visto atravès das suas cartas à família' in *Romantismo Figuras e factos da época de D. Fernado II*. Sintra, 1988 pp.9–14.

Estudos Orientais II: O legado Cultural de Judeus e Mouros. Lisbon, 1991.

Estrela, E. *Sintra, nossa terra, nossa gente*. Lisbon, 1997.

Etnografia de Região Saloia. Sintra, 1999.

Flor, J. *Sintra na Literatura Romântica Inglesa*. Sintra, 1978.

Fothergill, B. *Beckford of Fonthill*. London, 1979.

Francis, D. *Portugal 1715–1808*. London, 1984.

Freire, Anselmo Braamcamp *Brasões da Sala de Sintra*. 3 vols (1899) Lisbon, 1921.

Freitas, J. de S. de (et al.) *Trees of Monserrate*. Lisbon, 1997.

Garrett, Almeida J.B. da Silva *Travels in my Homeland* (trans. J.M. Parker) London, 1987.

Giraud, I. 'La réverie dans les jardins' *Romantismo*. Sintra, 1986 pp.65–87.

Glover, M. *Britannia Sickens. The Convention of Cintra*. London, 1970.

Guerra, A. *Plínio-o-Velho e a Lusitânia*. Lisbon, 1995.

Guerra, O. *Roteiro Lírico de Sintra*. Lisbon, 1940.

Hibbert, C. *The Grand Tour*. London, 1987.

Horace *The Odes of Horace* (trans. J. Michie) London, 1964.

Inchbold, A.C. *Lisbon and Cintra* (illus. S. Inchbold) London, 1907.

Jack, M. 'Monserrate: Beckford's Second Sintra House' *Beckford Journal*. Spring 1998, vol. IV pp.48–51.

—— 'Ramalhão: Beckford's First Sintra House' *Beckford Journal*. Spring 1997, vol. III pp.20–4.

—— 'The World of Beckford's Portuguese Palaces' in *William Beckford, 1760–1844: An Eye for the Magnificent* (ed. D. Ostergard) Catalogue of an Exhibition at the Bard Graduate Center for Decorative Arts, New York. 2001. New Haven and London, 2001 pp.88–97.

—— *William Beckford: An English Fidalgo*. New York, 1996.

Jackson, Catherine Charlotte, Lady *Fair Lusitania*. London 1874.

Jean Pillement & Landscape Painting in Eighteenth-Century Portugal. Catalogue of an exhibition at the Fundação Ricardo do Espirito Santo. Lisbon, 1997.

Juromenha, Visconde de *Cintra Pinturesca*. Lisbon, 1838.

Kennedy, H. *Os Muçulmanos na Península Ibérica*. (trans. M.G. Segurado) Mem Martins, 1999.

Kingsbury, I. *Castles, Caliphs and Christians: A Landscape with*

Figures. Monserrate. Lisbon, 1994.

Kinsey, W. *Portugal Illustrated in a Series of Letters.* London, 1828.

Le Roy Liberge, G. *Trois Mois au Portugal.* Paris, 1910.

Lino, R. *Os Paços Reais da Vila de Sintra.* Lisbon, 1948.

Livermore, H.V. *Portugal: A Short History.* Edinburgh, 1973.

Loução, P.A. *Os Templários na formação de Portugal.* Lisbon, 1999.

Luís, A.B. *João Sebastião.* Porto, 1981.

Macaulay, Rose *They Went to Portugal.* London, 1946

—— *They Went to Portugal Too.* Manchester, 1990.

Machado, Álvaro Manuel *Dicionário de Literatura Portuguesa.* Lisbon, 1996.

Marques, A.H. de Oliveira *História da Maçonaria em Portugal.* 2 vols Lisbon, 1996.

—— *História de Portugal.* 3 vols Lisbon, 1984.

Marques, J.M. da Silva *Sintra e Sintrense no Ultramar Português.* Sintra, 1949.

Marques-Gonçalves, J.L. 'Monumento préhistórico da Praia das Maçãs (Sintra) Notícia Preliminar' in *Sintria I–II. tomo I 1982–83.* Mem Martins, 1984–87 pp.29–57.

Massie, I. *Byron's Travels.* London, 1988.

McCarthy, M. *The Origins of the Gothic Revival.* Newhaven and London, 1987.

Mendanha, V. *O Esoterismo da Quinta da Regaleira.* Lisbon, 2000.

Moreira, J.M. (et al.) *O património florístico.* Instituto da Coversação da Natureza Sintra-Cascais. Lisbon, 1998.

Moreira, R. *Queijadas de Sintra.* Sintra, 1999.

Moreira, R. 'Novo dados sobre Francisco de Holanda' in *Sintria I–II tomo I 1982–83.* Mem Martins, 1984–7 pp.619–92.

Murphy, J. *Travels in Portugal.* London, 1795.

O Neomanuelino ou a Reinvenção da Arquitectura dos Descobrimentos. Instituto Português do Património Arquitectónico Lisbon, 1994.

Neves, V.M.L. Pereira *O Convento dos Capuchos*. Sintra, 1997.

Oliveira, F. & L. Martin A. 'O 25 de Abril e a terceira generação' *Jornal de Sintra*. Sintra, 23 April, 1999.

'Palacio Nacional de Sintra: Favourite Residence of King John I and Philippa of Lancaster'. *British Historical Society of Portugal*. Lisbon, 1987.

Parreaux, A. *Le Portugal dans l'Oeuvre de William Beckford*. Paris, 1935.

Paxeco, E. 'Adraga, Alvidar, Fojo, Sintra: Tentiva Justifactória de Etimologia' *Lingua Portuguesa*, vol. XIX. Lisbon, 1949.

Pena, A. (et al.) *Sintra A Borough in the Wild*. Sintra. (undated)

Pereira, A.D. *Sintra e suas Quintas*. Lisbon, 1983.

Pereira, D. (et al.) *Quinta da Regaleira, história, símbolo e mito*. Mem Martins, 1998.

Pereira, F.A. *Sintra do Pretérito*. Sintra, 1957.

Pereira, P. (ed.) *História da Arte Portuguesa*. 3 vols Lisbon, 1999.

Pereira P. & J.M. Carneiro *Pena Palace*. London, 1999.

Pessoa, F. *The Book of Disquiet* (trans. I. Watson) London, 1991.

—— *Selected Poems* (ed. & trans. P. Rickard) Edinburgh, 1971.

Picard, C. *Le Portugal Musulman. (VIIIe–XIIe siècle)*. Paris, 2000.

Pina, L. de. *Sintra O romantismo e o Cinema*. Sintra, 1985

Pires, M.L.B. *William Beckford e Portugal*. Lisbon, 1987.

Portugal From its Origins through the Roman Era. National Museum of Archaelogy and Ethnology. Lisbon, 1989.

Proença, M.C. *Eleições Municipais em Sintra 1910–1926*. Sintra, 1987.

Quadros, A. 'A Estranha Aventura de Sintra' *Panorama*, nos. 36 & 37. Lisbon, 1948.

—— *Portugal Razão e Mistério*, vol. I Lisbon, 1999.

Queirós, J.M. Eça de *O Mistério da Estrada de Sintra* Lisbon, 1884.

—— *The Maias* (trans. P.M. Pinheiro & A. Stevens) London, 1998.

—— *The Tragedy of the Street of the Flowers* (trans. M.J. Costa) Sawtry, Cambridge, 2000.

Quest-Ritson, C. *The English Garden Abroad.* London, 1992.

Redding C. *Memoirs of William Beckford of Fonthill.* 2 vols London, 1859.

Reed, J. *The Moors in Spain and Portugal.* London, 1974.

Ribeiro, J.C. (et al.) *Sintra: Património da Humanidade.* Sintra, 1998.

Ribeiro, J.C. (et al.) *Sintria I–II. tomo I 1982–83.* Mem Martins, 1984–7.

Ribeiro, M.L. (et al.) *Notícia Explicativa da Carta Geólogica simplificada.* Instituto da Conservação da Natureza, 1997.

Ribeiro, O. Portugal *O Mediterráneo e O Atlântico.* Lisbon, 1998.

Ribeiro e Costa, F.P. *Castelo dos Mouros.* Mem Martins, 1996.

Rodil, J. (ed.) *Serra da Sintra Poema Épico em Seis Cantos.* Sintra, 1993.

—— *Serra, Luas e literatura.* Sintra, 1995.

—— *Sintra na Obra de Eça de Queirós.* Sintra, 2000.

Russell, P. *Prince Henry 'the Navigator': A Life.* Yale, 2000.

Ruth, J.S. *Lisbon in the Renaissance.* New York, 1996.

Ruys, J. *Sintra O Encantado Monte da Lua.* Sintra, 1997.

Sabugosa, Conde de, *O Paço de Cintra.* Lisbon, 1903.

Salter, C. *Introducing Portugal.* Bristol, 1956.

Santos, P.B. (et al.) *Lisboa Setecentista Vista por Estrangeiros.* Lisbon, 1992.

Saramago, J. *Baltasar and Blimunda (Memorial do Convento)* (trans. G. Pontiero) London, 1998.

—— *História do Cerco de Lisboa.* Lisbon, 1989.

—— *Viagem a Portugal.* Lisbon, 1981.

Saraiva, A.J. & O. Lopes *História Literatura Portuguesa.* 17th ed. Porto, 1996.

Saraiva, J.H. *Portugal: A Companion History.* Manchester, 1997.

Serrão, V. 'A Pintura Maneirista em Portugal' *História da Arte Portuguesa* (ed. P. Pereira) 3 vols, vol 2 pp.429ff.

—— *Sintra.* Lisbon, 1989.

Silva, J.C. da & G. Luckhurst *Sintra. A Landscape with Villas.* Lisbon, 1989.

Sitwell, S. *Portugal and Madeira*. London, 1954.

Smith, R.C. *The Art of Portugal*. 1500–1800. London, 1968.

Sousa, M. de *Reis e Rainhas de Portugal*. Lisbon, 2001.

Southey, R. *Letters Written during a Short Residence in Spain and Portugal*. London, 1797.

Tabucchi, A. *The Case of the Missing Head of Damaceno Monteiro*. London, 1990.

Terra da Moura Encantada. Museu sem Fronteiras, Lisbon, 1999.

Vale, T.L.M. *O Beau Séjour: Uma Quinta Romântica de Lisboa*. Lisbon, 1992.

Veira da Silva, J. Custodia *The National Palace, Sintra*. London, 2002.

Vicente, G. 'Triunfo do Inverno' *Obras Completas* (ed. M. Braga) vol. 4 Lisbon, 1971.

Virgil: *The Aeneid, the Georgics, the Eclogues* (trans. J.A. Rhoades) Oxford, 1957.

Watson, W.C. *Portuguese Architecture*. London, 1908.

Wordsworth, W. *Poetical Works*. Oxford, 1966.

Zimler, R. *The Last Kabbalist of Lisbon*. London, 1998.

Index